FIRST EDITION

MACROECONOMICS: PRINCIPLES DECONSTRUCTED

By Brian A. Hunt

cognella® | PRESS

Bassim Hamadeh, CEO and Publisher
Kassie Graves, Director of Acquisitions
Jamie Giganti, Senior Managing Editor
Jess Estrella, Senior Graphic Designer
Zina Craft, Senior Field Acquisitions Editor
Gem Rabanera, Project Editor
Elizabeth Rowe, Licensing Coordinator
Berenice Quirino, Associate Editor
Brooke Knisley, Production Assistant

Printed in the United States of America

ISBN: 978-1-5165-1433-5 (pbk) / 978-1-5165-1434-2 (br)

cognella® | PRESS

For the love of my life, Emily, and our beautiful son, Cooper

TABLE OF CONTENTS

ACKNOWLEDGMENTS vii

CH. 1 MARKETS AND THE NECESSITY OF SCARCITY 1

1.0 Overview: The Concept of Scarcity 2
1.1 The Necessity of Scarcity for Markets to Function 2
1.2 The Systems-View Approach to the Market and the Butterfly Effect 5
Case Study: The Heritage Foundation's Annual Index of Economic Freedom for 2014 8
1.3 The Layers of an Onion: The Circular Flow of Income Model 12
1.4 Conclusion: The Importance of Micro Markets in the Study of Macroeconomics and Well-Being 14
Questions for Class Discussion 16

CH. 2 OPPORTUNITY COSTS AND PPFS: ALL CHOICES ARE BAD ONES, AND ALL BAD CHOICES ARE EXPLOITABLE 19

2.0 All Choices Are Bad Ones! 20
2.1 Measuring the Opportunity Costs of Trade-Offs 21
2.2 Working with the PPF under Constant Costs: Benefits of Specialization and Exchange 25
2.3 A Realistic Approach to the PPF and the Law of Increasing Costs 33
2.4 Conclusion: The PPF and the Macroeconomic Picture 36
Case Study: Canada's "Staples Trap": Consequences from an Overreliance on Production Specialization 37
Questions for Class Discussion 39

CH. 3 SUPPLY, DEMAND, AND THE "INVISIBLE HAND" 41

3.0 Trading Opportunity Costs in the Marketplace to Gain More 42
3.1 Demand: The Law of Demand and the Determinants of Demand 43
3.2 Supply: The Law of Supply and the Market Determinants of Supply 48
3.3 The Complete Supply and Demand Model 52

3.4 Short Run to the Long Run: Market Forces and Changes in Equilibrium Prices and Quantities 55
3.5 Conclusion: The Supply and Demand Model and the Macroeconomic Environment 60
Case Study: Application of Supply and Demand Analysis: Behavior of Copper Futures (1997–1998 Asian Financial Crisis) 61
Questions for Class Discussion 62

CH. 4 THE MACRO ECONOMY: PUTTING THE MACRO BUILDING BLOCKS TOGETHER 65

4.0 Overview: Packaging the Micro into Macro Bundles 65
4.1 The Circular Flow Again (Closed and Open Economy): The Players and the Markets 67
4.2 The Components of GDP and Its Measurement: The National Expenditure Approach 72
4.3 Nominal vs. Real GDP and the Consumer Price Index 84
4.4 The Price Index and the Inflation Rate 87
4.5 Conclusion: Finding the Elusive Elixir to Grow Real GDP 91
Case Study: Can GDP Tells Us Anything about Overall Life Satisfaction? 92
Questions for Class Discussion 94

CH. 5 ECONOMIC GROWTH: CAN AN ECONOMY ALTER ITS DESTINY WITH JUST INVESTMENT? 97

5.0 Overview 97
5.1 The Business Cycle, Unemployment, and Real GDP per Capita 98
5.2 The Production Function, Savings, and Investment 102
5.3 Conclusion: It Takes More than the Investment of Savings to Support Economic Growth 118
*Case Study: Africa An Awakening Manufacturing Giant: "Can Cheetahs Beat Tigers"? (*Economist*, February 8, 2014)* 120
Questions for Class Discussion 121

CH. 6 THE KEYNESIAN CROSS AND THE MULTIPLIER 125

6.0 Overview 126
6.1 The National Income Identity, the Keynesian Cross, and the Relevance of Multipliers 127
6.2 Conclusion: "In the Long Run, We Are All Dead" 138
Case Study: The Multiplier and the Services Economy 139
Questions for Class Discussion 139

CH. 7 THE AGGREGATE DEMAND AND AGGREGATE SUPPLY MODEL: SHORT RUN TO THE LONG RUN 141

7.0 Overview 142
7.1 Aggregate Demand 144
7.2 Aggregate Supply and Long-Run Aggregate Supply 145
7.3 Long-Run Adjustment from Changes in Short-Run Equilibrium Levels of Output 147
7.4 Demand and Supply Shocks 149
7.5 Conclusion: If Markets Can Take Care of the Correction, Then Why Is There Intervention? 152
Case Study: Final Note on the Aggregate Demand and Aggregate Supply Model 155
Questions for Class Discussion 156

CH. 8 FISCAL AND MONETARY POLICY: SHORT-RUN MANAGEMENT OF THE BUSINESS CYCLE 159

8.0 Overview 159
8.1 A Quick Overview of the 2007–2009 Recession 161
8.2 Fiscal Policy: Responding to Output Gaps through Changes in Government Spending, Taxes, and Transfer Payments 165
8.3 Fiscal Policy and Closing Output Gaps 168
8.4 Monetary Policy: Managing Aggregate Demand through the Money Supply and the Interest Rate 172
8.5 Conclusion: Boom and Bust Tendencies of Macro Policy's Dance with the Long-Run 175
Case Study: "Much Ado about Multipliers" (Economist, *September 24, 2009)* 176
Questions for Class Discussion 177

CH. 9 THE OPEN MACRO ECONOMY: A BRIEF SYNOPSIS OF THE WEDDED RELATIONSHIP OF INTERNATIONAL TRADE AND FINANCE 179

9.0 Overview 179
9.1 International Trade: Revisiting Tom and Hank from Chapter 2 180
9.2 Externally Financing Domestic Consumption, Investment, and Government Expenditures 181
9.3 Conclusion 183
Case Study: Global Monetary System "Thrills and Spills" (Economist, *October 3, 2015)* 186
Questions for Class Discussion 187

CREDITS 189

ACKNOWLEDGMENTS

Without the support of friends, family, and a great publisher, this first endeavor in writing a textbook would never have gotten off the ground. I want to first thank God for instilling in my heart a passion for economics and the privilege and responsibility to be influential to a world of students in the classrooms in which I have had the honor of teaching.

I want to thank Zina Craft at Cognella Publishing for opening a door to the chance to reinvent my career as an economist as a textbook author, and I want to thank my managing editors, Monika Dziamka and Gem Rabanera, and project manager, Seidy Cruz, for their patience and belief in me as an author for this endeavor. The talent, management, and production teams at Cognella Publishing are exceptional, and I also want to thank Jess Busch for the creation of a textbook cover that really captured the spirit and intent of this project.

Without the support of family and friends, the first words in the first chapter of this textbook would not have made it to the computer screen. I want to thank my parents for being the best dad and mom in the world. I love you so much.

I want to thank my in-laws for being a rock of support for my wife, son, and me through some turbulent times over the past year. I consider you both more as my best friends than just my in-laws. I love you both more than you know.

To my brothers-in-law and sister-in-law, I want to say thank you for being great friends and an uncles and aunt to my son.

Finally, this book is dedicated to my beautiful wife and my amazing son. Honey, I love you so much and you are my dearest and best friend. You are a rock and sanctuary in my life that I am so blessed to have. Words cannot express how much I love you. Just thank you for loving me, being the best mom to our son, and putting up with the craziness of our lives. You are my person!!! And, to my wonderful son, I love you to the moon and back. I love being your dad and I can't wait to see your dreams come true.

CHAPTER 1

MARKETS AND THE NECESSITY OF SCARCITY

Figure 1.0. Scarcity in action. Common problematic traffic congestion in Lagos, Nigeria. Such common traffic congestion affects and creates market rivalries and opportunities in an environment of scarcity.

1.0 OVERVIEW: THE CONCEPT OF SCARCITY

A cornerstone of economics is the study of choices in an environment of resource scarcity. At any given time, the economic environments in which we participate are constrained by a finite amount of resources available domestic and globally. There just are not enough resources to go around to satisfy the unlimited needs and wants of humans on this planet. Scarcity in its varying degrees is everywhere and inescapable. Even with the best market management of scarce resources and the scarce opportunities being produced from them, humans will always be confronted with economic scarcity. How we innovate to tackle this ongoing problem is important in the study of economic choices being made at every level for the improvement of human well-being in highly competitive environments. If the scarcity of resources makes goods and service scarce, then in all market environments there will be an unequal and finite amount of exploitable opportunities. The introductory image (Image 1.1) of daily traffic congestion in Lagos, Nigeria, illustrates the role scarcity plays in making market opportunities unequal and highly competitive as well for the creation of new market opportunities to be exploited. Scarcity is a set of economic constraints ready to be exploited.

Observable in the provided image is a road network without enough transportation capacity to handle the flow of people and traffic in and out of market centers. Daily traffic jams like the one in Lagos have the effect of a winter storm shutting down a major metropolitan city. The stoppage and congestion will decrease the potential transactions taking place in a given day, raise the cost of transportation and conducting business, contribute to costly inflation in the price of goods and services, and reduce the size of the economic pie. Yet the same traffic jam provides an exploitable opportunity for sellers in the pedestrian traffic. With the traffic jam delaying buyers and sellers from reaching the market center to conduct exchanges, sellers who are mobile can bring the market to buyers waiting in the cars and trucks. The scarcity in road space presents other exploitable opportunities that have the potential to reduce road congestion, make for better coordination of traffic flows, reduce transportation costs affecting delivery and final market prices for goods and services, attract new business development into the vicinity, raise returns to society, lift economic welfare, and so on. It is as if scarcity is a "necessary evil" for the sole purpose of supporting exploitable opportunities and sustaining market activity best suited to exploit such opportunities.

Economists want to study the approaches households, firms, and even governments take in addressing problematic situations like the daily traffic jam in Lagos. For example, what capital investments would need to be made in the existing road space to add capacity and better manage the flow of traffic? Or what new traffic and pedestrian laws (i.e., regulation) should be applied to encourage preferred traffic and pedestrian behavior that is favorable to market success and efficiency? In a constrained resource world, the economist will wish to examine the actions households, firms, and even governments execute in order to exploit opportunities, maximize the gains, and use the gains to leverage growth drivers. Using scarce resources and creating opportunities with them that are just as scarce, it is absolutely amazing how economic growth takes place in any form. Scarcity just might be one of the strongest human motivators to innovate and survive.

1.1 THE NECESSITY OF SCARCITY FOR MARKETS TO FUNCTION

If the goal of any economy is to create growth and translate such growth into the "lifting of boats" or the improvement of well-being for as many persons in the economic environment as possible, then there will be some difficult questions in need of answering to best determine how finite resources will be managed and used. What type of economic system(s) will be preferred to drive income growth and increase society's standard of living? How will finite resources be allocated for the best appropriate use, and how will it be ensured that such resources being allocated are used in the most productive way to add more to the marketplace for societies to work with? In all this, will economic goals trump societal goals, or will societal goals trump economic goals, affecting the trade-off between the efficient versus equitable allocation of resources for the creation of wealth? And how will markets function to transform wealth created into income flows that hopefully will be used to create more exploitable opportunities to the benefit of the lowest economic layers of an economy?

In these finite market environments, everyone will have choices requiring everyone to trade one set or sets of opportunities for another set or sets of opportunities. The trade-offs made will affect the benefits and costs of the choices being made to the decision maker as well as to society. Addressing scarcity in one area will create scarcity in other areas, thereby making scarcity inescapable. The presence of scarcity reinforces the incentives for human beings to exploit trade and exchanges that address scarcity and innovate ways to diminish it broadly. In sum, all choices are bad ones because all opportunities have costs. Yet the necessary evil of scarcity will support the signaling of market opportunities to incentivize humans to create and serve more. Without scarcity, humans would be incentivized to do things much differently and by far to do much less.

Defining a Market to Exploit Scarce Opportunities

In consideration of the above, there is a need to examine the function of markets for the coordination and exploitation of unlimited human needs and wants with finite resources. Using the web search engine Google, when "definition of market" is entered, 232 million results are found. According to *Dictionary.com®*, the definition of *market* as a noun is given as follows:

> An **open** place or a covered building where buyers and sellers convene for the sale of goods; a marketplace: *a farmers' market.*
>
> A store for the sale of food: *a meat market.*
>
> A meeting of people for selling and buying.
>
> The assemblage of people at such a meeting.
>
> Trade or traffic, especially as regards a particular commodity: *the market in cotton.*

According to these definitions provided on *Dictionary.com*, a market must be a physical location where goods are sold and persons assemble to meet and engage in trade for food and other commodities. However, on the website Investopedia, we are given the following definition of *market* as a noun:

> A medium that allows buyers and sellers of a specific good or service to interact in order to facilitate an exchange. The price that individuals pay during the transaction may be determined by a number of factors, but price is often determined by the forces of supply and demand.
>
> The general market where securities are traded.
>
> People with the desire and ability to buy a specific product/service.

According to these definitions, a market is a medium not limited by visible physical location. Exchanges in financial securities will take place as a function of prices, and these exchanges will be determined by market forces of supply and demand. In broad terms, this definition precludes a market as a general meeting place of persons. Rather, a market is a meeting place (physical or virtual) of persons that have both the willingness and ability to participate in the buying and selling of a specific product and/or service. Market outcomes will be dictated by participation, which penalizes nonparticipation.

So which definition is more accurate? With 232 million hits on the web for "definition of market," there is no clear consensus of what is an appropriate definition of the term. Markets vary in number, type, and functionality. Contract law between parties and court systems are used to narrowly or broadly define the terms and boundaries of a market and the expected market performance in which parties agree to operate.

In the United States, the US Census Bureau acts as the custodian of market definitions used in contract law. In a globalized economy, the most frequently used definitions have somewhat changed the classification of markets with the implementation of the North American Free Trade Agreement (NAFTA). The underlying logic for market classification as opposed to definition allows the Census Bureau to categorize the output of U.S. business into broad sectors of the economy: manufacturing, primary metals, agriculture, forestry, and so forth.[1] Each business output category is given a numeric code for use in the National American Industry Classification System (NAICS) as shown in the table below in Table 1.1. Each sector is subdivided and given a two-digit code, and each subdivided sector is subdivided further into three-digit, four-digit, five-digit, and six-digit code levels, with each additional digit added to represent a further subdivision of its initial classification.

The 20 Broad Sectors of the NAICS

Code	NAICS Sectors	Count
11	Agriculture, Forestry, Fishing and Hunting	553,708
21	Mining	37,975
22	Utilities	37,237
23	Construction	1,837,084
31–33	Manufacturing	762,527
42	Wholesale Trade	929,149
44–45	Retail Trade	2,206,681
48–49	Transportation and Warehousing	564,026
51	Information	410,057
52	Finance and Insurance	817,617
53	Real Estate Rental and Leasing	929,217
54	Professional, Scientific, and Technical Services	2,648,062
55	Management of Companies and Enterprises	53,806
56	Administrative and Support and Waste Management and Remediation Services	3,372,309
61	Educational Services	402,000
62	Health Care and Social Assistance	1,611,468
71	Arts, Entertainment, and Recreation	359,010
72	Accommodation and Food Services	869,948
81	Other Services (except Public Administration)	2,174,657
92	Public Administration	299,778

Table 1.1. The North American Industry Classification System (NAICS) categorizes the output of U.S. business into broad sectors of the macro economy. Source: North American Industry Classification System (2014).

This classification process permits the construction of data on industry output only, excluding consumer markets and deeper industry relationships that are reflected in horizontal and vertical relationships. This process of classification allows users to "define" a market as they see suitable in very broad or narrow terms. This is a useful approach since markets are not static and are always transforming in and beyond the scope of contractual arrangements used

[1] Pepall, L., Richards, D., and Norman, G. 2008. *Industrial Organization: Contemporary Theory and Empirical Applications*. 4th ed. Hoboken, NJ: Wiley-Blackwell.

to dictate market structure, behavior, and performance. Despite the large availability of data, economists continue to disagree on the appropriate merits that determine what a market is and continue their work without a clear consensus.

Since there are numerous "markets" around the world organized differently for different functions and needs, observing markets through a systems-view approach should help the understanding of the resource coordination problems economies face in their attempts to maximize gains from exploitable opportunities in an environment of scarcity while managing the delicate balancing act of economic goals with social ones.

This systems-view approach will not take a purist view of markets as limited to geography, products, industries, marketing channels, and so forth. In a modern global economy, multinational enterprises are not limited by geography. Industries today are a mix of vertical and horizontal integration along supply chains that bisect national boundaries and blur the boundaries between the firm and marketplace. And single products are more differentiated and segmented, adding depth, breadth, and variety through overlapping marketing channels.

Using a systems-view approach, this text will examine the macroeconomic environment as the whole market and like an onion, treating the overlapping layers of an onion as the overlapping micro economies that shape the macroeconomic picture of countries and the global economy. Connections will be treated as important, and choices made in any part of the globe will filter through the global economy, affecting everything and anything under the sun. By examining it all through the prism of the global economy, this will better prepare the user of the approach to examine the efficacy of policy approaches to macroeconomic goals and issues connecting us to the world stage and the players that are on it.

1.2 THE SYSTEMS-VIEW APPROACH TO THE MARKET AND THE BUTTERFLY EFFECT

The systems-view approach will provide better comprehension of the full complexities of the interconnected relationships of micro economies that shape macro economies and the performance of the broader global economy. To avoid the risk of looking at a macro economy in isolation from the world, or looking at a micro market in isolation from other micro markets, the systems-view approach will allow deconstruction of the macro view to a micro level. Since there is no clear consensus on what constitutes a market definition, a systems-view approach will better capture the variety of market descriptions, the interconnectedness, and reasons why predicted results of basic economic models and principles may exceed or fall short of what is expected to be observed.

Before Organizing a Market, There Are Some Questions to Ask and Answer

There are many questions that have to be answered regarding how best to organize an environment that will create numerous exploitable opportunities using finite resources available. At the core of addressing resource and opportunity scarcity are four basic questions asked first by an economy's participants. How these questions are answered in the private and public domain will shape responses to newer questions that often dominate the political-economy debate. The questions are:

What will be produced?

How will it be produced?

Who will produce it?

For whom will it be produced?

The systems-view approach demands different types of economic subsystems that will best organize market architecture and market activities to answer these four questions. In a complete system, will some subsystems be a composition of capitalist economic systems in which all four questions are answered through competitive rivalry in a private market? Or will some market subsystems be command economies in which the state—as the owner of the resources of production and the wealth created with them—answers these questions on the behalf of representation of its citizenry?

A Snapshot of a Capitalist Economy Subsystem

In a capitalist system, the role of government in the market place is limited. The government allows business to do what it does best so long as outcomes are efficient, market failure is minimal, and what market failure occurs will self-correct privately through exploitable opportunities. In such systems, property rights play the fundamental role in the creation, sale, exchange, and disposal of output and other forms of wealth. Legal claims on income (wages, interest, rents, and profits) are enforced through property contracts recognized under the rule of business and contract law and enforced by a mature and transparent court system. The high degree of competition in a supposed free or frictionless marketplace allows for a self-regulating market organized through formal and informal relationships balancing out cooperative and non-cooperative behavior in the interest of maintaining an acceptable normalized distribution of market power among participating economic actors (i.e., firms, persons, and so on).

The lack of regulated interference by government in a market that is expected to be self-regulating is expected to yield efficient outcomes that are both profit maximizing to the participants and welfare maximizing to society. Viewing scarcity as opportunity of unmet needs and wants, the capitalist serves society as a job creator, employing private labor with capital investments to produce output and paying labor the sellable market value of its production share. Self-interest and self-preservation will guide how each of the four questions will be answered privately to serve the self-preservation of many. Ownership is "king," and the creation of private security should strengthen public security by penalizing nonparticipation and free-riding behavior.

A Snapshot of a Command Economy Subsystem

In a purist command economy, the output of the economy is planned, and how resources are used and the gains rationed among society members will be dictated by a command authority that owns the resources on behalf of the public. Private property rights and private ownership of the factors of production are subordinate to the interest of the state and how it wishes economic scarcity to be managed. The state's ownership of the factors of production—land, labor, and capital—is legitimized through legal and sometimes illegitimate power.

Where the economic agents in a capitalist economy would answer those important four questions through private organization to meet private needs and wants, the nation-state answers the questions based on what it decides is best for its citizens and its own special interest. The production of output is planned and coordinated through state-owned enterprises to meet state goals and objectives first. Output and the income from it is rationed to persons or groups according to need or special interest, without reliance on a pricing mechanism to best ration scarce resources, scarce opportunities, and scarce goods to those most willing to pay for them and make productive use of them in alternative ways.

The profit motive in this system is deemphasized or nullified, and the equitable distribution of output and of income is seen as most important for the control of social mobility and the limiting of private opportunistic behavior that would raise personal welfare at the expense of society. Equitable outcomes are treated as paramount to efficient ones. Equitable redistribution of income and goods and services (decided by the state) is "king," and the marketplace is viewed as a welfare state with the assumption that economic actors will act first in the interest of the society before themselves.

The Alternative Market Mix and Market Principles

The provided choices of economic subsystems represent very extreme opposing ends of an economic spectrum reflecting an extreme management of self-maximizing, opportunistic human behavior in its organization and management of a system of choices (private and public) for the management, diminishment, and exploitation of resource scarcity. Each type of system in its purist form has shown through its own economic history to have experienced successes and failures. Pure capitalist systems are seen to be more prone to boom and bust business cycles amplifying income and wealth divisions in society, and pure command economy systems are seen to be more prone to market failure complemented by poorer growth derived from inferior consumption and investment, the lack of enforceable property rights (public and private), and lack of mature government institutions capable of delivering necessary public services (i.e., waste management, utilities [water and electricity], education, law enforcement, and so on).

Both economic systems favor certain types of opportunistic behavior for the exploitation of opportunities. Observations of countries in the global economy show that developed, developing, and emerging market economies are characterized by a mix of coordinated private and public elements to achieve outcomes representing the most optimal balance of trade-offs between efficiency and equity.

Each element is implemented in varying degrees across market spectrums to act as a "balance of power" check on human choice that is incentivized to varying degrees in each economic system. In any economy, the composition of the elements—the private marketplace versus the public marketplace and how the two will interact cooperatively or non-cooperatively—will vary in weight according to public and private preference, making economic and social goals mutually inclusive. Table 1.2 illustrates the concepts of the types of economic systems based on the treatment and freedom of human choice among individuals and firms in the marketplace.

Management of Economic Choices in the Marketplace	Type of Economic System
Customs	Traditional Economy
Consumers and Producers	Free Market/Capitalist
Government	Command/Socialist
Consumers, Producers, and Government	Mixed Economy

Table 1.2. A concept of different economic systems. Each economic system will emphasize which actors in the economy will be responsible for the management of choices in an environment of scarcity. The economic system type and its design will guide the actors in how four very important questions will be answered. These questions are: (1) What will be produced? (2) How will it be produced? (3) Who will produce it? (4) And, for whom will it be produced?

The mix of private and public market elements in a country's economy will be shaped by its economic history, culture, geography, availability of critical resources, level and path of development, historical government type, war, and so on. The degree and management of resource scarcity relative to geographical and population size will have a big influence on government type. Highly developed economies with more democratic-style governments have shown to be more organized around private elements, and less-developed economies with more authoritarian-style governments have shown to be more organized around command elements. This observation suggests that more-developed economies have a higher degree of freedom in economic choice, relative to less-developed economies. If this is the case, then this observation should hold in calculated economic freedom indices for countries.

CASE STUDY: THE HERITAGE FOUNDATION'S ANNUAL INDEX OF ECONOMIC FREEDOM FOR 2014

The Heritage Foundation's annual Index of Economic Freedom focuses on four key aspects of an economic environment that a country's government exercises some policy control over, affecting the type and behavior of the country's economic system and treatment of economic choices under its system.

The index measures ten specific components of economic freedom, and scores are scaled from 0 to 100. Scores of 50 to 100 indicate economies that are free, and scores of 0 to 49.9 indicate economies that are repressed. The identified ten specific components of economic freedom have been categorized into four key aspects of a country's economic environment that a country's government exercises control over (Table 1.3).[2]

Economic Environment of Policy Locus	Components of Economic Freedom Affected by Level of Policy Control
The rule of law	Enforcement and protection of property rights
	Freedom from corruption
Government size	Fiscal freedom
	Government spending
Regulatory efficiency	Business freedom
	Labor freedom
	Monetary freedom
Market openness	Trade freedom
	Investment restrictions
	Financial freedom

Table 1.3

Source: Heritage Foundation's 2014 Index of Economic Freedom.

A review of the Heritage Foundation's calculated economic freedom scores and country rankings for 2014 reveal some interesting results illustrated in Figure 1.1. Economies of Hong Kong (90.1, number 1), Singapore (89.4, number 2), Australia (82.0, number 3), Switzerland (81.6, number 4), New Zealand (81.2, number 5), and Canada (80.2, number 6) are highly developed and the most free. This is expected, since these countries favor democratic-style governments. However, none of these economies are even in the top ten largest economies in the world. Hong Kong's high openness to trade explains why its trade side elevates the country's calculated economic freedom index. Australia makes the list due to desolate geography and the economic activity of the country's largest cities: Sydney, Brisbane, Melbourne, and Canberra.

The economies of Chile (78.7, number 7), Ireland (76.2, number 9), United States (75.5, number 12), Bahrain (75.1, number 13), United Kingdom (74.9, number 14), Botswana (72.0, number 27), United Arab Emirates (71.4, number 28), and Columbia (70.7, number 34) are ranked as mostly free but also represent a diverse mix of economies in terms of market and resource size, participation in the global economy, and government system type from democracy to monarchy. The United States is the world's largest economy, with a 2013 Gross Domestic Product (GDP) of $16.8 trillion; Columbia is ranked number 30 in the world by economic size, with a 2013

[2] An explanation of the Heritage Foundation's methodological approach for this index calculation can be found at: http://www.heritage.org/index/book/methodology.

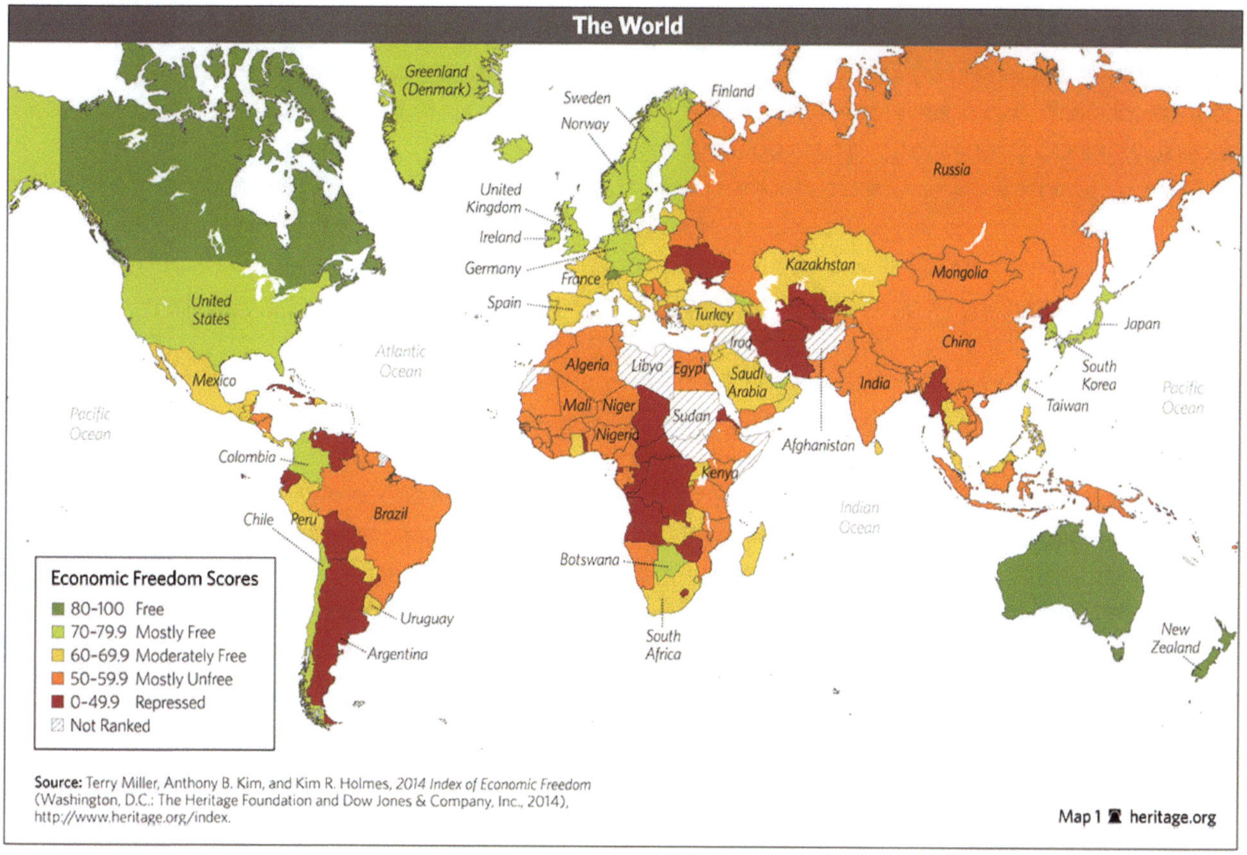

Figure 1.1. 2014 Index of Economic Freedom World Map.

GDP of $381.8 billion; and Botswana is ranked number 117, with 2013 GDP of $14.8 billion. With the exception of the United States, healthy economic freedom has not equivocally translated into larger economic size for all the economies ranked as mostly free. This suggests, outside of economic freedom and economic system type, a need to examine factors that are more responsible for a country's long-run growth potential and why countries ranked as mostly free economically may grow more slowly than those countries ranked as mostly unfree economically.

The above inference is further supported when examining the economic freedom rankings of the world's second-, eighth-, and eleventh-largest economies ranked as most unfree economically. China, with a 2013 GDP of $9.3 trillion, is the world's second-largest economy. The country's government is a single-party Communist government system with little more than 80 percent of its domestic output produced by state-managed firms. The economy's market privatization schemes are quite tied into the country's centrally planned elements as reflected in its industrial policy. China has a 2014 economic freedom score of 52.5 and an economic freedom ranking of number 137. India is the world's eighth-largest economy and world's largest democracy by geography and population size. It has an economic freedom score of 55.7 and an economic freedom ranking of number 120. And finally, Russia, the world's eleventh-largest economy, with a 2013 GDP of $2.1 trillion, is a former Communist command economy with a parliamentary-style government that is more autocratic. Russia has an economic freedom score of 51.9 with an economic freedom ranking of number 140.

All three economies are geographically large, have large resource bases, are large global recipients of foreign direct investment (with China being the largest), and are highly integrated into the world economy through trade and international finance. For these economies, the size of their respective resource endowments and their economic systems that manage and exploit these endowments play a more fundamental role in their economic strength, geopolitical reach, and potential size. This does not mean that lacking a high degree of economic freedom will necessarily handicap the long-run growth path of these economies.

Our most economically repressed economies are Iran (40.3, number 173), Eritrea (38.5, number 174), Venezuela (36.3, number 175), Zimbabwe (35.5, number 176), Cuba (28.7, number 177), and North Korea (1.0, number 178). Economies that were not ranked were Liechtenstein and the war-torn economies Afghanistan, Iraq, Kosovo, Libya, Somalia, Sudan, and Syria. Of our most-repressed economies, Iran and Venezuela are oil-rich economies with highly mismanaged administrations that have burdensome subsidization schemes and penalizing economic sanctions. Cuba and North Korea are the most isolated countries by choice and international embargoes and economic sanctions. All these economies have highly autocratic governments that are, by any simple measurement, economically repressive under rule of law and political corruption.

Figures 1.1 and 1.2 help illustrate that countries with a higher degree of economic freedom experience higher degrees of standard of living as reflected in higher GDP per-capita (per person) statistics. This means that countries with more repressive economic systems will experience a higher degree of poverty intensity across their population. Figure 1.2 suggests that mostly free economies should experience GDP per-capita some 130 percent higher than moderately free economies and 582 percent higher than mostly unfree economies.

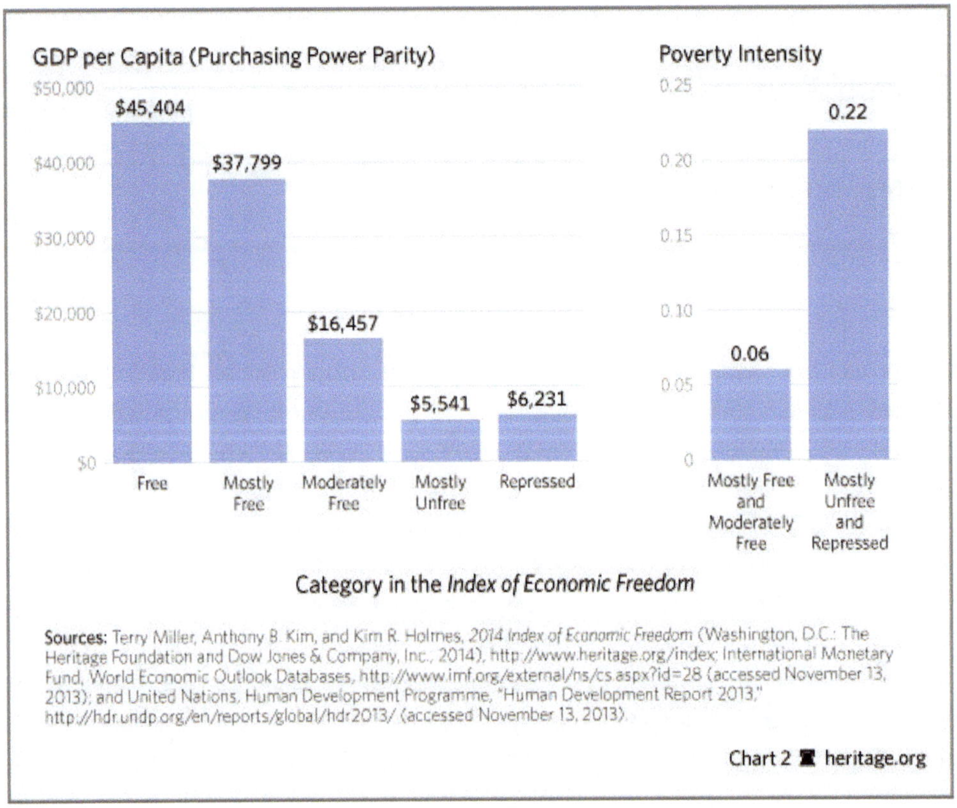

Figure 1.2. Economic Freedom, Standard of Living, and Poverty.

Sources: Terry Miller, Anthony B. Kim, and Kim R. Holmes, 2014 Index of Economic Freedom (Washington DC: The Heritage Foundation and Dow Jones & Copmany, Inc. 2014) http://www.heritage.org/index; International Monetary Fund, World Economic Outlook Databases, http://www.imf.org/external/ns/cs.aspx?id=28 (accessed November 13, 2013); and United Nations, Human Development Programme, "Human Development Report 2013," http://hdr.undp.org/en/reports/global/hdr2013/ (accessed November 13, 2013).

The Function of Markets in Principle for the Efficient Exploitation of Scarce Resources and Scarce Opportunities

Without diving into the politicized discussion of private versus public economies, a mixed marketplace should function along four tenets:

1. Serve as a medium to coordinate activities in response to private and public incentives signaling unlimited needs and wants in a resource-constrained environment.
2. Serve as a medium for the allocation of scarce resources through the use of a pricing mechanism (regulated or non-regulated) or adoption of some acceptable private and/or public practice.
3. Make use of a pricing mechanism for the allocation of scarce resources or adoption of some type of acceptable private or public practice for the allocation of resources—land, labor, and capital—to persons or entities that will make for the most productive use of such resources.
4. Create exploitable trade and exchange opportunities for participants that will maximize private and public gains and returns to society.

At first glance, the four listed tenets of the principle function of markets sound quite ideal and orderly. This would work well in a marketplace providing 100 percent public disclosure of perfect information; all potential gains and potential losses are accounted for to participants; and economic participants could not exercise any degree of market power to gain an advantage at the expense of other participants. Our world, in which we attempt to demonstrate the idealism of these tenets, is much different. The world is chaotic, guided by a different underlying order that humans often attempt to control.

The systems view of the marketplace and the broader global economy must take into account an orderly chaos that surrounds market activity. This is better known as the *butterfly effect*. According to *Merriam-Webster Dictionary* the butterfly effect is described as follows:

> *"a property of chaotic systems (as the atmosphere) by which small changes in initial conditions can lead to large-scale and unpredictable variation in the future state of the system".*[3]

The Butterfly Effect in an Example

Consider the following hypothetical situation to apply the concept of the butterfly effect. Let's say in country X the predominant output of the country is coffee, and during the course of a year, climate or weather changes in country X have now yielded much lower than expected coffee harvests. This has resulted in a higher price of coffee per pound in country X and a higher domestic level of inflation. Since the coffee industry is the predominant employer of resources and output of country X, this situation will affect the overall level of aggregate prices in country X.

Country Y is a large importer of coffee and other goods from country X, and these goods and coffee from country X enter country Y via maritime trade. As the price of coffee in country X rises, it also raises the value-to-weight ratio of what is moved on a tanker ship from country X. Observing the increase in the inflated value of coffee, maritime shipping firms moving coffee out of country X will raise their price to ship coffee in order to capture a share of the increase in the nominal market value of coffee. This causes the maritime transport costs from country X to Y to rise and makes all goods on the ship more expensive when entering country Y before any import tax is applied.

---

[3] The name of the effect was coined by meteorologist, Edward Lorenz. Working with a simple heat convection model, Lorenz discovered of a level of unpredictability in the model. He ascertained this level of unpredictability would make long-range weather forecasting impossible. He illustrated this point using the example of how the flapping of a butterfly's wings would alter atmospheric conditions and change weather patterns. Source: https://www.technologyreview.com/s/422809/when-the-butterfly-effect-took-flight/

Once country Y imposes its tariff on imported coffee from country X, coffee is even more expensive, as evident from the double-markup effect of the higher transport costs and import tax.

Not only has coffee entered country Y more expensive, but so have the remaining goods from country X arriving on the same ship. The higher price of coffee in country X, the higher transport costs from the nominally higher value-to-weight ratio, and the import tax will show in higher retail prices for coffee and coffee products downstream in country Y.[4]

On the consumption side, let's say the rise in the price of retail coffee and coffee products now rivals or equals the price per gallon of gas domestically in country Y. In response to higher coffee prices and the necessity to drive, consumers spend less on coffee and everything else, since more expensive coffee has raised the overall price level in country Y. Let's also finish the example and armchair analysis and say that country Y is a large importer of goods from country Z. With consumers in country Y cutting back on consumption due to a decrease in purchasing power created from higher import prices driven by higher imported coffee prices from country X, this will translate into weaker exports to country Y from country Z, where country Z's export industries constitute the biggest source of employment of country Z's middle class. As a result, the purchasing power and earnings to the middle class in country Z will be reduced in a marginal way.

In the constructed hypothetical example, the butterfly effect helps explain why a small change in one variable in one part of the world (the rise in coffee prices in country X) sets off a chain reaction of events. The transmission of new information signals through marketplaces altered the consumption patterns of participants in an import country (country Y) and affected the overall welfare of workers in a third country (country Z). The change in initial conditions in coffee prices in country X set off a chain of events that altered conditions in the market for all things in countries Y and Z and resulted in a new equilibrium condition that becomes a new initial steady state from which the economy starts.

The events above in our hypothetical butterfly effect example are connected like layers in the onion analogy that best describe the systems-view approach. Each onion layer's integrity is affected by the integrity of other layers; just as rot in one onion layer will spread through other layers and spoil the entire onion. With the onion layers acting as the market architecture, each overlapping layer creates a final system, which will be the macro economy.

1.3 THE LAYERS OF AN ONION: THE CIRCULAR FLOW OF INCOME MODEL

An important goal of the systems-view approach to the macro economy is the ability to deconstruct the macro market into a multitude of micro market segments that can be examined independently or interconnected through respective market relationships. The analogous use of an onion as a macro economy will treat the fibers of each layer of the onion as a web of micro markets made up of participating economic agents whose behavior, needs, and wants are driven by incentives that are coordinated through well-organized market structure(s). The circular flow of income (CFI) diagram demonstrates a useful visual of the overlapping elements much like the layers-of-an-onion analogy (Figure 1.3).

The CFI Diagram (Closed Economy)

The CFI diagram illustrates the transactions that take place in the broader economy by mapping the flow of income and payments among the interactive participation of economic actors around a circle. For simplicity, the

[4] Assuming country Y's export prices have not risen, its terms of trade and purchasing power have worsened, since import prices have risen relative to earned export prices.

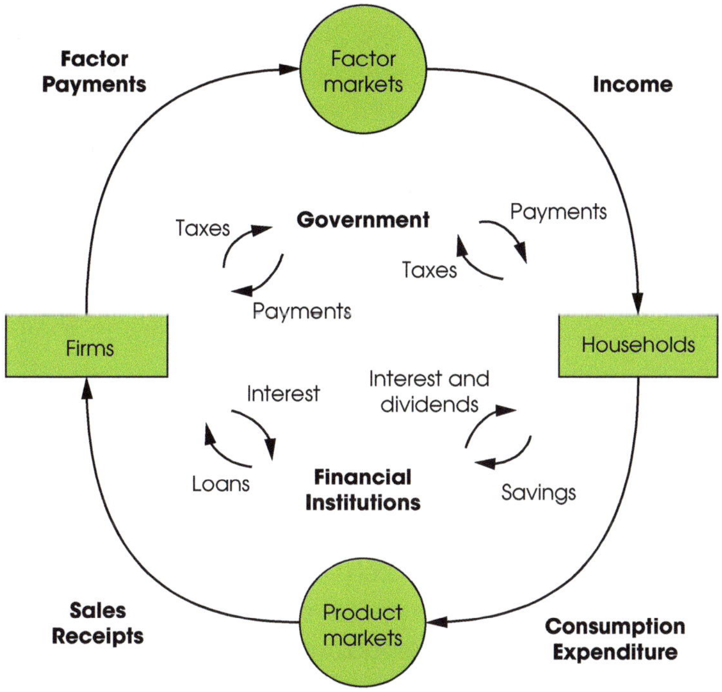

Figure 1.3. A. diagram of the circular flow of income between households and firms via factor and product markets. Savings as a fraction of wages, interest, rent, and profits earned will be translated into loanable funds via indirect and direct financing channels to be used for consumption and investment (public and private). A share of the income stream captured by households and firms will be collected as taxes by the government and used for government purchases of private goods and services; it will be redistributed to households and firms through a tax system (if there is one) and social insurance schemes.

above diagram treats the overall macroeconomic system as a closed economy with no trade.[5] In the diagram, the broader economy will be one ring (the macro economy) as the summation of various interconnecting rings (the many micro markets), with each ring mapping the flow of income and payments among participants in a given ring and across rings.

In the model of a closed macroeconomic system, the simple economy of overlapping micro markets is made up of four organized inhabitants—households, firms, government, and financial institutions—and will constitute the building blocks of the economic aggregates for the national income identity introduced in Chapter 4. Any domicile made up of one or more group of persons that share income is a household. In most but not all cases, this will be a family. And, any organization employing the factors of production supplied by households for the production and sale of goods and services in exchange for payments (wages, interest, rent, and profits) will be a firm.

For a closed macro economy, there will be no trade and no cross-border inflows and outflows of payments and income such that expenditures on final goods and services stay domestic. The inhabitants—households and firms—interact with each other between two different markets: a factors (resources) market and a market for goods and services.

Households will be the owners of the factors of production: land, labor, and capital. Households will supply these factors of production to a factors market, and firms will enter these markets to pay for the employment of these factors

[5] In future chapters, this CFI diagram will be expanded to an open economy that allows for the flow of goods, services, payments, and income across borders.

to be used to produce output that will be supplied to goods and services markets for members of households to expend on and consume.

In exchange for the employment of resources (factors) used to produce output, households are paid income based on the market value of the share of output they produce. These payments (constituting a share of sales revenue and borrowed funds) will take the form of wages, interest on borrowed funds for production assets owned, rental payments on the use of capital that is leased, and dividends as a share of paid profits not reinvested by firms. Households will use these payments to purchase goods and services they have produced, and firms will earn sales revenue that they will use to pay out on the employment of their resources and pay back borrowed funds used to pay for the employment of resources and to make investments.

In the middle of the CFI diagram are the remaining two inhabitants—government and financial institutions. In the model, the government acts an economic agent in three forms: buyer, taxer, and regulator. As a buyer, the government purchases from the private market goods and services paid for with taxes earned on income streams of households and firms. Of the taxes collected and not spent on final goods, remaining taxes are redistributed to households and firms for allocation to consumption and investment spending. In the case of financial markets, the income—wages, rent, interest, and dividends—that households do not spend on goods and services will be saved and translated into loanable funds loaned to firms to pay out current and future income contracts to households, pay out tax obligations owed and coming due (households will also borrow for the payment of taxes), and to invest in capital for added production capacity.[6]

An interesting observation from Figure 1.3 depicts the government as a buyer of goods and services and a redistributor of taxes collected on earned income by households and firms. Unlike firms, the government in the CFI diagram is not depicted as a producer of goods and services, and unlike households it is not an owner/supplier of the factors of production. Placing the government in the middle of the diagram makes it a competitive borrower of scarce savings in the marketplace.[7]

Providing a frictionless marketplace, the CFI model illustrates that (for closed and open economies) output produced and translated into a flow of income streams is simply recycled through market participation (directly and indirectly) so that total expenditures will equal total output and income in the long run. Yet in an environment of economic scarcity with resources being finite and thereby making the availability of economic opportunities to be exploited unequal, users of the CFI diagram will want to know more about how well micro markets across the broader macro economy allocate the distribution of gains as wells as losses among households and firms, affecting the performance of micro markets that will shape the performance of the macro economy.

1.4 CONCLUSION: THE IMPORTANCE OF MICRO MARKETS IN THE STUDY OF MACROECONOMICS AND WELL-BEING

Scarcity exists, and when capitalized on in efficient ways, exploitable opportunities will emerge that create wealth. In a well-functioning economy with well-functioning markets, such wealth can be translated into income streams raising income per person and standard of living per household. In an odd way, scarcity creates opportunities for growth, reinforcing the human incentive to create and add more, as will be seen in Chapter 2 and Chapter 5.

---

[6] For later chapters in the text, the function and role of financial markets and financial intermediaries to economies for the transformation of savings into investment will be examined.

[7] In the chapters covering savings, investment, and fiscal policy, the impact of government borrowing on domestic and world interest rates affecting investment will be discussed.

The choice of economic system for the management and exploitation of scarcity will greatly impact the role choices (private and public) will have on individual well-being, employment, wealth and income creation, composition of transactional and transformation activities, inflation, and sustainability (resources, environment, debt, and so on). Outside of the defense-driven economic growth rates of the United States and former Soviet Union during the Cold War years (and each country experienced consequences—good and bad—from the mobilization of resources around a defense output race), command economic systems in the purist state-centric form have shown to be the worst performing across many statistical measurements.

Figure 1.4 highlights the grave economic performance difference between the neighboring economies of South Korea and North Korea. The figure illustrates the consequence North Korea's militarized and closed command economy has had on the performance change in its real output per-person as reflected in the persistent severe economic scarcity being reinforced but never allowed to be capitalized on and exploited to raise well-being.

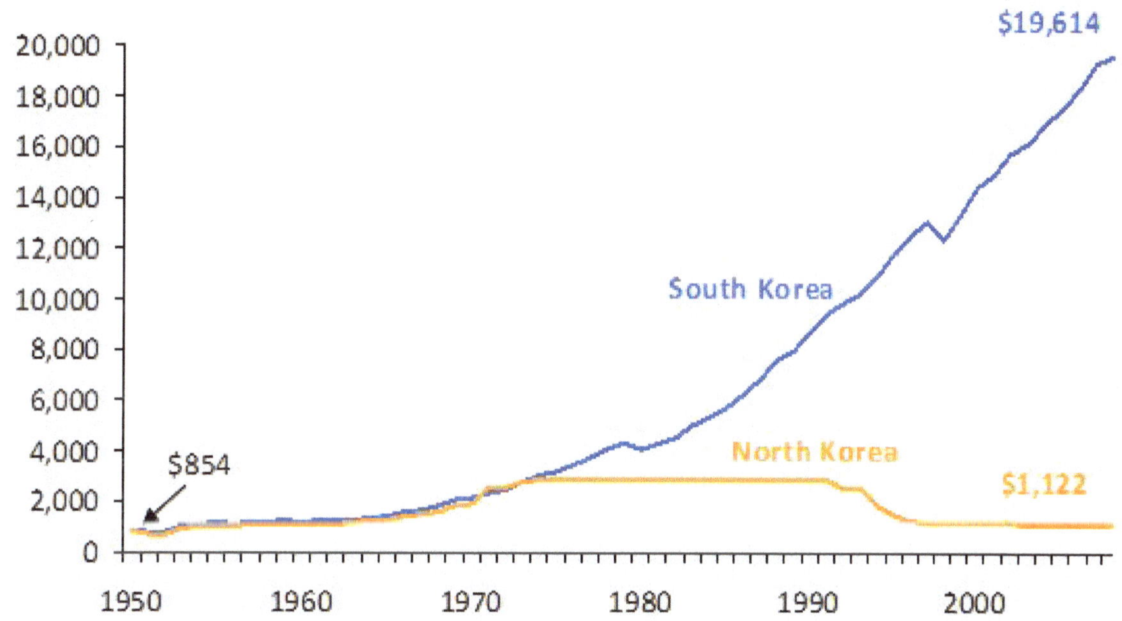

Figure 1.4. Institutions Matter: Real Per Capita GDP in North and South Korea (1990 International Dollars).

Source: www.intellectualtakeout.org/library/chart-graph/institutions-matter-real-capita-gdp-north-and-south-korea

The costs associated with scarcity cannot be extinguished, just diminished through innovative changes in how humans use resources, produce, transact, travel, live, and so on. As the CFI model illustrates, through the competitive interaction of economic actors around scarce income streams from scarce opportunities, the costs and benefits of scarcity are just being shifted here and there through a competitive rationing called a marketplace. Outcomes may be considered efficient in aggregate market terms but highly inequitable at a number of socioeconomic and micro market levels.[8]

[8] It should be noted here that a market experiencing a wealth and income divide might actually constitute a market working well and efficiently. A discussion of trade-offs and associated opportunity costs in the next chapter will shed light on this statement and help show how the measurable outcomes of the trade-offs made will best improve the allocation of scarce resources for future use.

The CFI model makes evident and argues that a study of the macro economy and macroeconomic policies cannot be done without a full understanding of how aggregate economic behavior filters down to the numerous micro markets levels, and likewise how activities at the numerous micro market levels shape the aggregate building blocks of the macro economy. From a policy perspective, an attempt to study fiscal, monetary, and other public policy in isolation of micro markets would fail to address why expected outcomes from the models constructed fall short of the intended target. In today's world, where costs become mistaken for benefits and benefits mistaken for costs and the concept of scarcity can be quickly forgotten or shifted out of view, one can better understand why what is wished to be observed simply does not happen or would likely have happened had a deconstructive approach of macroeconomics been prescribed with a heavy dose of critical thinking of the microeconomics behind it.

QUESTIONS FOR CLASS DISCUSSION

1. Economics and scarcity are everywhere. This chapter argues that scarcity is a necessary condition for the creation of markets and exploitable opportunities.
   a. Describe a past or more current market observation or event in which scarcity in a resource, good, or service supported the creation of an exploitable market opportunity.
   b. Before the scarcity was addressed, what impact did it have on private and public economic well-being? How was the scarcity addressed and diminished?
   c. What market emerged to address the scarcity, and what were the consequences (good and bad) to private and public economic well-being? How clear are the consequences?
   d. How important are economic and noneconomic incentives in addressing scarcity and capitalizing on exploitable opportunities? How might certain incentives deter human motivation to act on scarcity, thereby preventing an exploitable opportunity and subsequent organized market from following?
2. Because scarcity exists, every society is faced with the challenge of the most appropriate way to ration scarce resources, goods, services, and income. Therefore, each society will choose an economic system (or a hybrid or mixture of multiple economic system characteristics) that will best maximize and balance the competing interests (private versus public economic well-being) of society members.
   a. Compare and contrast the pros and cons of capitalist, command, and mixed economies and what economic and noneconomic incentives are supported and discouraged in each.
   b. What are the more common successes and failures of each?
   c. What factors (economic, historical, cultural, governmental, geographical, degree of economic openness with the world, and so on) would greatly influence a society's choosing of one form of an economic system over another?
3. The chapter demands that a global systems view be used in analyzing the impact of economic events on a country's economic performance and how impacts on such performance will impact the performance of other economies with which the country participates. For each scenario, apply a global systems view and describe how you and your classmates would expect the scenario to play out through the global economy.
   a. Great Britain votes to exit the European Union.[9]
   b. China abandons the fixed exchange rate arrangement the Chinese Yuan has with the U.S. Dollar.
   c. A precipitous fall in global oil prices raises the risk of default on sovereign debt issued by large oil-producing economies highly dependent on oil revenue from past high oil prices per barrel.
   d. An explosion in three-dimensional printing occurs in highly developed manufacturing economies.

[9] On June 23rd, 2016, Great Britain in a public referendum voted to exit the European Union.

IMAGE CREDITS

- Table 1.1: http://www.naics.com/history-naics-code.
- Table 1.2: Adapted from into table from Fig. https://wikis.engrade.com/economicsystems.
- Fig. 1.1: Terry Miller, Anthony Kim, Kim Holmes, "2014 Index of Economic Freedom World Map," http://www.heritage.org/index/images/book/2014/in-2014-region-map-web-world.jpg. Copyright © 2014 by The Heritage Foundation.
- Fig. 1.2: Terry Miller, Anthony Kim, Kim Holmes, "Economic Freedom, Standard or Living and Poverty," http://www.heritage.org/index . Copyright © 2014 by The Heritage Foundation.
- Fig. 1.3: Copyright © Le0t (CC BY-SA 3.0) at http://commons.wikimedia.org/wiki/File:Circular_flow_of_income.png.
- Fig. 1.4: "Institutions Matter," www.intellectualtakeout.org. Copyright © by Intellectual Takeout.

CHAPTER 2

OPPORTUNITY COSTS AND PPFS: ALL CHOICES ARE BAD ONES, AND ALL BAD CHOICES ARE EXPLOITABLE

Figure 2.0. An environment of finite opportunities available for a finite amount of time influences human beings to trade away one set of opportunities for another to maximize their level of happiness and welfare. For every opportunity taken, an alternative opportunity that could have been exploited must be forgone. As the image suggests, if people do not act now before time expires, they will miss out on an opportunity that will no longer be in the marketplace to exploit and will be left with alternatives not as exploitable.

2.0 ALL CHOICES ARE BAD ONES!

In the initial chapter, a bold assumption was made about scarcity being an exploitable opportunity. Scarcity—this author states—is a "necessary evil" for the creation of exploitable opportunities using a marketplace to coordinate and maximize the self-interest of parties involved. So with all the scarce opportunities that exist in marketplaces, then as the Image 2.1 suggests, "Act now!! Time is running out!!" If you don't act now, the opportunity will be gone!!

The above caption begs some important questions about the availability and exploitability of finite opportunities, resource scarcity, and the role innovation has played in generating more workable opportunities in a resource-constrained world. With all the scarce opportunities in the marketplace, why do some people pass up opportunities and others take them? How might some opportunities—such as public health care and education treated as universal rights in the political sphere—be provided universally to society in a marketplace if we do not fully understand the resource and funding constraints we are tasked with operating within? How are exploitable opportunities used to create an enlargement of market opportunities that may raise society's standard of living?

This chapter will examine choices made in an environment of resource scarcity and the importance of incentives in guiding the direction of private and public choices. Using a descriptive model of an economy's production possibilities frontier, trade-offs will be made among available but unequal opportunities to determine which opportunity or combination of opportunities will yield the economy its best welfare gain to society as a whole. For such possible welfare gains to be maximized, an economic system is needed to coordinate competing private and public interest in the use of scarce resources. Will the system value the private management of choice and the maximization of self-interest in an attempt to maximize society's overall well-being? What consequences will this yield? Or will choices be severely limited in the public domain, with government management determining what is the best use of resources that will benefit nation-state goals first; making private goals of households and firms now subordinate. In the end, there will be a trade-off between efficiency and economic equity, creating an environment of winners and losers.

"There Is no such Thing as a Free Lunch!!"

This simply means all opportunities are costly, and costs will be borne directly by the decision maker, shared and leveraged between parties, and/or shared broadly directly or indirectly across participation in private and public marketplaces. An opportunity cost will be defined as something(s) that has to be forgone in order to obtain and enjoy the benefits of an obtained opportunity. In all: All choices are bad ones.

Here is a classic example of opportunity cost. As a university student, in the morning you can choose to sleep in or go to class. If you choose to sleep in, you miss class and miss out on the opportunities available in class that morning. These classroom opportunities you miss out on are non-recoverable, but you enjoy any physical and mental health benefits extra sleep affords to you. In this choice scenario, if you elect to sleep in versus going to class, you are communicating to the marketplace that the discounted value of future benefits enjoyed from going to class are worth much less to you than the discounted value of future benefits you would receive from extra hour(s) of sleep.[1] On the other hand, if you choose to go to class, you enjoy the benefits of being in class (hopefully, useful information you learn), but you miss out on the value of the health benefits that extra sleep would afford to you. In this case, you are communicating to the marketplace that the

[1] The concept of the time value of money implies that the value of a Dollar today is worth more than the value of the same Dollar to be used in the future. This same approach can be used for discounting future benefits earned but not received.

discounted future value to you of going to class is worth more than the discounted future value you would receive from sleeping in.

All choices derive benefits to the individual and society (directly and externally), and these same choices yield costs to the same individual and society (directly and externally). Using a systems approach, the user can examine where the gains and costs of private and public choices accrue directly and externally throughout the economy domestically and globally.[2] For example, the systems approach will allow the user to examine if certain economic trade-offs made as a result of a public policy shift are explaining why some areas of a metropolitan city are experiencing a higher concentration of lower economic activity and lower income earned when similar trade-offs are being made in other areas of the city. All costs and gains from exploited choices are not spread uniformly. The same goes for economic growth, globalization, innovation, and so on. Resources and/or funds linked to resources used will have to be allocated away from other activities in pursuit of present ones.

2.1 MEASURING THE OPPORTUNITY COSTS OF TRADE-OFFS

All choices are a reflection of opportunistic behavior; including selfless actions. And all choices, when made, bear an opportunity cost. In what form gains and costs materialize, where such gains and costs accrue, and who bears them constitute an important study by economists and policy makers. Economists will study the accrual of such gains and costs for the purpose of optimal welfare maximization in an economic system designed to apportion society's wealth.

Up front, all this sounds like demonizing profitable exploitation, but it is not. Recall that scarcity requires profitable exploitation in order for individuals and society to benefit and have more of something than there was before.[3] For markets to function and even exist, the existence of scarce opportunities and the differing opportunity costs expected to be incurred from such opportunities will form a basis of trade and exchange. Even the existence of costs generated from exploitation provides other exploitive opportunities for the management and diversification of such costs in a profitable way. As humans, it is in our nature to be exploitive in the interest of self-preservation.

Costly Choices as a Basis for Market Exchange: Absolute Advantage vs. Comparative Advantage

This section will serve as an application of the production possibilities frontier (PPF) model, which is used in all economics courses to cover the concept of opportunity costs in a set of production choices exploitable for exchange opportunities to be created. Suppose there are two persons living on opposite sides of a deserted island. Let's call these two persons Jack and Jill.

[2] See coverage of the butterfly effect from Chapter 1.

[3] As defined and measured, an opportunity cost is what you give up in order to have an alternate opportunity. This implies that creating more that is deficient in amount will create a larger deficiency amount over time in all other production opportunities, provided resource amounts available and technology stay unchanged. This also means that if resource amounts stay unchanged, then all production occurs in an increasing-cost environment, and the cost of an opportunity in terms of the alternate good(s) will increase at a rate up to a maximum limit. In more intermediate and advanced microeconomics literature, production and cost theory examines ways to create decreasing cost environments (economies of scope) such that the increase in the output of one good (exhibiting strong economies of scale in production) in terms of another good(s) lowers the average cost of production of all other complementary goods produced along with it.

On this deserted island, Jack and Jill have two activities: fishing or harvesting coconuts.[4] Of the resources available, Jack and Jill each have their own labor skill sets and ingenuity to work with and will be constrained by an eight-hour workday.

Both and Jack and Jill will do the following:

1. *Fully utilize all working hours*
2. *Leave no working hours unemployed*[5]
3. *Use a fixed level of technology (their own ingenuity), and their own labor will be the only factor of production available to be employed in the production of either good*[6]

Considering Jack and Jill's labor as the only resource equally suitable to produce both fish and coconuts allows for the examination Jack and Jill's production environments as constant opportunity cost environments. Constant opportunity costs will imply that any single amount of one good produced will come at a constant opportunity cost in terms of a fixed amount that is always given up for the other good. For Jack and Jill, the opportunity cost they will each bear producing any combination of fish and coconuts will be a constant amount expressed as a domestic rate of exchange of one good in terms of another in their own individual market environments.

In a marketplace, one will be able to examine whether the true opportunity costs borne will be adequately reflected in goods prices.[7] A final assumption of our example will treat transportation and all possible transaction costs (i.e., taxes and other fees) within their individual markets and those that may be present in an exchange opportunity between Jack and Jill as zero.

Jack and Jill Produce and Face Opportunity Costs

Jack and Jill on their respective sides of the island will in an eight-hour workday produce only fish, produce only coconuts, or produce a combination of the two that maximizes their level of happiness. This working example will be used to determine how scarcity and different opportunity costs Jack and Jill bear will determine a basis of trade of coconuts for fish and vice versa between these two on the deserted island.

Using the PPF model of constant costs, it is here that the concepts of absolute and comparative advantage are introduced and why comparative advantage is a better explanation for a basis of exchange and trade as opposed to absolute advantage. Table 2.1 shows the maximum amounts that Jack and Jill can produce of a single good in an eight-hour workday.

	Fish	Coconuts
Jack	24	40
Jill	16	32

Table 2.1. The maximum amounts of fish and coconuts Jack and Jill can produce if 100 percent of their labor hours each day are devoted to the production of either fish or coconuts.

[4] A similar example of this and results can be found in Krugman, P., and R. Wells. 2012. *Macroeconomics*. 3rd ed. New York: Worth. For the Jack and Jill example, different maximum production values of fish and coconuts are used.

[5] To keep our analytical exercise simple, assume Jack and Jill's individual marketplaces are perfectly competitive. Using a perfectly competitive environment in the model for simplicity will treat each of them as: (1) price takers with neither of them large enough so that their production and consumption choices will influence a market price that is favorable to one of them and unfavorable to the other, (2) treating the goods they produce as identical, and (3) having no prohibitive barriers (tax and/or regulatory) that will add costs to trade and exchange between them.

[6] Realistically, the production of fish and coconuts uses land and capital along with labor. For this example, the assumption is that production of both goods is 100 percent labor intensive, so that an examination of opportunity costs can be done in a constant cost environment.

[7] In an analysis later in this chapter, the same PPF model will be used to examine an increasing cost environment for Jack and Jill when their labor hours are employed with land and capital for the production of fish and coconuts.

During an 8-hour workday, Jack can either produce 3 fish per hour for a maximum of 24 fish in an 8-hour workday or 5 coconuts per hour for a maximum of 40 coconuts in the same workday. Jill can produce either 2 fish per hour for a maximum amount of 16 fish in an 8-hour workday or 4 coconuts per hour for a maximum of 32 coconuts.

On a per hour level, Jack is marginally more productive with his daily labor hours in producing both goods. For every hour that Jack works to produce fish, he makes a marginal contribution toward his total daily output of 3 fish per hour, which is greater than Jill's marginal contribution toward her daily output of 2 fish per hour. In terms of coconut production, Jack makes a marginal contribution of 5 coconuts per hour, and Jill makes a marginal contribution of 4 coconuts per hour.

The Concept of Absolute Advantage First

Since Jack is marginally more productive at producing both goods on a per hour basis than Jill, Jack is said have absolute advantage in the production of both goods. Absolute advantage is based on differences in marginal productivity as affected by differences in technology. In this case it is how different Jack and Jill's ingenuity is in how they use their labor to produce coconuts and fish.

In this problem, the basis for absolute advantage lies in the level of hourly labor productivity as a function of "good old know-how." In short, absolute advantage is based on technological prowess. Whoever is "better"—marginally more productive—at producing a good(s) is said to hold an absolute advantage in the production of that good(s).[8] So will Jack's absolute advantage in the production of fish and coconuts be a basis for exchange with Jill? If so, would this encourage Jack to specialize his labor efforts in either one of these goods?

It's All about Differing Comparative Advantage to Create an Exploitable Opportunity

Suppose Jack and Jill encounter each other on the island and provide complete information to one another on the single maximum amounts each can produce of fish and coconuts in a single day. From this encounter, Jack learns he is marginally more productive on a per hour basis in producing fish and coconuts. Based on the concept of absolute advantage, Jack's productivity advantage provides no incentive for him to specialize in fish or coconuts and exchange or trade with Jill. This problem suggests that highly productive economies would have no basis to trade or exchange with less-productive economies. If this is the case, then why in the real world are less-productive economies trading and exchanging with economies that are relatively more productive or technologically advanced? The answer to this question can be best explored in the concept of comparative advantage as basis for trade and exchange versus absolute advantage. The definition of comparative advantage is:

> *A person, firm, or economy is said to hold a comparative advantage in the use of resources for the production of a good for which it forgoes less of its next available opportunity for which those same resources may be used as compared to another person, firm, or economy using similar or identical resources for the production of the same good and similar alternatives.*

That description is a mouthful, so in a more simplified statement, whomever gives up the least amount of opportunity for a given activity (production or otherwise) using existing resources is said to hold a comparative advantage in that production or activity. Those who sacrifice less will obtain more in exchange and trade and will see a greater improvement in their economic well-being. If comparative advantage holds and markets work well in communicating opportunity costs (i.e., reflected in different prices, returns, risk, and so on), then the market should communicate

---

[8] In the real world, a sustained absolute advantage may show up in the micro marketplace as a monopoly advantage supported by economies of scale and scope. This is the ability to produce a large range of output over a fixed amount of inputs that drives down the average fixed cost per unit and average total cost per unit.

an incentive to specialize production in what that person, firm, or economy is comparatively better at producing at a lower opportunity cost in terms of an amount(s) give up of other opportunities.[9]

Using Comparative Advantage as a Basis for Jack and Jill to Trade/Exchange

Comparative advantage as a basis for trade requires an examination of the opportunity costs Jack and Jill bear in their constant costs environments when they trade away one production opportunity for another (fish versus coconuts). Recall that opportunity cost is defined as what must be traded away for a given opportunity. For Jack and Jill, of interest to each of them would be the amount of fish (or coconuts) traded away for a single unit amount of coconuts (or fish).

Jack and Jill will hold a comparative advantage in the production of those goods for which the opportunity cost of using their fixed amount of labor hours is the lowest. Table 2.2 illustrates the opportunity costs Jack and Jill face in their respective constant cost environments when they each make choices of how to allocate their daily labor hours exclusively between the production of fish and coconuts.

	Opportunity cost of producing 1fish in terms of coconuts	**Opportunity cost of producing 1 coconut in terms of fish**
Jack	$^5/_3$ of a coconut forgone	$^3/_5$ of a fish forgone
Jill	2 coconuts forgone	½ of a fish foregone

Table 2.2. The amount each good Jack and Jill forgo when each makes a production choice of producing either fish or coconuts.

In Jack's economy, he will always incur a constant opportunity cost of $^5/_3$ of a coconut forgone for every 1 fish he produces with his labor, and he incurs a constant opportunity cost of $^3/_5$ fish forgone for every 1 coconut he produces with his labor. Over in Jill's market, for every 1 fish she produces with her labor, she forgoes 2 coconuts, and for every 1 coconut she produces with her labor, she forgoes ½ fish.

Despite the fact that Jill is less productive at every margin with her labor hours than Jack and holds no absolute advantage in either good, Jill does command a comparative advantage in at least one good, which is coconuts. From the table, it is observable at a comparative level that Jill gives up .10 fewer fish (Jack's opportunity cost less Jill's opportunity cost) than Jack when she produces a coconut. Because Jill has a lower opportunity cost in producing every fish than Jack, she holds a comparative advantage in fish.

As well, despite the fact that Jack holds an absolute advantage in the production of both goods because he is marginally more productive with every hour available to him when he produces either fish or coconuts, he only holds a comparative advantage in one good, which is fish. From the table it is observable that Jack gives up .3333 fewer coconuts (Jill's opportunity cost less Jack's opportunity cost) when he produces each fish versus Jill. In a two-good model, a person, firm, or economy can hold an absolute advantage in both goods but can only hold a comparative advantage in at least one. So how do the differing opportunity costs between Jack and Jill serve as basis for specialization and trade?

The action of specialization creates scarcity and the incentive to trade/exchange to cover it

Thinking in terms of how choices in a resource-constrained environment creates scarcity in opportunities forgone, using Table 2.2 the opportunity costs that Jack and Jill incur when they each choose to produce only fish or coconuts creates scarcity in their markets of workable opportunities that would have been available in the other goods

9 This is not free of dilemmas, as the case study in this chapter will show.

had they been produced. Whether they produce more fish and fewer coconuts or more coconuts and fewer fish, their individual welfare may be affected by producing too much of one good and too little of another. As closed markets (for the time being), Jack and Jill can only consume what they produce. But the existence of differing opportunity costs provides them an opportunity to specialize in what they are comparatively better at; allowing the other person to produce more of the other good for them to address scarcity in that other person's market at a lower opportunity cost.

An intuitive example is the fast-food industry. The existence of fast-food markets and the broader fast-food industry suggests the menu items the restaurants produce can be done so at a lower opportunity cost in terms of time and place for those who want to consume them without having to bear the opportunity cost of forgone opportunities to produce them. The Dollars that consumers pay for the menu item(s) represent the other goods in the marketplace that the fast-food restaurants in the industry have a very high opportunity cost of producing and so do not produce. As such, there is an incentive to specialize in the comparative advantage good and trade it for the other good(s) that there are very high opportunity costs in producing. Such an intuitive example on a global scale aids the explanation for the reasons of outsourcing and offshoring as means for firms to exploit different comparative advantages to their benefit and cost to obtain larger gains than they would otherwise realize had they not.

For Jack and Jill, the concept of comparative advantage suggests Jack should specialize completely in fish production and Jill should specialize completely in coconut production. For the action of specialization to be beneficial, the amount of fish and coconuts available between them should be much larger than if they elected to produce coconuts and fish in isolation of one another. The next section, working with a different example with the same assumptions under constant conditions as in the Jack and Jill case, will illustrate how the incentive to specialize according to comparative advantage will yield a trade/exchange opportunity to allow the participants to end up with more and be better off marginally than without specialization and trade. In this section the graphical representation of the production possibilities frontier will be introduced.

2.2 WORKING WITH THE PPF UNDER CONSTANT COSTS: BENEFITS OF SPECIALIZATION AND EXCHANGE

The use of the production possibilities frontier provides a visual reference of the production possibilities available using a finite amount of a resource(s). The provided graphical representation will show for a given amount of labor and level of technology the maximum amounts of individual goods that can be produced and show the opportunity costs incurred when labor is allocated between the productions of two goods.[10] The graphical model provides visual affirmation of the concept of scarcity and opportunity cost.

For simplicity, there is an individual named Tom using his own labor, no other resources, and his own level of ingenuity in an 8-hour workday to produce either yards of cloth or bushels of wheat. On any given day, using 100 percent of his labor, Tom can produce either a maximum of 30 yards of cloth, 40 bushels of wheat, or a limited number of maximum combinations of yards of cloth and bushels of wheat. Figure 2.1 depicts Tom's production possibilities frontier drawn for his environment of constant opportunity cost using his labor as his only resource and level of ingenuity as the current level of technology in his economy.

[10] When the use of only one resource allocated between the production of two different goods is examined in the model (i.e., labor), all opportunity costs incurred will be constant. The graphical PPF frontier will be drawn with a constant slope, where the slope of the frontier will be the opportunity cost (trade-off) of producing one more good on the x-axis in terms of the amount of the good on the y-axis that is given up. In a perfectly competitive marketplace, this opportunity cost will be the relative price of good X in terms of good Y.

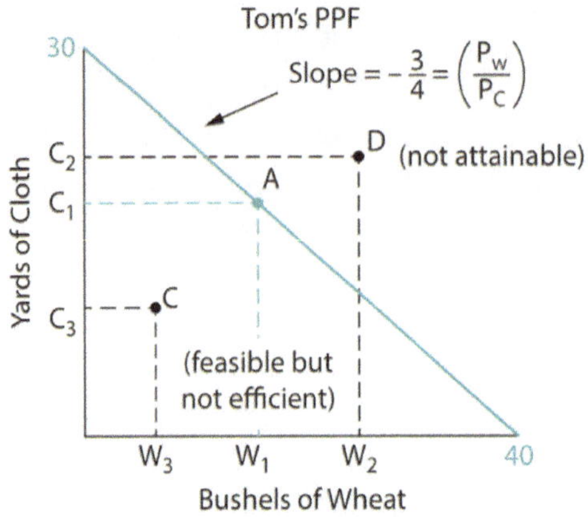

Figure 2.1. The slope of Tom's production possibilities frontier demonstrates for a constant cost environment his opportunity cost for every bushel of wheat produced will be a constant ¾ yards of cloth forgone.

From Figure 2.1, Tom's PPF illustrates the production constraint he faces with an 8-hour workday having to allocate his scarce time between the production of yards of cloth and bushels of wheat. Because Tom's labor is the only resource he his using (coupled with his ingenuity), his labor will be treated as equally suitable in producing either yards of cloth or bushels of wheat for producing different constant amounts of yards of cloth and bushels of wheat per hour. As well, Tom's maximized consumption will be any maximized combination of yards of cloth and bushels of wheat he chooses to produce in a given workday that makes him the happiest.[11]

Tom's PPF also shows some very important information about his production/consumption constraints. First, the PPF is drawn according to the maximum amounts of yards of cloth or bushels of wheat he can produce should he choose to allocate 100 percent of his labor to either task. From the graph, in a given 8-hour workday, he can a produce a maximum of 30 yards of cloth or 40 bushels of wheat. The slope of the PPF is equal to –¾, which gives us the constant opportunity cost of ¾ a yard of cloth forgone for every 1 bushel of wheat he produces.

This slope communicates a constant rate of exchange of 1 bushel of wheat: ¾ of yards of cloth. At any combination level of yards of cloth and bushels of wheat he chooses to produce, Tom will incur this constant rate of exchange, which will also be equal to the relative price of a bushel of wheat in terms of yards of cloth: Pw/Pc = ¾ yards of cloth. Taking the reciprocal of the slope of his PPF, the domestic relative price of a yard of cloth in terms of bushels of wheat for any combination of yards of cloth and bushels of wheat he produces will be Pc/Pw = $^4/_3$.

Tom's PPF also depicts a boundary limit of a limited number of possible maximum combinations of yards of cloth and bushels of wheat he can produce and consume with his labor and level of ingenuity. These combinations are attainable, provided the ratio of the output he produces along his PPF is equal to slope of the PPF, which is –¾. If Tom is able to fully utilize his labor hours in a given day across the production of yards of cloth and bushels of wheat, there will be a limited number of possible maximum combinations of these two goods he can produce.

According to Figure 2.1, point A on the curve, where Tom produces C_1 of yards of cloth and W_1 of bushels of wheat, represents one of the possible combination available to him within his constraint of an opportunity cost of ¾ yards of cloth for each bushel of wheat of the total amount he produces. Point A on the curve is just as efficient as any other point of possible production on the curve. Point A and other possible points of production on the curve represent possible maximum production outcomes providing a full utilization of his labor hours in a given workday. An important assumption of our model is Tom is acting rationally and will utilize all his working

[11] In microeconomics, this optimal amount produced will the combination of goods X and Y as a point on the PPF tangent to the highest attainable indifference curve. This point of tangency will represent the highest level of utility (satisfaction) than can be obtained from producing and consuming the optimal mount of goods X and Y where the slope of the PPF at that point is equal to the marginal rate of substitution between both goods.

hours in a given day and produce his preferred combination of yards of cloth and bushels of wheat that makes him the happiest. Facing no obstructions in his market that would prevent him from allocating his full workday between both types of production, Tom will always produce a combination of the two goods that lies on his PPF.[12]

Observable in the provided figure is point D (C_2, W_2) of a combination of yards of cloth and bushels of wheat that is desirable to Tom but unattainable. Without freeing up additional labor hours or making innovative improvements in how he produces either good, this point and all other points outside the PPF are unattainable. However, further exploration of this example will show that an opportunity to trade with another actor will allow Tom to consume combinations of yards of cloth and bushels of wheat far greater than what his production constraint allows for. This will allow Tom to improve his welfare through higher consumption supported by a higher value on what he specializes to produce and trade making himself better off than he would be without trade.

Finally, the figure also shows point C (C_3, W_3) combination of yards of cloth and bushels of wheat he can produce. This point and all other production and consumption points inside the curve are attainable but technically inefficient. Such production choices represent a non-full utilization of Tom's labor. For example, if on a given workday Tom values leisure over work, then his output combination(s) will be less than any maximum and derive him a lower level of welfare. As such there may also be other factors in Tom's market that prevent him from producing a maximum combination of yards of cloth and bushels of wheat. For instance, if Tom were to incur a nonzero switching cost between producing either yards of cloth or bushels of wheat, such as a cost he may incur to transport himself from one production area to another, then the additional cost he incurs would place him at a production and consumption point inside the curve.

Doing better than 100 percent self-sufficiency

So can Tom do any better than what his production and consumption constraint allows for? To illustrate this opportunity, we need to provide Tom with a basis for trade with another actor in the marketplace.

We do know that without trade, Tom can only consume what he produces, which limits the maximum welfare gains available to him. This would be that combination of goods when produced and consumes which makes him the happiest. Suppose nearby to Tom is a person named Hank. Hank will also produce identical yards of cloth and identical bushels of wheat. For simplicity let's also assume that Hank will use his labor and level of ingenuity exclusively for the production of identical cloth and wheat. And, like Tom, Hank is constrained by an eight-hour workday. For comparison, Figure 2.2 depicts Hank's and Tom's respective PPFs.

For a fixed 8-hour workday, Figure 2.2 illustrates the single maximum amounts of yards of cloth and bushels of wheat Tom and Hank can produce on their own. Also shown in the figure are the chosen production and consumption amounts made by Tom and Hank for the same 8-hour workday. Tom will produce and consume 9 yards of cloth and 28 bushels of wheat and incur a constant opportunity (the slope of his PPF) of ¾ yards of cloth for each bushel of wheat he produce and consumes in lieu of yards of cloth. Hank will in his workday produce and consume 8 yards of cloth and 6 bushels of wheat at a constant opportunity cost of 2 yards of cloth for each bushel of wheat he produces and consumes.

It is also shown in the figure that Tom holds an absolute advantage in the production of both goods. Both Tom and Hank are identical in every respect except for the level of ingenuity they use. This difference in ingenuity shows up as different maximums each can produce and different corresponding constant opportunity costs. Tom has an absolute advantage in both goods because at a technological level, Tom is marginally more productive with his labor than Hank.

[12] If there were more information about Tom's preferences (level of utility or satisfaction) for a given combination of yards of cloth and bushels of wheat, and treating his PPF as his budget constraint, then an empirical determination could be made as to the best possible combination of these two goods he would produce without trade that would maximize his welfare at some point in time.

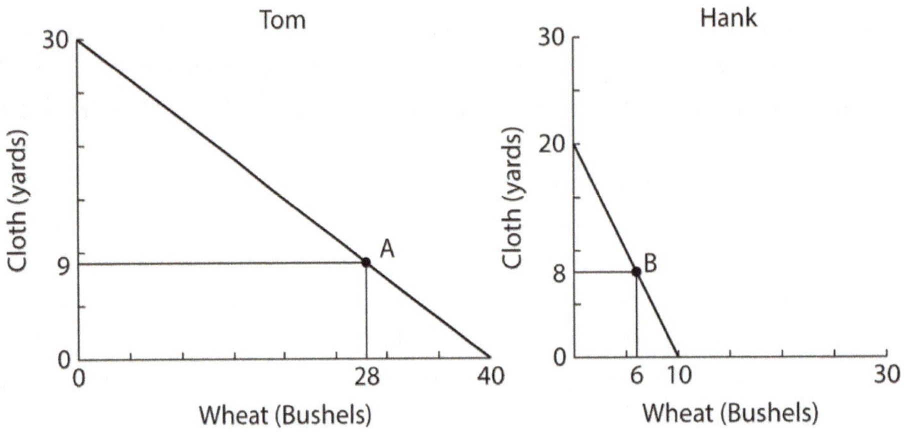

Figure 2.2. The PPFs for both Tom and Hank. The figure illustrates the maximum amount of yards of cloth and bushels of wheat they each can produce in any eight-hour workday using their own labor and level of technology exclusively. Both Tom and Hank produce identical goods, and as illustrated, they each incur different constant opportunity costs (slopes of their PPFs) when they allocate their labor between the production of yards of cloth and bushels of wheat. It is observed from Tom's PPF that he incurs a constant opportunity (slope of Tom's PPF) of ¾ yards of cloth for each bushel of wheat produced, and Hank incurs a constant opportunity cost (slope of Hank's PPF) of 2 yards of cloth for each bushel of wheat he produces.

Again, comparative advantage is a basis for specialization and trade

If absolute advantage was a basis for trade, then in this case, trade would not be beneficial because Tom can produce greater amounts of both goods. However, Tom and Hank incur differing opportunity costs, suggesting that both Tom and Hank hold a comparative advantage in at least one good, and this will be the good they will each have an incentive to specialize in.

Before considering the incentive to specialize production in a good, consider the goods Tom and Hank hold comparative advantages in. The Table 2.3a depicts the opportunity costs that Tom and Hank incur when they each allocate their labor hours between the production of yards of cloth and bushels of wheat.

	Opportunity cost of producing 1 bushel of wheat	**Opportunity cost of producing 1 yard of cloth**
Tom	¾ yards of cloth foregone	$^4/_3$ bushels of wheat foregone
Hank	2 yards of cloth foregone	½ bushel of wheat foregone

Table 2.3a. Tom's and Hank's opportunity costs in producing either yards of cloth or bushels of wheat as illustrated by their respective PPFs derived from Figure 2.2.

Based strictly on the opportunity costs of production, Tom's opportunity cost of producing a bushel of wheat is 1.5 fewer yards of cloth given up than Hank. So bushels of wheat production will be the production activity that Tom holds a comparative advantage in. On the other hand— and despite not holding an absolute advantage in either good— Hank holds a comparative advantage in the production of yards of cloth. He forgoes .833 fewer bushels of wheat than Tom. With differing opportunity costs that reflect what Tom and Hank are comparatively better at in producing, why will this be enough to specialize their time and labor exclusively in the production of that good?

Differing Opportunity Costs and the Corresponding Incentive to Specialize

First, for Tom and Hank to specialize completely in the production of the good they hold a comparative advantage in, doing so should show there will be more yards of cloth and bushels wheat between them to trade. Table 2.3b illustrates this with an extra 3 yards of cloth and 6 bushels of wheat available for them to trade than would be without production specialization.

	Output Before Specialization		**Output Post-Specialization**	
	Yards of Cloth	**Bushels of Wheat**	**Yards of Cloth**	**Bushels of Wheat**
Tom	9	28	0	40
Hank	8	6	20	0
Totals	17	34	20	40

Table 2.3b. Tom and Hank's output outcomes with and without specialization.

If efficiency drives the maximization of welfare gains and the minimization of welfare losses in a market environment, then it makes sense that Tom and Hank specialize in the production of the good they hold a comparative advantage in. If the goods they produce are identical, and Tom and Hank can obtain goods from one another through trade, then why would Tom continue to produce yards of cloth on his own and bear the higher opportunity cost of doing so when he can obtain the same yards of cloth from Hank at a lower opportunity cost (lower relative price)? And the same goes for Hank in terms of bushels of wheat. So that resources are allocated to the use exhibiting the lowest possible opportunity cost, it demands the user of the resources to specialize in the production of the good they hold a comparative advantage in. The act of specialization on both their parts increases the output of yards of cloth between them by 3 additional yards (a 17.65 percent increase) and 6 more bushels of wheat (an 11.11 percent increase).

Complete specialization adds to total output in the market and makes for more available to trade. But as stated in this chapter and Chapter 1, scarcity is a factor that is necessary to facilitate the incentive to exchange. Here, specialization is adding more to the market, not less! So how can trade or exchange between Tom and Hank be facilitated if there is less scarcity between them?

1. ***The act of specialization by one creates scarcity and an exploitable opportunity to capitalize on by another***

First, it is correct to say more being added to the market from Tom's and Hank's specialization has diminished the amount of scarce yards of cloth and bushels of wheat between them. *However, Tom's and Hank's specialization in their comparative advantage goods has created scarcity in the alternate production they are forgoing by focusing more on the production of those goods they have the lower opportunity cost in producing.* Tom creates complete scarcity in yards of cloth since his act of 100 percent specialization in bushels of wheat production completely eliminates, by choice, his cloth-producing activity. Hank creates complete scarcity in the production of the bushels of wheat, specializing 100 percent completely in the production of yards of cloth. *It is the scarcity that Tom and Hank create in the other good in their marketplaces that facilitates the basis to exchange their comparative good (that the other will value more) for the good that they have completely forgone producing.*

2. ***The degree of scarcity will affect the value you place on trading/exchanging for it***

For example, Tom will want Hank to release a yard of cloth to him for a bushel of his wheat, of which Hank has no production. Since Tom has no cloth and only bushels of wheat, to obtain one yard of cloth, Tom must value each yard of Hank's cloth by more than Hank's opportunity cost in bushels of wheat to make it. This means that Tom will be willing to give up to Hank more bushel(s) of wheat for each yard(s) of cloth than what Hank gave up in the way of bushels of wheat to produce the same yard of cloth.

Since yards cloth are scarce to Tom, each yard is more valuable to Tom in bushels of wheat to exchange for than what Hank values each yard of cloth for in terms of wheat. This same logic will apply to Hank's valuation of each of Tom's bushels of wheat for one of his yards of cloth.[13] Let's review again the opportunity costs that Tom and Hank bear in their own marketplaces before specialization as shown in Table 2.3c.

	Opportunity cost of 1 producing bushel of wheat	**Opportunity cost of 1 producing yard of cloth**
Tom	¾ yards of cloth foregone	$^4/_3$ bushels of wheat foregone
Hank	2 yards of cloth foregone	½ bushel of wheat foregone

Table 2.3c. Tom and Hank's opportunity costs under production specialization and trade.

With Tom specializing completely in the production of bushels of wheat, for Tom to release a bushel of wheat to Hank, Hank will need to value each bushel of wheat from Tom by more than what Tom values each bushel in his marketplace. Without any trade, Tom already pays (i.e., pays himself implicitly) ¾ a yard of cloth for each bushel of wheat he produces and supplies. For Tom to supply a bushel of wheat, Hank would need to value each bushel of wheat from Tom for at least ¾ a yard or cloth or greater, so Tom would still earn the same benefit or more for every bushel of wheat.

For Hank to buy a bushel of wheat from Tom, Hank will want to pay equal to or less than what he already incurs for having the same bushel of wheat in his economy, which is 2 yards of cloth. As such, for Hank to release a yard of cloth to Tom, Tom will need to value the identical yard of cloth from Hank by at least equal to or greater than what Hank values the yard of cloth at ½ bushel of wheat.

Scarcity of yards of cloth in Tom's marketplace and scarcity of bushels of wheat in Hank's marketplace cause both of them to value the good the other has more of in terms of the amount of the good each is producing under specialization and willing to trade away for. As a result, the trade of yards of cloth and bushels of wheat between Tom and Hank will bid up the price (value per unit) of the good they have specialized in, and each will be better off for it in terms of how much more they will be able to consume from trading with each other as opposed being 100 percent self-sufficient.

The Benefits When Trade Takes Place...

With different opportunity costs expressing different domestic market prices for each good in terms of the other in Tom's and Hank's markets, coupled with the scarcity created from specialization, there is now a recipe for an exploitable trade opportunity between Tom and Hank that will make them better off. This "better off" situation will be the outcome of the exchange rate of bushels of wheat to yards of cloth, improving Tom's and Hank's consumption profile of both goods above what they would just consume without trade.

Just as in any buy-and-sell environment, for both buyer and seller to transact, the rate of exchange or market price must be no greater (the buy side) and no less (the sell side) than the opportunity costs already incurred.

[13] The different values each will place on other's comparative advantage good will affect the equilibrium price and quantity of that good in their respective marketplaces. This will be shown in an illustrated example in Chapter 3, applying the concepts learned from supply and demand analysis. In the long run, trade of yards of cloth and bushels of wheat between Tom and Hank (applying the assumption of this perfectly competitive free trade model of identical goods) will converge the domestic relative market prices in their respective markets to an equilibrium trade price. Once this convergence process is completed, the international trade price will prevail as the uniform price in their respective economies, making trade between their markets no longer beneficial.

In the example, Tom will not release a bushel of wheat to Hank if he cannot receive at least ¾ or more of a yard of cloth from it as payment from Hank. Hank will not accept a bushel of wheat from Tom if he has to pay more than 2 yards of cloth for it. So, with a possible rate of exchange ranging from 1 bushel of wheat for at least ¾ yard of cloth and no more than 2 yards of cloth, how is this rate of exchange determined?

The rate of exchange that would make trade beneficial for Tom and Hank and raise their consumption profile to point(s) outside their PPF can be determined via the following:

3. *The outcome of the market forces of supply and demand (which will be covered in Chapter 3) trending toward an equilibrium exchange rate that is optimal for Tom and Hank to maximize their overall level of happiness.*[14]
4. *With or without revealed preferences, Tom and Hank would negotiate for a rate of exchange that would be joint-welfare maximizing between them.*

Assume for the moment that Tom and Hank meet and share with each other complete information on the respective opportunity costs they incur when each produces either yards of cloth or bushels of wheat. From their discussion, both recognize that the difference in opportunity costs they incur presents an exploitable, arbitrage opportunity to specialize production and trade.

For simplicity, assume that explicit and implicit costs to trade between them are zero. Suppose Tom and Hank come to an agreement to specialize their individual production in the good they are comparatively better at producing and trade bushels of wheat for yards of cloth at a rate of exchange of 1 bushels of wheat for 1 yard of cloth. According to our analysis and concept of comparative advantage, Tom will specialize in and export bushels of wheat and Hank will specialize in and export yards of cloth in order to capture the higher price for their good than what they would receive just on their own.

At a rate of exchange of 1 bushel of wheat for 1 yard of cloth, the benefits are as follows:

1. *Tom will gain ¼ extra yards of cloth for every bushel of wheat he trades with Hank.*
2. *Hank will save 1 yard of cloth in payments for each bushel of wheat he obtains in trade from Tom.*
3. *As well, Tom will gain ½ more bushels of wheat for each yard of cloth he trades with Tom, and Tom will save $^{1}/_{3}$ bushels of wheat for every yard of cloth he obtains from Hank.*
4. *The gains and savings in trade between Tom and Hank will show up as an improved consumption profile for both with their existing production constraints. Figure 2.9 takes the PPF graphical analysis one step further, illustrating the improved gains in consumption for Tom and Hank with trade when they participate at the agreed exchange rate: 1 bushel of wheat: 1 yard of cloth, or Pw/Pc = 1.*

Provided that the rate of exchange lies between their domestic relative prices without trade, all other trade costs and obstruction to trade are zero, and the market environment is perfectly competitive, there is zero opportunity for Tom or Hank to act opportunistically in a way that would shifts gains from one to another. Trade and/or exchange will be beneficial and gains will be maximized.

Tom and Hank Exploiting Their Self-Interest through Trade and/or Exchange

In Figure 2.3, we see that Tom and Hank will each produce at respective point P on their PPF, where point P denotes production under specialization. Without trade, each would trade bushels of wheat for yards of cloth (and vice versa) along their domestic PPF at the respective constant opportunity costs they face (Tom: ¾ yards of cloth for each bushel of wheat; Hank: 2 yards of cloth for each bushel of wheat). With specialization and trade, each would produce and supply their comparative advantage good and exchange it for the alternate good along the trade line of P^{w} = Pw/Pc = 1.

[14] For us to know what exchange rate this would be, we would need to know more about Tom's and Hank's preference and level of utility in order to solve for Tom's and Hank's best post-trade consumption bundle of yards of cloth and bushels of wheat; as well, the market between them would have to be perfectly competitive with perfect information.

Before trade, we see in Figure 2.4 that Tom produces and consumes 28 bushels of wheat and 9 yards of cloth. Hank will produce and consume 6 bushels of wheat and 8 yards of cloth. With specialization and trade, Tom will produce 40 bushels of wheat and 0 yards of cloth. Keep in mind that Tom is supplying 40 bushels of wheat at a price of 1 yard of cloth versus ¾ of a yard of cloth.

Of this amount produced, Tom consumes 30 bushels of wheat, leaving him with 10 bushels which he will exchange for 10 yards of cloth at the exchange rate of 1 bushel of wheat: 1 yard of cloth. Because at this exchange rate Hank is participating at, Hank is valuing each bushel of Tom's wheat by ¼ more yards of cloth than what Tom values it. Because the rate of exchange used in this trade scenario increases the value of Tom's bushels of wheat in terms of yards of cloth, he is able to obtain under trade ¼ more yards of cloth than we he could exchange by himself at a domestic exchange rate of 1 bushel of wheat: ¾ yards of cloth with no trade. The extra 10 bushels of wheat that Tom has left over after consuming what he needs is exchanged for 10 yards of cloth. The outcome for Tom under trade with Hank is 2 more additional bushels of wheat and 1 more additional yard of cloth consumed.

In the same figure, Hank will gain as well. Assume of the yards of cloth Hank produces under specialization, he consumes what he needs, which is 10 yards of cloth. This leaves 10 extra yards of cloth for Hank to trade for bushel of wheat he does not have. On his own, Hank values each yard of cloth he produces at ½ bushels of wheat.

At the given exchange rate, Tom values each yard of cloth from Hank at 1 yard, or ½ yard more. Rather than exchange his yards of cloth domestically at an internal exchange rate of 1 yard of cloth for ½ bushels of wheat, Hank will produce under specialization 20 yards of cloth and supply them at the exchange rate of 1 yard of cloth: 1 bushel of wheat. After Hank consumes the 10 yards of cloth he needs, he trades his 10 extra yards yard for 10 bushels of wheat. The outcome for Hank under trade with Tom is 4 more additional bushel of wheat and 2 more additional yards of cloth consumed.

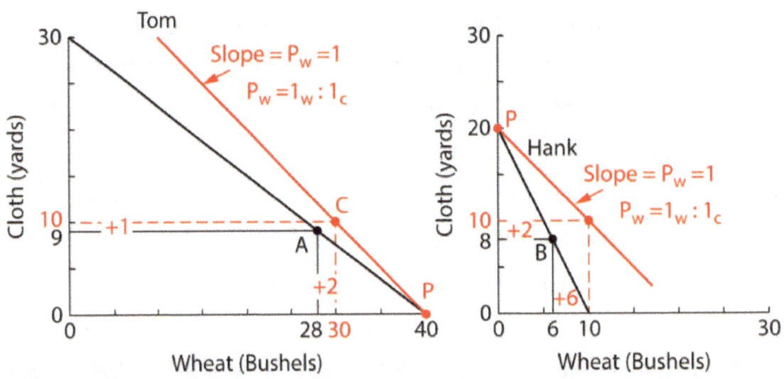

Figure 2.3. The consumption gains from trade for Tom and Hank when they trade bushels of wheat for yards of cloth at 1:1. So long as the rate of exchange falls between their domestic relative prices and there are zero other costs and obstructions that would diminish gains or shift gains away from one party to the other, trade will be beneficial and both parties involved should realize gains from trade through improved consumption opportunities.

The Basic Trade Model Is Powerful but with Problems from Limiting Assumptions

From this basic trade example, not only is scarcity a powerful economic motivator to promote specialization and trade, the consumption profiles of the trade participants can also be improved to achieve consumption combinations possibly greater than what their production constraint allows for. The model and example also suggests that the right amounts are produced and everyone involved is a winner (but in all trade cases this is not so). Tom and Hank gain only with the dynamics of trade covering up their up-front losses when each specializes. However, are these realized gains shown more of a causal outcome from the limiting assumptions placed on the problem?

For example, how realistic is it to consider a production environment of constant costs only? What happens to the descriptive PPF model and opportunity costs when considered are additional resources used with labor, such as land and capital? What about economic growth?

In our trade problem, no economic growth takes place, so how is the macroeconomic picture improved with just Tom and Hank trading? How would economic growth look in the model, and how might this affect the difference in opportunity costs and the benefits to trade? Finally, is it realistic to assume that trade/exchange costs are zero and there are zero other obstructions that would prevent an efficient production outcome, preventing the full gains on consumption to be realized? If assumptions made were relaxed and costs introduced, would the model lose any of its utility for use at the microeconomics and macroeconomic level? Let's consider a more realistic example in which opportunity costs are not constant but are increasing as more of one good is produced in lieu of the other.

2.3 A REALISTIC APPROACH TO THE PPF AND THE LAW OF INCREASING COSTS

The Tom and Hank example considers some given assumptions that are quite limiting and unrealistic. The reason for fixed assumptions is to examine the behavioral changes in a given independent variable(s) and see how such changes in those variables affect the behavior of the dependent variable(s) while holding all factors not accounted for constant.

Problems in the Hypothetical Model

In the hypothetical example, labor was considered as the only resource used in production when allocated between two production choices. This is an assumption that is not quite realistic, giving the model some problems that must be accounted for.

1. *There were no other resources being employed. It is as if the example is saying that output produced is 100 percent labor intensive.*
2. *Labor was considered perfectly mobile between industries, with zero obstructions in the way of this mobility (i.e., distance, transportation, regulations, and so on).*
3. *It was also assumed with this perfect mobility of labor between both modes of production there were zero capacity constraints in either production activity that would prevent full employment of labor hours and labor units for production specialization.*
4. *Complete production specialization in the model fully absorbed all available labor hours and labor units. In this regard, competition from imports created no injury to labor, since 100 percent of the employment of labor hours and labor units was in the production of the alternative good that would be traded for the import.*

Realistically, for any given two goods chosen to produce (including yards of cloth and bushels of wheat), it should be observed that more than one resource would be employed with labor (i.e., land and capital) and each of our three resources would be employed in specific input amounts to produce any single unit of goods in the two-good model. If some of the above assumptions are relaxed, a market environment of constant opportunity costs is abandoned, and the market now experiences an environment of increasing opportunity cost in which as more of one good is produced or opportunity is pursued in lieu of the next best alternative(s), the opportunity cost of the good being produced increases in terms of the other good or opportunity forgone.[15]

[15] This does not suggest that all production environments will be increasing cost environments, since the relevance of economies of scale and scope that are specific for a firm may allow for a decreasing cost environment for the production of two or more goods. The examination of firm-specific internal economies of scale and scope in production can be left to studies in intermediate microeconomics.

Relaxing some of the assumption in the Tom and Hank example and working with the following new assumptions for the new economy of TOM (a macro economy) with a fixed amount of labor units employable between products of yards of cloth and bushels of wheat, the following points are illustrated for a more realistic scenario.

1. *In addition to labor units and a fixed amount of labor hours, suppose that land and capital resources (tools, equipment, and machinery) are employed with labor to produce yards of cloth and bushels of wheat.*
2. *Assuming new resource suitability constraints, land is specific to the production of wheat but not the production of yards of cloth, and capital is specific to the production of yards of cloth but not the production of bushels of wheat.*
3. *Each of these specific resources has a maximum amount of labor/labor hours that can be employed with it and a limited amount of capacity to support employment of labor units.*
4. *For simplicity, the assumption is maintained that labor is perfectly mobile between both production activities and there are zero obstructions in the market that will prevent the total amount of labor from being fully employed between cloth and wheat production.*

Labor can be used to produce either good, but some labor is better suited to producing yards of cloth and some to producing bushels of wheat. This is due to differences in the efficiency of which working knowledge is employed by labor in either activity and how labor will use either land for the production of wheat or capital for the production of yards of cloth.

5. *The employment of labor between cloth and wheat production is subject to diminishing returns as opposed to constant returns in a constant cost model. Diminishing returns implies that as more of a variable input (labor) is employed over a fixed amount of input (land or capital), each additional unit of labor employed will increase output by a positive decreasing marginal amount up to the maximum amount that can be produced.*
6. *The economy of TOM has a comparative advantage in the production of bushels of wheat.*

So what would the new PPF look like for the economy of TOM endowed with a given amount of labor units, land units (specific to wheat production only), and capital units (specific to cloth production only)? Figure 2.4 provides an excellent illustration of what this two-good product environment would look like, using our PPF model as a graphical description.

Using the new assumptions and constraints, Figure 2.4 describes the production environment for the TOM economy as one of increasing opportunity costs. In Figure 2.5, TOM is able to produce the same given maximums of yards of cloth and bushels of wheat (30 yards of cloth and 40 bushels of wheat) under PPF1. Unlike the PPF for constant costs that is drawn with a constant slope for when labor is the exclusive resource used, the new PPF1 is drawn concave to the origin to reflect an increasing cost environment that is an outcome from the diminishing returns to labor as it is allocated to the production of one good versus and another.[16]

Realistically, TOM can't specialize completely when opportunity costs are not constant

Suppose that TOM, operating along PPF1, chooses to produce 25 yards of cloth and 20 bushels of wheat. TOM then forgoes 5 yards of cloth. The labor resources employed with capital in yards of cloth production that would have been used to produce these 5 yards are traded away for a gain of 20 bushels of wheat. In terms of allocation, the labor employed in yards of cloth production but better suited to producing bushels of wheat are employed in wheat production, and we see an increase in return of 20 additional bushel of wheat. The allocation of labor will be reflection of the type of economic system the TOM economy is in.

[16] In Chapter 5, covering economic growth, the concept of diminishing returns and its impact on output potential and distribution of income is covered in more detail.

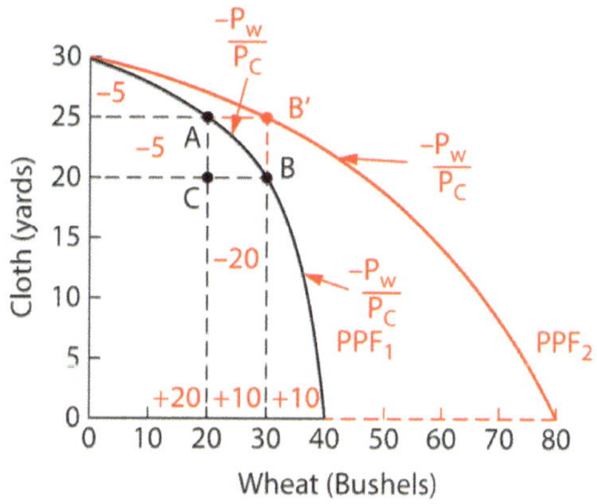

Figure 2.4. PPF profile for the economy of TOM describing an increasing opportunity cost environment for producing yards of cloth and bushels of wheat. The fixed amount of labor in the economy can be employed as a variable input between production of yards of cloth and bushels of wheat. Land and capital are also used but as fixed inputs and specific to one type of production activity. Land is specific to the production of bushels of wheat, and capital is specific to the production of yards of cloth. Labor is completely mobile between industries. Land and capital are completely immobile. The figure also shows that over the long run, additional land resources or an innovative change in how wheat is produced will shift TOM's PPF outward along the wheat-production axis to PPF2. This new production profile for the economy of TOM will reflect a lower opportunity cost in producing bushels of wheat in terms of yards of cloth than as shown in PPF1.

The slope of the line drawn at point A in the Figure 2.4 is equal to the relative price of a bushel of wheat in terms of yards of cloth given up. If TOM increases its production outcome to point B in order to have 30 bushels of wheat and 20 yards of cloth, the opportunity cost of the additional 10th bushel of wheat for 30 bushels is much higher than the additional 20th bushel obtained at point A. The figure shows these 10 additional bushels of wheat cost an additional 5 yards of cloth, where previously the same 5 yards traded for 20 bushels of wheat!! So what has happened?

As more wheat is produced, more labor is needed to work the land, and this labor will come from the cloth industry. Due to the assumption of diminishing returns, the additional labor that would have produced 5 yards of cloth is now employed with other labor on a fixed amount of land, leaving fewer acres available to each unit of labor to work, thereby increasing the amount of bushels of wheat added to the economy by a smaller marginal increase.

Because the increase in the additional amount of wheat obtained in terms of the 5 yards of cloth forgone is less than the initial amount of bushels of wheat obtained (20 bushels) when the same 5 yards of cloth was traded away for bushels of wheat, the opportunity cost of each additional bushel obtained up to 30 has increased by more than the opportunity cost of obtaining the 20th bushel!

In the end, TOM would never fully specialize in the production of bushels of wheat because the next 10 additional bushels would cost 20 yard of cloth forgone! As such, since the amount of land available to produce bushels of wheat is fixed and has a capacity level for a maximum amount of labor it can employ, at some point this limit is reached, and what remaining labor not employed in wheat production will be employed in cloth production.

Although complete 100 percent specialization in the production of wheat is too costly, TOM will partially specialize in the production of wheat and produce more bushels relative to yards of cloth. TOM will still export bushels of wheat for yards of cloth and will still obtain gains in consumption from trading according to comparative advantage. But unlike the initial constant cost environment where all the gains accrued to Tom's own labor producing only bushels of wheat, seen in this TOM macro economy there will be a much different distributional welfare effect from trade that will be reflected in dispersed level of income inequality and purchasing power within the labor force.

Economic Growth for TOM in the Model

Finally, it is important to note that in Figure 2.4 is a PPF2 for the TOM economy. This new PPF2 curve is drawn outside TOM's initial PPF1 curve. Suppose the TOM economy obtains more land specific to wheat production or adopts new production methods/technology (i.e., mechanized farming) that raises the productivity of each existing acre and new acres of land employed, so now a maximum of 80 bushels of wheat can be produced. With more land and better technology used to farm the land, TOM's PPF curve will rotate out along the horizontal axis to reflect the new maximum of bushels of wheat that can be produced, leaving the maximum amount of yards of cloth that can be produced unchanged.

This rotation of the PPF out and along the horizontal axis to give a new PPF2 illustrates the new maximum production possibilities available to TOM and new opportunity costs incurred between the productions of each good. The economic growth in the wheat industry from more land obtained or innovation in wheat production has given TOM a much flatter PPF that is more biased toward wheat production, suggesting the opportunity cost of producing any amount of bushels of wheat has fallen relative to every yard of cloth produced! Resource expansion or technology acquisition changing production methods in the wheat industry not only has supported expansion of the industry (which is growth positive in total output for the TOM economy), it also has decreased the opportunity of using resources employed in wheat production by the flatter slope of the price line at point B' along PPF2 as compared to point B along PPF1.

2.4 CONCLUSION: THE PPF AND THE MACROECONOMIC PICTURE

In summary, the use of the PPF model in both constant and increasing opportunity cost terms reinforces the necessity of scarcity to create exploitable opportunities for trade and exchange according to differing opportunity costs between economic actors: persons, firms, and the economies of countries.

The existence of different opportunity costs and other trade-offs in the marketplace support the notion that at best, scarcity is useful in its utility as an economic motivator and drives specialization and a more efficient allocation of resources to the most productive, lowest opportunity cost areas to maximize exploitable trade and exchange opportunities. Even with economic growth from resource acquisition and technological advancement, which will redistribute the gains and costs unequally across the broader marketplace, the action of exchange and trade following the concept of comparative advantage will at best diminish product/ resource scarcity but not fully eliminate scarcity. The elimination of scarcity, although desirable, only creates scarcity in other areas, ever changing the incentives and the motivation of actors in the marketplace. This statement does beg a word of caution to economies that have chosen to over-specialize their production assets around a source of comparative advantage. The case study at the end of this chapter highlights the consequences to Canada's economy from overspecialization in the extraction and export of its natural resources.

At the macro level, the PPF provides a picture of the potential output possibilities of an economy, suggesting the opportunity costs of resources to be used and the type of economic system being preferred for the best allocation of resources. Any point on a PPF curve represents an output combination representing a part or total of the whole macroeconomic pie (i.e., GDP). The observable and sometimes not so observable changes in opportunity costs will be reflected in the changes of prices for single goods in our two-good model. When expanded to include all other goods, this will shape discussions on macroeconomic policy addressing items such as the trade-offs between inflation and unemployment.

Although this chapter shows the gains from trade and how economic growth and can affect the future potential of an economy and the costs to be internal or shared externally with other partners, more explanation is needed for the market forces overall that are putting pressure on opportunity costs to rise and fall, and consider if such opportunity costs are adequately reflected in all prices. Scarcity, although not desirable but essential, should be reflected in the changing of prices (including interest rates in a loanable funds markets) acting as a mechanism to reflect the degree of scarcity, profitability of exploitable opportunities, and the rationing of scarce resources, goods and services, and economic opportunities.

What's next?

The next chapter will build on the Tom and Hank model and consider the market forces between facilitating trade and exchange by applying a supply and demand analysis approach. The analysis will be important in determining not only the factor(s) that change overall market demand and supply but also the changes in overall final prices and quantities shaping the overall macro output picture, employment of resources, inflation, interest rates, and distribution of income. Suggested in the onset of this text that scarcity is a "necessary evil" to be an effective economic motivator to drive exchange and trade, it will be shown in the supply and demand model that disequilibrium will be preferred to equilibrium in order to sustain ongoing exploitable opportunities for exchange and trade.

CASE STUDY: CANADA'S "STAPLES TRAP": CONSEQUENCES FROM AN OVERRELIANCE ON PRODUCTION SPECIALIZATION

Canada is a rich country by world measurements relying heavily on the exploitation of its natural resources, or so-called staples, for export.[17] The country's reliance on the exploitation of its natural resource endowment has given the country a specific political-economy character providing insight into Canada's future growth path. The country's heavy reliance on the export of natural resources as an economic driver is a concern. Declines in global demand and increases in global staple supplies now pose a challenge to Canada's political economy in finding a new economic base that will sustain Canada as a wealthy developed economy.

An important question to ask is: Why does a rich country such as Canada devote so much continued attention to natural resources at a time when employment growth in the country's resource sector has slowed and declines in global commodity prices since mid-2014 have caused a pullback in resource sector investments?[18] Similar to economies with development underpinnings tied to the extraction and export of natural resources, Canada's geographical composition of its natural resources remains a cornerstone of the country's political economy via a staples export-dependent model. The location, extraction, and export of natural resources through mature market channels continues to be the lifeblood of the many provincial centers spread out across Canada's expansive geographical area. According to notable resource economists, Canada's climate and topographical challenges prevented the nation from undergoing a development process similar to its southern neighbor, the United States. The climate and topographical challenges necessitated the need to invest heavily in transportation and logistical

[17] The government of Canada estimated in July 2015 that Canada's natural resources accounted for 20 percent of the total contribution to the country's nominal GDP in 2014, with forestry (1 percent), minerals and metals (4 percent), and energy (10 percent) accounting for 15 percent of the direct impact of the total contribution. In 2014 Canadian exports were valued at $259 billion, with forestry, minerals and metals, and energy accounting for more than 53 percent of Canada's merchandise exports. The United States, Great Britain, and China are the three main export destinations of Canada's natural resource exports, with 97 percent of energy, 66 percent of forest products, and 52 percent of mineral and metal of total Canadian natural resource exports destined for the US market. Source: http://www.nrcan.gc.ca/publications/key-facts/16013.

[18] The government of Canada estimated in July 2015 that natural resource sectors in Canada contributed 1.8 million jobs to total national employment in 2014. Between 2010 and 2014, employment in forestry, fishing, mining, quarrying, oil, and gas grew at an annualized rate of 3.5 percent, accounting for 2.09 percent of total employment in 2014. Source: http://www.statcan.gc.ca/tables-tableaux/sum-som/l01/cst01/econ40-eng.htm.

infrastructure networks to serve staple-importing industrial economies at the consequence of underinvestment in manufacturing.[19]

Canada's attention on natural resources as staples for export provides a unique glimpse of Canada's cultural trait termed as *statism*, which is described as the handling of social and economic development questions through the government's involvement in the process of exploiting resources over the continent. Canadian political power is heavily influenced by domestic business and political elites serving as agents of interests in targeted industrialized countries importing Canadian staples. The goal of this heavy involvement by Canada's government is to spread the economic welfare effects of its export sectors broadly across the country's provincial areas having strong dependency on income from natural resources. The table in Table 2.4 illustrates the heart of the Canadian provinces' dependency on staples exports.[20]

	Revealed Comparative Advantage	Export Dependency
British Columbia	1.87	75.87
Alberta	1.97	79.95
ASkatchewan	2.19	88.56
Manitoba	1.42	57.41
Ontario	0.46	18.60
Quebec	0.99	39.99
New Brunswick	2.24	90.60
Nova Scotia	1.59	64.30
Prince Edward Island	1.94	78.76
Newfoundland and Labrador	2.38	96.48
Yukon	2.13	86.20
Northwest Territories	2.45	99.08
Nunavut	2.46	99.64

Table 2.4. Canada's Dependency on Staples Exports.

Source: Canada Department of Foreign Affairs and International Trade, 2003.

With the exception of Ontario and Quebec, all other provinces are highly dependent on natural resource sectors, with sources of dependency highly differentiated among them. For example, oil and natural gas dominates Alberta's natural resource sectors (as evident with the cross-border investment with the United States in the Keystone Pipeline Project), and agriculture is the leading sector in ASkatchewan.

Against the global backdrop of an oil price shock that has taken its toll on oil-producing economies, Canada's current experience shows economic growth for the provincial economies tends to be divided between oil-producing provinces and oil-consuming ones. The plunge in global oil prices since mid-2014 has, according to the Royal Bank of Canada, dimmed the economic outlook for the oil-producing provinces of Newfoundland and Labrador, Alberta,[21] and ASkatchewan. Although lower oil prices are clearly a negative for oil-producing provinces in Canada,

[19] Wellstead, A. 2007. "The (Post) Staples Economy and the (Post) Staples State: A Historical Perspective." *Canadian Political Science Review* 1 (1): 8.

[20] The table shows the revealed comparative advantage, the ratio of the provincial share in resource trade to the national share of resources in total trade. If the revealed comparative advantage as a statistic is greater than one, then that province trades more in natural resources than it does for all other commodities.

[21] The oil sands in Alberta have been coined Canada's "Great Wall of China" and will constitute the lion's share of oil exports to the United State via the Keystone Pipeline Project. Lower per barrel oil prices will curb the purchasing power of Alberta's production.

lower oil prices should provide Canada with a weaker Canadian Dollar, helping boost the economy's manufacturing export sector.

Despite having a reduced share of the Canadian economic footprint, 50 percent of Canadian manufacturing sales are exported, with 80 percent of those sales destined for a strengthening US market. This is a welcomed reprieve for an economic sector that has been struggling to capture gains from US import growth since the turn of the century, but this has at the same time raised doubts as to how much manufacturing exports can offset a weaker oil and natural gas sector that will remain weak for the remainder of the year and into 2016.[22]

Years of overinvestment in natural resources, or staples, has created an underinvestment in manufacturing capacity. Economists consider this to be problematic in the sector's ability to respond to normal drivers of economic activity and respond to stronger US demand and a weaker domestic currency to capture an export advantage. Because resource export dependency is differentiated and varies from province to province, the regional impact from lower oil and commodity prices will be felt in a substantial variation between oil-producing and non-oil-producing provinces; while the aggregate impact on the Canadian economy will be minimal.

The most significant problem for Canada's provinces is an export dependency that has become a "staples trap," creating a reluctance to focus on domestic development and rely more on the importing country's dependency on the provinces' exports. Resource economists argue the Canadian state and Canadian finance overinvest in discovering and exploiting resources already having established resource markets. It is very much evident how much resource exports have been a cornerstone of economic growth for the Canadian provinces. However, with declining global demand and increases in global supplies, Canada will need to set a new political-economy trajectory that replaces staples-dependent activities or augments them with value-adding, transformational activities.

QUESTIONS FOR CLASS DISCUSSION

1. The model of trade and exchange presented in this chapter is a simplified model to illustrate the basis for trade and exchange (according to comparative advantage) when there are exploitable differences in the opportunity costs between the parties involved. However, the assumptions of the constant cost model are unrealistic when reconciled against management and regulations of trade and exchange between countries and individuals in the real world. In class, discuss which assumptions of the model are unrealistic and why, and reconcile the basic trade model against real-world observations in the marketplace. If free trade is desirable and said to be welfare maximizing, then why are such activities regulated and managed, thereby affecting the distribution and maximization of gains from trade and exchange between parties involved?
2. Less-developed economies are more often trade protectionist than developed economies, which have mature market systems to diversify and trade risk in market transactions between parties (providing other wealth-creating opportunities). Discuss reasons why such lesser-developed or poorer economies (those you and your classmates choose) should or should not be more open to free trade. List the pros and cons. Are such pros and cons you and your classmates listed an example of trade-offs incurred when engaging in free trade or not?

[22] *RBC Economics Research*, "Will Lower Oil Prices Provide a Boost to Canadian Manufacturers?," February 2015.

3. Over the course of history, poorer and lesser-developed economies have used more openness to trade and the rest of the world as a catalyst for economic development, to attract capital investments, raise living standards, and so on. Yet the results have shown to be successful for some and unsuccessful for others. Under free trade, consider reasons why such economies (for the ones you and your classmates choose) have or have not become more developed.

IMAGE CREDITS

- Image 2.0: Copyright © Depositphotos/roxanabalint.
- Tbl. 2.4: Brian Hunt, "Canada's Dependency on Staples Exports," Canada Department of Foreign Affairs and International Trade, 2003.

CHAPTER 3

SUPPLY, DEMAND, AND THE "INVISIBLE HAND"

Figure 3.0. Open-air spice market in Dubai (August 2008).

3.0 TRADING OPPORTUNITY COSTS IN THE MARKETPLACE TO GAIN MORE

In the previous chapters, the role of scarcity was examined as an economic motivator to drive the basis for exchange and trade to satisfy unlimited needs and wants with finite resources and opportunities. The Tom and Hank trade example in Chapter 2 applied this concept to show the different opportunity costs each faced when making choices in the allocation of their scarce labor between the production of yards of cloth and bushels of wheat. The differing opportunity costs Tom and Hank faced, as a reflection of differing labor productivities, facilitated the basis for production specialization and exchange to exploit an opportunity between them to satisfy needs and wants above and beyond their production potential.

In a free market environment, Tom and Hank were able to exchange some amount of yards of cloth for bushels of wheat at a rate of exchange better than their respective internal rates of exchange. This trade at the better rate of exchange allowed both to consume more of both goods than they were able to do under self-sufficiency. Following the principle of specialization and comparative advantage, Tom and Hank created immense scarcity in the good they needed, and then they each traded the good they specialized in at a higher market value to obtain the alternate good at a lower opportunity.

A helpful model to explain the dynamics of Tom's and Hank's exchange is the model of supply and demand. What does this model describe well in terms of the observable behavior in the marketplace between Tom and Hank? What does it not describe well? How useful will this model be in explaining the final quantities and prices prevailing in their markets and those that may or may not be observed in the real world markets?

Supply and Demand in a Dubai Spice Market

Image 3.1 at the start of this chapter is a single photo this author took of spices being sold in an open-air market during a trip to Dubai, United Arab Emirates, in August 2008. While browsing the spices in the open-air market, observable were the dynamics of supply and demand between buyers and sellers. In this spice market, prices are not posted but rather negotiated through a process called haggling. The seller of the spices has a maximum reservation price in mind for selling a quantity of a spice to the buyer. The buyer has in mind a maximum reservation price for demanding a quantity of spice at.

Through the haggling process, market forces are at work between buyer and seller that will determine a final price—that lies between the maximum reservation prices of the seller and buyer—for a final quantity of spice that will be demanded and supplied. Spices are allocated to buyers who are willing to pay the most in terms of time, place, and use. There is an assumption: Those who are willing to pay more for a good are also more likely to use the good in a more valuable way than someone who values the good less.

So how can a supply and demand model be used to illustrate the behavior of prices and quantities of spices throughout a normal market day, and would gains from such exchange be fully maximized and exhausted between buyer and seller? Would the model best describe through the behavior of prices the true opportunity costs in the trade-off of opportunities?

Navigating the Nuances of Supply and Demand in This Chapter

To start, the demand side of the market will be examined. Next will be an examination of the supply side of the market. Finally, supply and demand will be integrated together, and the concept of equilibrium and how changes in overall demand and supply affect final equilibrium prices and quantities will be covered.

For subsequent chapters, supply and demand analysis will be useful at the macro economy level to consider the following:

1. *How final quantities and final prices for all goods in the marketplace shape a final market value of what is produced as total output for the entire economy*
2. *How the behavior of prices in the marketplace shape inflation and price indexes*
3. *How final quantities and final prices support the employment of resources—land, labor, and capital—and the income paid to said resources*

3.1 DEMAND: THE LAW OF DEMAND AND THE DETERMINANTS OF DEMAND

Adam Smith (c. 1723–1790), the father of classical economics, in his famous book, *The Wealth of Nations* (1776), explained his conception of market behavior and the function of nation-states in the wealth-building process. Deriving a better understanding of the behavior of market prices and corresponding market quantities, Smith introduced two important laws of economics: the law of demand and the law of supply.

The law of demand in its simplest form is this:

> *As the price of a good increases (or decreases,) the quantity demanded of the good decreases (or increases), holding all other non-price determinants of demand constant.*

The law of demand essentially examines how a change in the price of a good affects the quantity demanded of that good only. This is completely different from a change in overall demand, where there is some observed increase (or decrease) in demand at some given price in the marketplace. A behavioral change in overall demand will be explained by changes in the non-price determinants of demand independent of changes in prices. It is important here to note a change in quantity demanded is differentiated from a change in overall demand.

As stated, the law of demand examines the relationship of a change in the price of a good only and the corresponding change in quantity demanded from the change in price; holding all other non-price determinants of market demand constant. When the price of a good increases or decreases, holding all other factors constant, a change in the quantity demanded will be observed but not a change in overall demand. Using Tom's individual market again from Chapter 2, Figure 3.1 illustrates the law of demand as an inverse relationship between the change in the price of the good and the change in the quantity demanded while holding all other non-price determinants of demand constant.

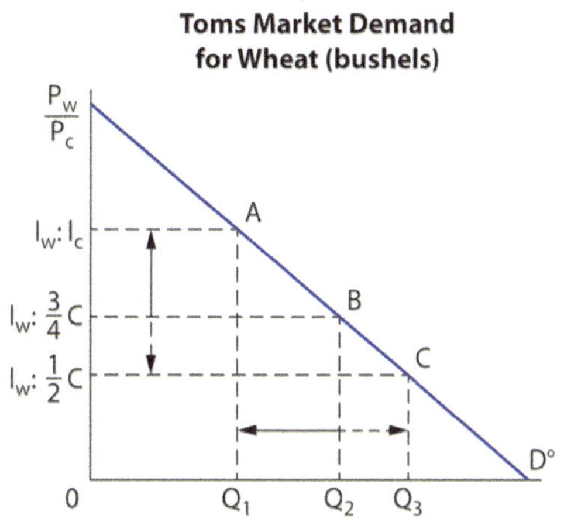

Figure 3.1. Tom's market demand for wheat (bushels).

Tom's demand for bushels of wheat

Tom from Chapter 2 is back again, and he is producing bushels of wheat and yards of cloth in an environment of increasing cost as opposed to a constant cost environment. As Tom elects to produce more bushels of wheat, the opportunity cost of each bushel increases at a faster marginal change (opportunity cost) in terms of yards of cloth forgone. Correlating the change in the opportunity cost of each bushel of wheat in his economy to an equal change in the price per bushel, the law of demand as applied will show the inverse relationship between the quantities of bushels of wheat Tom demands at different prices.

Tom's increasing opportunity cost experience in the production of wheat shows every bushel produced becomes more expensive in terms of cloth forgone. If Tom were to purchase the wheat he produces, he essentially would have to pay a price at least equal to the opportunity cost of the last bushel in order for that last bushel to be released to himself. Tom's individual demand curve for wheat is also his market demand curve for wheat, since he is the only buyer of wheat in his own market. Holding all other non-price determinants of demand for Tom's wheat constant, observed in Figure 3.1 will be his quantities demanded of bushels of wheat at different prices or opportunity costs he faces in production. At a price of 1W = ¾C (or ¾ yards of cloth trades for 1 bushel of wheat), Tom demands a quantity of Q_2 bushels of wheat.

At a higher per bushel price of 1W:1C (or 1 yard of cloth trades for 1 bushel of wheat), Tom's quantity demanded is Q_1 bushels of wheat, which is less than the Q_2 bushels of wheat he is demanding at the lower per bushel price of ¾ yards. In this case, Tom's quantity demanded for bushels of wheat has decreased at the higher market price (opportunity cost) per bushel. At a market price of 1W = ½C (or ½ yards of cloth trades for 1 bushels of wheat) Tom's quantity demanded of Q_3 bushels of wheat is greater than his quantity demanded at the price of ¾ yards of cloth for 1 bushel of wheat. While holding all other market non-price determinants of demand constant, higher market prices for bushels of wheat translate into lower quantities demanded for bushels of wheat, and lower market prices per bushel of wheat translate into a larger quantities demanded for bushels of wheat.[1]

Differentiating a change in quantity demanded from a change in overall market demand

Figure 3.2 also shows that as a market price for bushels of wheat adjusts higher or lower, the change in the market price and the inverse corresponding change in the quantity demanded constitutes a movement up (or down) along the market demand curve. Any change in market price only, while holding everything else constant, will keep market demand unchanged. Essentially, the only change expected to be sees with a change in price only is a change in the quantity demanded for bushels of wheat and the same for any good or service in the market.

The key concept here is that any change in market price only (holding everything else constant) will result in a change in quantity demanded of some amount for the good, but no change in overall market demand for the good. In our market for Tom's wheat, for there to be an overall change in market demand for Tom's wheat, he must be demanding more bushels of wheat at the initial market price and at every higher and lower price in the price schedule.[2]

So ... what constitutes a change in overall market demand: an increase or decrease? Students often mistakenly believe that a change in the price of a good will result in an increase or decrease in overall demand for the good. This is incorrect. A change in price only will constitute a change in quantity demanded only; not a change in

[1] In special cases, there are goods for which, over a specific range of higher market prices, a greater quantity is demanded for the goods, and at prices above the range the quantity demanded begins to decrease. These types of goods are called Giffen goods; they have price offer curves that exhibit a positive slope over the range of higher prices where quantity demanded increases and a negative slope above that range of higher prices where quantity demanded begins to decrease.

[2] A price schedule is a schedule of prices showing the corresponding quantities demanded and supplied of the good at each scheduled market price.

overall demand. Increases or decreases in overall market demand will be the result of changes in the non-price determinants of demand. Figure 3.2 examines changes in Tom's overall market demand for wheat at a current market price as opposed to changes in his quantity demanded for wheat.

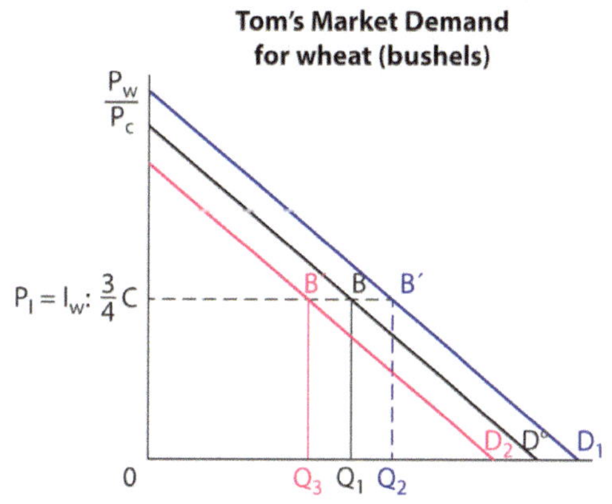

Figure 3.2. Tom's increases and decreases in overall demand for bushels of wheat.

Figure 3.2 shows the price of a bushel of wheat set in Tom's marketplace at P_1 = 1W:¾C (or ¾ yards of cloth trades for 1 bushel of wheat). Also shown is Tom's initial demand curve for wheat, D_0, at the market price demanding a quantity of Q_1 bushels of wheat at point B. The figure also illustrates two different cases for Tom: an increase in his market demand for wheat or a decrease in his market demand for wheat at the current market price, P_1 = 1W:¾C. His increase in demand for bushels of wheat is represented by rightward shift of his demand curve from D_0 to D_1, and his decrease in demand for bushels of wheat is represented as a leftward shift of his demand curve from D_0 to D_2.

Suppose Tom's initial demand curve, D_0, shifts out and to the right to D_1 at the current price, P_1 = 1W = ¾C. Initially, Tom was demanding a quantity of Q_1 bushels at the current price, and he is now demanding a greater quantity of Q_2 bushels at the current price (at point B′) and also demanding greater quantities of bushels of wheat at every higher and lower price along our price axis.

If his initial demand curve, D_1, shifts out and to the left to D_2 at the current price, P_1=1W=3/4C, observed is a decrease in Tom's market demand for bushels of wheat to Q_3 (at point B″) at the current price and all prices higher and lower along the price axis. How is this different from what was observed applying the law of demand?

Recall that the law of demand considers the change in quantity demanded only when there is change in price only at some current level of market demand. This change in quantity demanded in response to a change in market price will be represented as a movement up or down and along the market demand curve. The law of demand also assumes that in order to observe the change in quantity demanded with a change in market price, all other non-price determinants of demand must be held constant. In Figure 3.2, we see the opposite: Market price is held constant, allowing all other observable non-price determinants of market demand to change and influencing the overall level of market demand at a current price in the market.

Shifts in Market Demand: Changes in the Non-Price Determinants of Market Demand

In Figure 3.2, Tom either experiences an increase in overall demand for bushels of wheat or a decrease in overall demand for bushels of wheat at the current price. The visible shifts in his market demand curves in the figure do not provide enough information as to what demand factor(s) are changing and causing Tom to respond with greater or lesser participation as a buyer in his wheat market. What might the changes in the non-price determinants of market demand be, and can these changes in non-price determinants of demand be applied for a broader examination of any micro market with more than one buyer? The following are a list of market demand non-price determinants. When these non-price determinants are applied in a general way, changes in them best explain the following:

1. *Expected observations of greater or weaker demand in a market at some existing market price.*
2. *The predicted change in the equilibrium market price and equilibrium market quantity.*

Changes in income (normal vs. inferior goods)

If a buyer(s) in a given market experience a rise in income, the predicted observable result will be an increase in market demand for goods that are normal goods and a decrease in market demand for goods that are inferior goods. A normal good is one that buyers will consume more of as their income level rises and less of as their income level falls. Inferior goods are ones consumers purchase more of as income declines and demand less of with a rise in income.

Qualified buyers in a market must have the willingness and ability to participate. Buyers may have the willingness to participate but not the ability as defined by income level. As a buyer's ability to participate in more market transactions is improved with increases in income, demand for normal goods will increase and demand for inferior goods will decrease. An example of a normal good would be new luxury makes of certain types of cars. As income rises and the demand for goods like luxury cars (and other luxury items) increases, the market demand for other goods may decrease, since the increase in buyer income has negatively affected the demand for such goods.

Take for example a public transportation system in a metropolitan area that is treated as an inferior choice to private transportation.[3] As buyers in a market make more income and the increase in income gives buyers more transportation opportunities to participate in, demand for public transportation—the use of buses for transportation—can decrease. This is provided there are available private transportation substitutes that provide highly competitive market access and choice to the user. In this market example, public transportation goods are considered inferior and treated as an inferior choice or preferences as buyer income increases.[4]

Changes in tastes and preferences

If a buyer(s) tastes or preferences for a good become much stronger or more positive—the good is preferred more relative to other substitute goods—then overall demand for the goods(s) will increase. If a buyer(s) tastes or preferences become more negative or overall weaker—the good becomes less preferred to other substitute goods—then overall demand for the good will decrease. Factors influencing buyers' tastes and preferences include but are not limited to culture and cultural changes, changes in education and occupation, demographic changes, advertising (all mediums), social group affiliation, and socioeconomic standing.

In consumer theory, consumers will choose the goods or bundles of goods that will derive them the highest level of satisfaction (i.e., utility) and prefer less goods or bundles of goods that will derive them lower levels of satisfaction. When income and market prices for goods and services change, buyers will adjust consumption quantities and substitute between goods and services to preserve (improve on) an existing level of satisfaction.

---

[3] In a number of US metropolitan areas, public transportation is seen as a highly competitive substitute in price and service to private transportation substitutes; provided that public transportation options deliver the same level of depth and breadth to market access that private transportation would. However, public transportation can be viewed as an inferior good, provided that the depth and breadth of public transportation limits a person's access to markets and employment opportunities. For instance, persons who use bus lines as their primary source of transportation will typically live and work closer to areas that have a high connectivity with bus routes.

[4] Goods and services that are normal goods will have a calculated value of income elasticity that is positive and greater than zero. Goods and services that are inferior will have calculated values of income elasticity that are negative and less than zero.

Changes in expectations about future prices

If buyers expect the market price of a good to rise in the future, these same buyers will go out and demand more of the good today—participating more in the marketplace to secure the good—at the current price, causing demand to increase.

For example, if buyers expect a gasoline shortage and gasoline prices to increase in response to the shortage, these buyers will demand more gasoline in gallons at the current price at the pump and enter the market in large numbers in response to this expectation about the future. This will result in an increase in market demand for gasoline and will put pressure on market gasoline prices to rise. If buyers expect lower prices in the future, then these same buyers will participate less at the current price or hold back their spending plans. This will result in a decrease in market demand for gasoline and put pressure on market gasoline prices to fall. As a result of herding effects by buyers following the action of other visible buyers with equal or similar expectations about the future, the expectation about future market prices becomes self-prophetic.

Changes in the number of buyers entering and exiting the market

Changes in costs—prices, fees, and/or taxes paid—of entering and exiting a market and changes in market regulation affecting costs of entry and the number of qualified buyers able to participate will affect overall demand for a good. Changes in income and transportation will also impact the number of buyers entering and/or exiting a marketplace.

For example, if the income of existing and potential buyers rises, this will provide improved market participation for existing market opportunities and market opportunities once foreclosed to buyers at lower income levels. Changes in transportation design and transportation infrastructure impacting the mobility and transactions costs of buyers entering and exiting markets will affect overall demand through participation (entry and exit). For instance, expanded public transportation options will have an impact of opening market access (entry) to buyers that once had limited market access limited by public transportation routes.

Changes in the price of related goods (substitutes and complements)

Overall demand for goods in the marketplace will increase or decrease in response to a change in the market price of a related good or service: substitute or complement.[5] Goods and services can be substitutes to one another in terms of the following:

1. *Price*
2. *Tastes and preferences*
3. *Risk and uncertainty*

Substitutes

For example, suppose goods A and B are perfect substitutes—can be exchanged at a rate of 1:1—and the prices of both goods are equal. When the price of good A increases relative to good B, the quantity demanded for good A decreases. There is no change in the overall demand for good A because there has been a change in price for the good. But the overall demand for good B will increase by some amount at the current price and all prices in the good's price schedule.

[5] A good is a substitute to another good in terms of price when the calculated cross-price elasticity between the two goods is greater than zero and positive. A good is a complement to another good terms of price when the calculated cross-price elasticity between the two goods is less than zero and negative.

Buyers equally preferring good A and good B are consuming some amount of both goods. As the price of good A rises, buyers reduce their quantity demanded of good A, substitute good B, and increase their consumption amount of good B at the current price in order to keep their level of satisfaction unchanged. The opposite will be true for a decrease in the price of good A: Quantity demanded of good A will increase and the overall demand for the now expensive substitute—good B—will decrease at the current market price for good B.

Complements

Goods considered to be complements are consumed together. Basic examples of such goods would be coffee and cream, hot dogs and hot dog buns, peanut butter and jelly, and tennis rackets and tennis balls. As the price of one of these goods rises relative to the other, the quantity demanded will decrease and the overall demand for the good's complement will decrease. The opposite would occur for a decrease in the market price of one these goods relative to its complement.

By how much demand will increase or decrease for good in response to a change in price of its substitute or complement will be influenced by the market treatment of the pair of goods. For instance, the strength of price substitution between two goods will vary depending on the distance between the goods in the marketplace and the degree of product differentiation that substantiates the price points of the goods.

Changes in taxes and subsidies

Taxes (of any kind) are regressive and will result in observable decreases in market demand (and associated deadweight losses in market welfare) for an increase in taxes on consumption (an excise tax). An example of a tax on consumption (excise tax), or so-called sin tax, is the tax on cigarettes (and ad valorem tax) that is designed to increase the overall price per pack a consumer pays in order to decrease the quantity of cigarettes consumed and decrease overall tobacco use.

All subsidies designed to increase buyer participation in the market act as income received but not earned. One designed purpose of the subsidy is to increase participation in the market for a targeted consumable good (i.e., health insurance and health care). An example of a subsidy that is a monetary transfer in kind would be Social Security, and an example of a subsidy that would be considered a transfer of a good in-kind would be food stamps.

All taxes on consumption are a way to curb consumption or substitute consumption away from one type of consumable to a consumable that is taxed less or not at all. This will result in decreases in overall demand. All subsidies are designed to support existing participation and/or increase the participation among existing and new buyers to enter the marketplace and will result in increases in overall demand.[6]

3.2 SUPPLY: THE LAW OF SUPPLY AND THE MARKET DETERMINANTS OF SUPPLY

Like the law of demand, the law of supply looks at the relationship between a change in market price and the quantity of the good supplied while holding all other non-price determinants of supply constant.

[6] Subsidies act as a "negative tax."

Holding all other non-price determinants of supply constant, the law of supply illustrates an observable change in the price of the good with an observable change in the quantity supplied.

> *If the price of a good increases—holding all other non-price determinants constant—the seller will respond with a greater quantity supplied. If the price of a good decreases—holding all other non-price determinants constant—the seller will respond with a lower quantity supplied.*

Unlike the law of demand that describes an inverse relationship between market price and quantity demanded, the law of supply describes a positive relationship between market price and quantity supplied.

Tom's PPF and supply curve

Let's get back to Tom again. Suppose Tom is producing only yards of cloth and 0 bushels of wheat. If Tom elects to trade away 5 yards of cloth to produce and supply a quantity of 20 bushels of wheat, he does so at an opportunity cost of ¼ yards of cloth for each bushel of wheat he produces to supply as shown in Figure 3.3.[7] In his market, each bushel of wheat of the 20 bushels will be supplied at a domestic price equal to his opportunity of each bushel, which is Pw/Pc = 1W:¼C = slope of the line segment.

If Tom chooses to produce and supply a greater quantity of bushels of wheat—an additional 10 more bushel for a total of 30 bushels produced and supplied—the additional 10 bushels he produces and supplies comes at an opportunity of 5 more yards of cloth.[8] The market price at which Tom will supply 30 bushels of wheat must be at least equal to his opportunity of the 30th bushel, Pw/Pc = 1W:½C = slope of line segment AB.

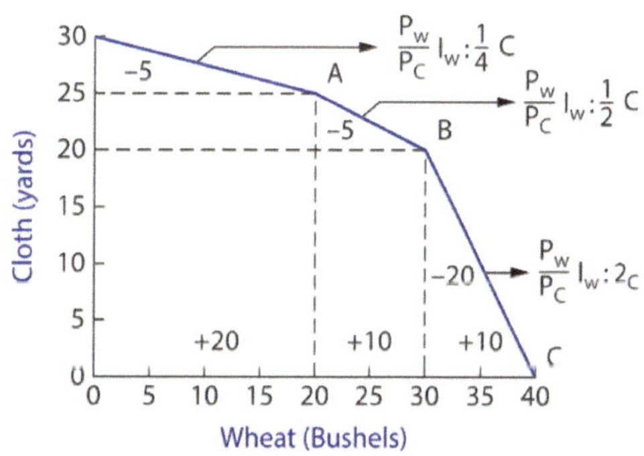

Figure 3.3. Tom's PPF for yards of cloth and bushels of wheat in an increasing cost environment.

Finally, if Tom wishes to produce and supply 10 more bushels of wheat to have a total of 40 bushels of wheat supplied in quantity in his market, it will cost him 20 yards of cloth. To cover his opportunity cost of producing and supplying the 40th bushel in his market, Tom must supply each bushel of the 40 bushels at a rate of exchange at least equal to the trade-off he makes, which will be Pw/Pc = 1W:2C = slope of line segment BC.

From this increasing cost environment, Tom produces and supplies a greater quantity of bushels of wheat at higher prices. From a seller viewpoint, the incentives to supply a greater quantity must be at a higher market price equal to or greater than the opportunity cost incurred to produce and supply the given quantity. The information

[7] Figure 3.3 shows four connected straight line segments—of increasing slope—creating Tom's PPF for yards of cloth and bushels of wheat. Each line segment represents a constant opportunity cost of bushels of wheat in terms of yards of cloth. At production point A, Tom produces 20 bushels of wheat and 25 yards of cloth. The opportunity cost of the 20th bushel of wheat supplied is equal to the slope of the line segment, –¼, from the intercept of the y-axis to point A. As a price taker, Tom's quantity supplied price is ¼ yards of cloth for 1 bushel of wheat. Each remaining line segment has a steeper slope forming Tom's PPF and indicating that greater quantities produced of bushels of wheat will be supplied at higher prices reflecting higher opportunity cost.

[8] Figure 3.3 shows diminishing returns to scale for Tom's labor.

in Tom's PPF can be used to create a supply curve (Figure 3.4) for the quantity of bushels of wheat he will supply at different prices and show the law of supply in practice.

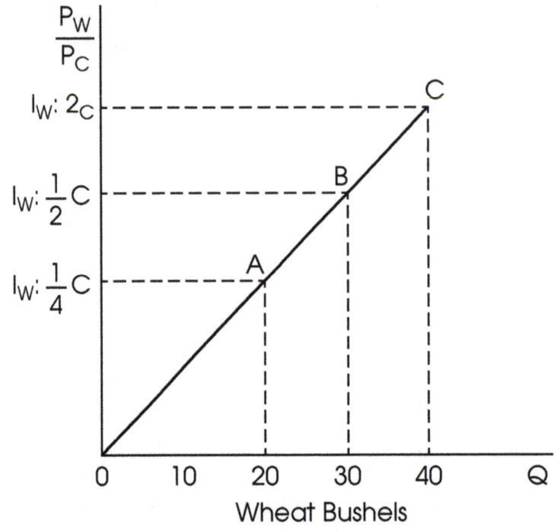

Figure 3.4. Tom's market supply curve for bushels of wheat, with market prices expressed in terms of yards of cloth. Because of rising opportunity costs incurred over different output ranges for producing additional quantities of bushels of wheat, as a producer/seller, Tom will supply greater quantities of bushels of wheat at higher market price to at least cover his incurred opportunity cost (in terms of yards of cloth given up) for the marginal increases of bushels of wheat he is supplying to the marketplace.

Shifts in Market Supply: Changes in the Non-Price Determinants of Market Supply

So, what if Tom is able to supply more bushels of wheat at a current price and at every price level in terms of yards of cloth in his marketplace? In this case changes in the non-price determinants of supply will describe Tom's ability and reasons for supplying more (or fewer) bushels of wheat at the current price and every price in the overall marketplace. Figure 3.5 depicts the increase (or decrease) in Tom's supply of bushels of wheat in the market at the current price, Pw/Pc = 1W = ½C in response to a change(s) in non-price determinants impacting his overall market supply at the current price. What are these non-price determinants of market supply that when changed result in overall increases or decreases in the market supply at a current market price?

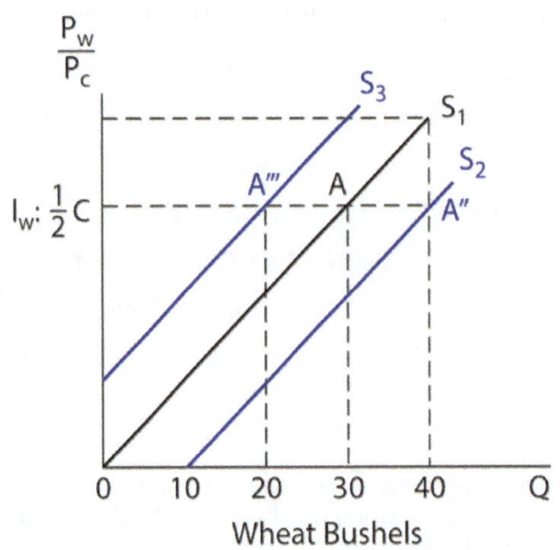

Figure 3.5. Shifts in market supply curve for Tom's wheat.

Changes in technology

If Tom is able to adopt new production methods that are time saving and will increase his output of bushels of wheat for every hour of his employed time, he will be able to supply more bushels of wheat at current market prices. Production innovation has a positive impact on market supply (always an increase). This will be denoted as a rightward shift of Tom's market supply curve from S_1 to S_2, increasing his market supply of bushels of wheat from 30 bushel to 40 bushels.

Changes in input prices

Changes in input costs (including labor costs) are a major factor impacting the overall costs of production and final output supplied. If Tom were to experience an increase in the cost of the inputs he uses to produces bushels of wheat, and he is unable to raise his price in the market to cover this rise in cost, he will respond by decreasing his market supply as denoted by a leftward shift of his market supply curve from S_1 to S_3, resulting in 10 fewer bushel of wheat being supplied in the market at the current market price.

As such, any decrease in the cost of inputs he uses will result in savings for him, and such savings can be invested in new production capacity and will allow for him to increase his market supply of bushels of wheat from S_1 to S_2, an increase of 10 additional bushels of wheat at the current price.

In the real world, changes in costs of inputs sourced domestically or through trade will affect overall production costs and the overall market supply by the firm. This is why global supply chain management is important to firms. As well, changes in market regulation may affect the availability of critical inputs and costs of procuring such inputs, thereby having a favorable or unfavorable impact on market supply. For example, in January 2016 the US government lifted its export ban on domestic oil. This addition of US domestic oil produced from fracking will now be added to the global marketplace. The result of this lifting of the US export ban on domestic oil will result in increased global oil supplies being traded and will lead to a lower US Dollar price per barrel.

Changes in the number of sellers in the marketplace

If Tom's production of wheat is profitable and the costs of entry into his market are minimal, more outside sellers of wheat may enter Tom's market. The increase in the number of sellers will add more wheat to market supply and will be reflected as a rightward shift of the curve with more being supplied at the current price.

On the other hand, if the profitability of the wheat market becomes unfavorable and/or costs of operations in the market rise to levels causing profits to decline and losses to emerge, then sellers of wheat will exit the wheat market; provided exit costs are negligible. In this case an overall decrease in the market supply of wheat will occur as sellers exit, and the market supply curve will shift leftward and less will be supplied at the current price.

Changes in the price of related goods in production

For Tom, if the market price of yards of cloth were to rise above the market price of wheat per bushel, Tom would decrease his supply of wheat at the current market price and increase the quantity supplied of yards of cloth at the higher prices.

The decrease in Tom's market supply of wheat (leftward shift in his market supply curve) is the result of Tom allocating his labor (and any other mobile resources) away from the production of bushels of wheat to the production of yards of cloth. If the market price of yards of cloth were to decline, Tom will allocate his labor hours (and any other mobile resources) away from yards of cloth production to be employed in wheat production adding more bushels of wheat to the market at the current bushel price.

Changes in seller expectations

If Tom expects higher prices in the future that he can supply and sell his wheat at, he will supply fewer bushels of wheat today at the current price. If he expects lower prices per bushel of wheat in the future, Tom will supply more wheat at the current price in order to get ahead of the fall in price. Just as the expectations of future prices among buyers are self-prophetic, the expectations of future prices among sellers are self-prophetic (Figure 3.6).

Changes in taxes and subsidies

If Tom were to be taxed on each bushel of wheat that he produces—assuming Tom is a price taker and unable to raise price in the market to shift a share of the tax or the full tax into a higher price for consumers to pay—he will supply less at the current price. The regressive nature of production taxes will not just negatively affect the production supply and profits after taxes, it may also negatively affect the employment level of resources used in production. If Tom were to experience a subsidization of his production and input costs—cover some share of his costs of production paid for by borrowed money or taxes collected—he will be expand his market supply of wheat.

Changes in climate or weather

A change in climate, such as drought conditions, would reduce the overall supply of wheat at all prices. Favorable weather conditions may translate into higher yields per acre and effectively add to the total market supply at every price. Changes in weather conditions not only benefit and/or adversely affect the overall supply of agriculture goods, but also affect the transportation (logistics) of non-agriculture goods and services.

For example, the severe winter weather experienced in the United States in 2014 and along the Eastern Seaboard in January 2016 affected both ground and air transportation. The impact of such severe winter weather impeded the timely delivery and available supply of key goods and services. Due to severe weather, if air travel is limited and ground transportation by truck is affected negatively by hazardous road conditions, this will cause temporary supply disruptions and be reflected as a decrease in the market supplies for those goods not being shipped.

3.3 THE COMPLETE SUPPLY AND DEMAND MODEL

Integrating both sides of the market together, the concept of equilibrium and how changes in market demand and market supply affect equilibrium prices and quantities will be examined. Figure 3.6 describes a market situation for Tom in equilibrium where an amount of Q^* is being both supplied and demanded at the equilibrium market price of $(Pw/Pc)^* = 1W = \frac{3}{4}C$.

If a market is in equilibrium, the market will experience no shortage or surplus of the good. However, in equilibrium all exploitable opportunities in terms of price are accounted for and all potential gains between buyers and sellers are exhausted. In a state of equilibrium, there will be no further incentives to specialize and trade/exchange as all potential gains have been arbitraged out between buyers and sellers.

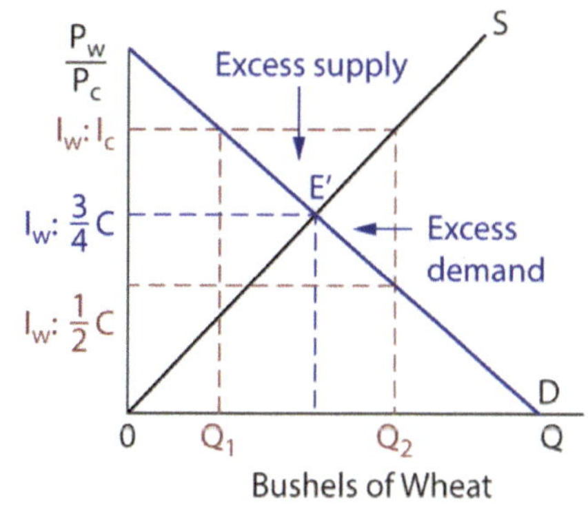

Figure 3.6. The figure illustrates a complete supply-demand graphical representation of Tom's wheat market in equilibrium with quantity, Q*, demanded and supplied at the equilibrium price of (Pw/Pc)* = 1W = ¾C. Holding market demand and market supply constant, at market prices above the equilibrium price, the market experiences an excess supply of wheat of $Q_2–Q_1$. At per bushel market prices below the equilibrium price, the market experiences a shortage $Q_1–Q_2$ of bushels of wheat.

Recall from the example in Chapter 2, Tom without trade with Hank produced quantities of both bushels of wheat and yards of cloth. In the example, Tom produced and supplied 28 bushels of wheat at a domestic price equal to his opportunity cost of ¾ yards of cloth for each bushel of wheat. Since Tom was consuming what he produced, this domestic market price in terms of yards of cloth, Pw/Pc = 1W:¾C, will be the equilibrium price, and 28 bushels of wheat will be the equilibrium quantity in the marketplace. In Figure 3.6 this equilibrium point is at the intersection of his market demand and market supply curve, with quantity Q* = 28 bushels of wheat being supplied as well as demanded.

Equilibrium as a concept of what markets naturally trend to

The concept of equilibrium is an important one. Allowing a market to operate in the most efficient way possible, an equilibrium condition—in which no more is being supplied than is being demand—is efficient because all the potential gains from exchange/trade between buyers and sellers willing and able to participate at the equilibrium price have been exploited and accounted for. Keep in mind that in the real marketplace prices paid are not equilibrium prices. As such, these prices are an outcome of organized market structures and profit maximizing levels of output by firms.

Holding demand and supply constant in Tom's market, if the market price were below the equilibrium price, Pw/Pc = 1W:½2C, the quantity demanded of bushels of wheat at Q_2 would be greater than the quantity supplied at Q_1. The difference between the quantity supplied and the quantity demanded would reflect excess demand and a shortage of the bushels of wheat in Tom's marketplace. At Pw/Pc = 1W:½C, let $Q_1 = 30$ and $Q_2 = 40$. In this case, at the lower market price below equilibrium, Tom experiences a market shortage of 10 bushels of wheat. Without importing the difference at the current price of Pw/Pc = 1W:½, this markets shortage is only able to clear out through a rise in market price.

How does this price rise so that the shortage clears and for the market to return to equilibrium? It is very simple. Treating wheat as a good that is both rivalrous in consumption and excludable to those who choose to not pay the price, buyers in the market begin to bid up the price for every bushel of wheat to encourage sellers to supply a greater quantity of wheat at higher prices.

As the market price rises, the price mechanism is acting as a rationing mechanism to allocate wheat to those buyers who value it more than Pw/Pc = 1W:1/2 and no less than Pw/Pc = 1W:3/4C. Sellers of wheat will allocate bushels of wheat to those buyers willing to pay higher prices. Holding supply and demand constant, the rise in the market price results in a decrease in quantity demanded and offset by an increase in the quantity supplied.

If markets work efficiently—supply and demand curves are clearly defined, all available information in the marketplace is visible and accounted for, and holding all non-price determinants constant—the market price rises and returns to its initial equilibrium point. This is considered a short-run to long-run market correction in price needed to return the market to a natural state where there is no market disequilibrium.

What if the market price is set above equilibrium? If the market price is set above equilibrium, and holding market supply and market demand constant, an observable excess supply or surplus of bushels of wheat will emerge in the marketplace. Returning to the Tom and Hank trade example in Chapter 2, when Tom and Hank opened to trade and agreed to exchange bushels of wheat for yards of cloth at Pw/Pc = 1W:1C, Tom was incentivized to specialize in the production of wheat—his comparative advantage good—and supply greater quantities of wheat at the higher trade price as opposed to his domestic no trade price of ¾ yards of cloth.

Again referring to the graphical example from Chapter 2, with specialization, Tom supplied 40 bushels of wheat at the new trade price offer of Pw/Pc = 1W:1C. At this price only 30 bushel of wheat were demanded and consumed by Tom, leaving 10 bushels in excess to be traded for 10 yards of cloth from Hank. In Figure 3.7, at the market price Pw/Pc = 1W:1C, quantity Q_2 is being supplied and quantity Q_1 is being demanded.

At this price point, the difference between the quantity supplied and quantity demanded is greater than 0. In our Chapter 2 example, this was represented as the excess supply of 10 bushels of wheat traded for 10 yards of cloth. If Tom is able to export his excess supply of bushels of wheat at the higher market price, then the higher market price will be persistent in his market. But what if Tom has no outside buyer to purchase his excess supply? How will the market adjust to clear out the market surplus for wheat and return to equilibrium?

Unlike excess demand with a market shortage, where a rise in the market price is necessary to clear out the shortage through a competitive rationing process between buyers and sellers, with excess supply there is competitive bidding down of prices buy the sellers to incentivize buyers to demand a greater quantity of the output unsold.

With the excess supply of a good going unsold, the firms(s) holding excess inventory will begin to lower the price on the inventory in order to incentivize buyers to demand a greater quantity. The idea is to turn over inventory and get idle inventory sold. And if markets work efficiently—all available public and private information is accounted—and buyers and sellers are price takers (the same conditions in the excess demand example)—the fall in price will adjust the market to a return to equilibrium. This will also be considered a short-run long-run correction in the market price to return the market back to a natural state of no disequilibrium.

The "invisible hand" and the perfectly competitive ideal

An important tenet of the supply and demand model and how markets clear out disequilibrium in markets is the presumption of perfect flexibility of prices in the marketplace and the nonexistence of any buyer or seller influential enough to influence or obstruct the market adjust process and keep the price in their favor. All buyers and sellers in the supply-and-demand model are presumed to be price takers, not price setters.

The concept of the "invisible hand" suggests it's the aggregation of individual choices and firms choosing to respond the same way to disequilibrium in the market causing the market price to rise or fall and adjust the responding changes in quantities demanded and supplied to return the market to its equilibrium state.[9] Even without the assumption of perfect competition holding true, the model is still a useful guide to predict what observable result(s) will be if market prices are set above or below market equilibrium.

In the examples provided so far, only considered was the position of the market price to the equilibrium price and how shortages and surpluses were "cleared" out through the rationing process using a mechanism of flexible price adjustments; along with the treatment of holding market demand and market supply constant. However, all markets are in constant flux. This means in any micro market, market demand and supply are changing by overall

[9] The end of this chapter will briefly reconcile the assumptions of the supply and demand model with the observable real world; accounting for what the model does and does not account for.

amounts over time, and this means equilibrium prices and quantities are also changing. How might these changes be observed, and what can be predicted as the outcome of market equilibrium prices and quantities? And will this beg the question of whether equilibrium prices and quantities in the marketplace will ever be realized? Are markets trending toward equilibrium but never getting there?

3.4 SHORT RUN TO THE LONG RUN: MARKET FORCES AND CHANGES IN EQUILIBRIUM PRICES AND QUANTITIES

The previous section demonstrated that for a market price set above equilibrium, a market surplus would emerge, and for market prices set below equilibrium, a market shortage would emerge. In order for such market surpluses and shortages to clear out and the market to return to its initial equilibrium price and quantity—holding demand and supply constant—the market price for the good would either rise (to clear out the market shortage) or fall (to clear out the market surplus). The market adjustment process in the price mechanism assumes enough perfect flexibility in market prices to complete the rationing process.

However, market demand and market supply cannot be held constant. As well, an assumption of our supply and demand model is that buyers and sellers are price takers and not price setters and take prices as given throughout the market adjustment process. The market as is in the supply and demand model assumes a perfectly competitive environment, with unhindered trade/exchange between buyers and sellers, to allow this adjustment process to unfold in an efficient way.

Realistically, markets are always in a constant state of flux such that changes in overall market supply and market demand that will cause the market to deviate from an initial equilibrium level and trend to a new one. This section will examine the changes in the non-price determinants of market demand and market supply and, using provided examples, will conclude with what is predicted to be the new equilibrium level in market price and quantity.

Table 3.1 provides a summary of how a change in non-price determinants will affect overall increases (or decreases) in market supply and demand. A few examples will be provided to illustrate cases of behavioral changes in the non-price determinants and illustrate graphically the expected observation over time of what the new equilibrium price and quantity should in the marketplace. This is overall important in the study of macroeconomics, since changes in equilibrium prices and equilibrium quantities in all micro markets will shape the overall market value of an economy's national output (GDP), its domestic price level, domestic rates of inflation, and employment of the domestic factors of production.

Non-price determinants of market demand	**Non-price determinants of market supply**
Changes in consumer tastes and preferences for goods	Changes in the cost and availability of production inputs and resources
Changes in buyers income (normal vs. inferior good)	Advances in technology
Changes in the price of related goods (substitutes and complements)	Changes in taxes and subsidies
Changes in the number of buyers entering/exiting the marketplace	Changes in the number of sellers entering/exiting the marketplace
Changes in buyers expectations about future prices	Changes in sellers expectations about future prices
Changes in taxes and subsidies	Changes in the price of related goods in production (substitutes and complements)
	Changes in climate and weather

Table 3.1. Summary of the non-price determinants or market supply and market demand when changing will over time produce observable in increases (or decreases) in market demand and market supply.

Increases in Market Demand Holding Market Supply Constant

Figure 3.7 shows a market for a given good with a schedule of prices and quantities demanded and supplied. The initial demand and supply curves of D_0 and S_0 respectively show an equilibrium price of $40 and equilibrium quantity of 500 units at point A.

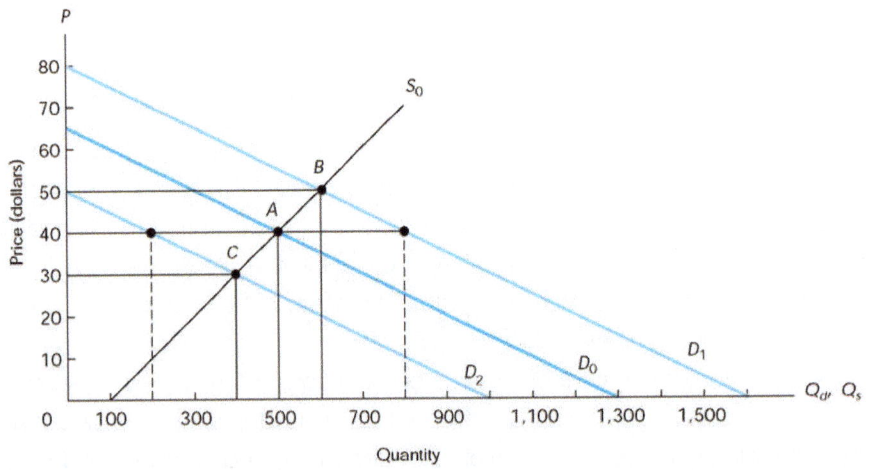

Figure 3.7. Increases and decreases in market demand for a market with supply constant. The graph shows the resulting changes in equilibrium price and quantity for increases and decreases in overall market demand. The increases and decreases in overall demand show a deviation away from the initial equilibrium price and quantity at point A.

Source: Adapted from Farnham, P.G. 2006. Economics for Managers. Upper Saddle River, NJ: Prentice Hall.

Suppose there is a change in one, some, or all of the non-price determinants of demand. For example, an increase in income (normal good), an increase in the number of buyers entering the market, a change in the expectations of a higher future price among buyers, an increase in subsidies into the hands of buyers to participate more in the market at the current price and all prices, an increase in the price of a substitute good, and so on. Then observed will be a rightward shift of the market demand curve at the current price from D_0 to D_1, with 800 units now being demanded at the current price of $40 but with the same initial quantity supplied of 500 units.

As a result, a shortage of 300 units emerges, and in order for the shortage to clear, the market price will need to rise. The rise in the market price will incentivize sellers to supply a greater quantity, and the increase in price will decrease the quantity demanded; rationing the increase in the quantity supplied to buyers willing to pay a higher market price. The market demand curve's shift to the right, in response to a change(s) in a non-price determinant(s), is a movement up and along the market supply curve. Allowing for perfect flexibility in market price and unhindered trade/exchange between buyers and sellers, the long-run adjustment will be the higher equilibrium price of $50 and a higher equilibrium quantity of 600 units.

A change in a non-price determinant(s) of demand having a negative impact on the market demand for this good—i.e., a decrease in income of buyers for the good if it's a normal good, buyers exiting the market, buyers being taxed on their per unit consumption of the good, expectation that prices will be lower in the future for this good to participate at, and so on—then the market demand curve shifts to the left and down and along the market supply curve, leading to a lower equilibrium price of $30 and a lower equilibrium quantity of 400 units. Prior to the price adjustment, the decrease in demand relative to supply causes a market surplus of 300 units, and this visible market surplus puts downward pressure on the market price to fall to a lower equilibrium level ($30) for a new lower equilibrium quantity (400 units).

Example #1: A report by the surgeon general provides conclusive evidence that drinking more than one cup of coffee a day provides important health benefits to brain function and longevity. The result will be an increase in preferences toward the consumption of coffee and less consumption of coffee-drink substitutes. The demand for coffee drinks and coffee overall will increase and over time will lead to a higher equilibrium per cup and a higher equilibrium quantity.

Example #2: Evidence emerges in the marketplace that bone meal in cattle feed shows to be linked to the cause of mad cow disease. The purchasers of cattle feed are now encouraged to substitute away from cattle feed with bone meal and use cattle feed containing soybean. The demand for cattle feed with bone meal would decrease, and this will lead to a lower equilibrium price and quantity for cattle feed with bone meal. As well, the overall demand for bone meal as input in the production of cattle feed would decrease, and the market demand for the substitute input soybean would increase.

Increases in Market Supply Holding Market Demand Constant

Figure 3.8 illustrates the impact on market equilibrium price and quantity for an increase in market supply or decrease in market supply only while holding demand constant. Working with changing non-price determinants of supply at the current equilibrium price of $40 and current equilibrium quantity of 500 units at point R, an increase in market supply will result in a lower equilibrium price and higher equilibrium quantity.

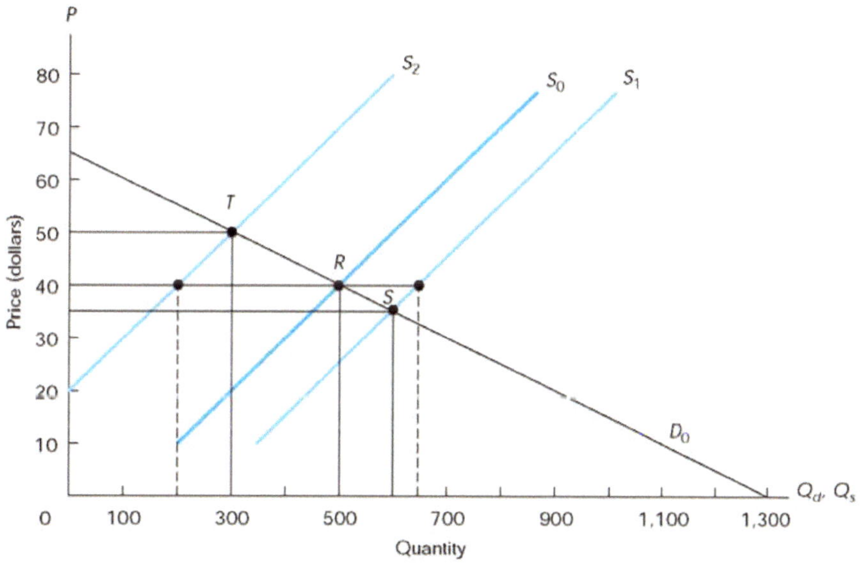

Figure 3.8. Increases and decreases in market supply while holding demand constant. An increase in market supply (holding demand constant) will lead to lower equilibrium prices and a higher equilibrium quantity, and a decrease in market supply will lead to a higher equilibrium price and lower equilibrium quantity.

Source: Adapted from Farnham, P.G. 2006. *Economics for Managers*. Upper Saddle River, NJ: Prentice Hall.

Suppose on the supply side of the market there is an adoption of technology that raises the productivity of existing resources through a change in production methods, more sellers enter the marketplace, sellers expect lower prices to sell at in the future, and production costs are subsidized, and so on. Then the result will be a rightward shift of the supply curve from S_0 to S_1 and a movement down and along the market demand curve.

The increase in market supply from S_0 to S_1 shows a greater amount of units supplied at the current price of $40, which is 500 units. The resulting market surplus at the current market price will be communicated to buyers in the market and pressure will be put on the market price to fall in order to clear out the excess supply. Graphically, this increase in market supply will lead to a lower equilibrium price and quantity as shown from the movement from equilibrium point R to point S.

As well, changes in non-price determinants of supply that are a negative—such as sellers exiting the market, changes in regulation that increase the cost of inputs used, unfavorable weather conditions creating supply disruptions, expectations of higher future prices sellers can sell at, and so on—will cause the market supply curve to shift to the left (S_0 to S_2) and up and along the market demand, moving our equilibrium point from R to T for a higher equilibrium price and lower equilibrium quantity (P = \$50 and Q = 300 units). The rise in the market price from a decrease in market supply is designed to clear out the market shortage that emerges when supply decreases at the initial equilibrium level.

Example #1: Changes in business regulation in a given market raises the cost of input prices and affects the profitability of producers causing profits to decline and loses to emerge. In response, sellers exit the marketplace.[10] The reduction in the number of sellers in the market leads to a leftward shift of the market supply curve and results in a higher equilibrium price and lower equilibrium quantity.

Example #2: Severe drought conditions emerge in the Midwest of the United States, where a large percentage of the nation's wheat is produced. Such drought conditions reduce the overall yield per acre and result in less wheat harvested. Futures markets for wheat predict future wheat price per bushel will be significantly higher. The result of these events will be a leftward shift of the market supply curve, leading to a lower equilibrium market quantity of bushels of wheat and a higher equilibrium market price per bushel.

Simultaneous Shifts in Market Demand and Market Supply

Unlike previous examples, where behavior on one side of the market was held constant in order to observe the change in equilibrium price and quantity from a behavioral change in the other market, in the real world the selling and buying sides of the marketplace are not held constant. Buying and selling markets are integrated and respond to all sorts of market events, information, and signals, and this means markets are experiencing, over time, simultaneous shifts in market supply and demand of varying degrees.

In Panel A of Figure 3.9, market supply and market demand increase. The new equilibrium quantity will be known, but the new equilibrium market price will be non-determinant, since more information is need as to how much market demand and market supply increased by in percentage terms.

If market supply increases by more than the increase in market demand, the equilibrium market price will be lower with a higher equilibrium quantity. If market demand increases by more than the increase in market supply, the equilibrium price will be higher with a higher equilibrium quantity. Without knowing more information as to how much market demand and market supply increase by, the change in equilibrium price from demand side and supply side effects may be lower, higher, or unchanged.

In panel B, market supply and market demand shift in opposite directions. The new equilibrium market price will be known, but the new equilibrium quantity may be lower, higher, or unchanged. In Panel B, if market demand decreases by more than the increase in market supply, there will be a lower equilibrium quantity and lower equilibrium price. If market supply increases by more than the increase in market demand, there will be a lower equilibrium price and a higher equilibrium quantity.

---

[10] In a supply and demand model, the market is assumed to be perfectly competitive. With this market condition, it is assumed that costs and entry and exit that sellers and buyers face are zero.

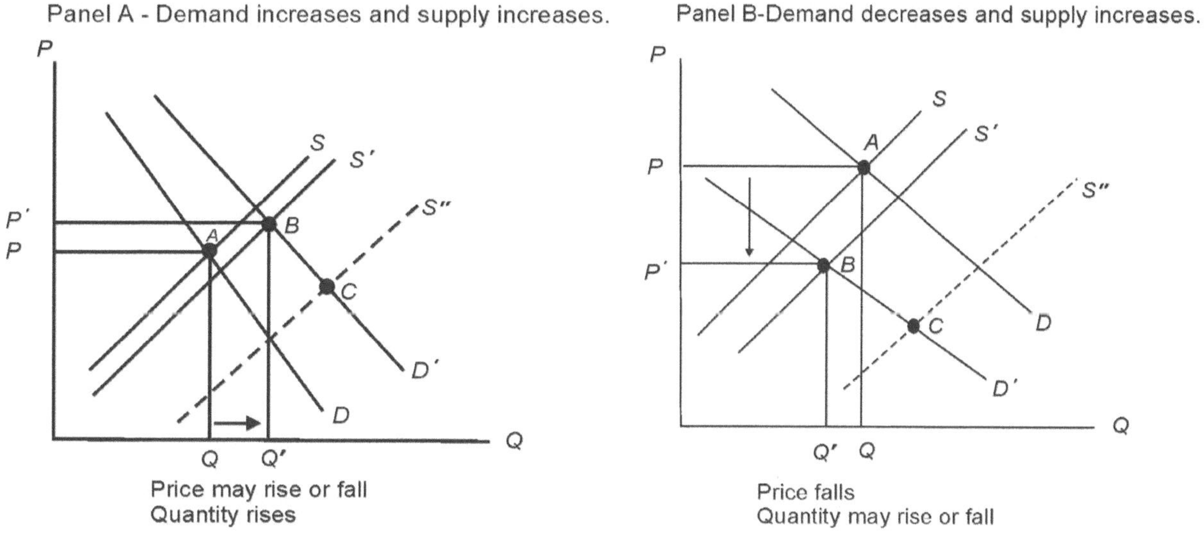

Figure 3.9a-b. Simultaneous shifts in market supply and demand. Panel A and Panel B show case(s) where the changes in equilibrium price or equilibrium quantity are non-determinant.

Source: Adapted from "Economics for Managers", 1st ed. (Farnham, 2006).

Example #1: A local movie theater company decides to open new locations, adding more seats available for moviegoers in its marketplace. At the same time, the theater company cuts concession prices by 50 percent. What is expected to happen to the equilibrium price and quantity of a movie ticket?

The first event of opening new theater locations is reflected as an increase in market supply as more theater seats are added to the overall supply in the marketplace (treating all the seats as identical). That event alone would lead to a lower equilibrium price and higher equilibrium quantity of movie tickets.

The simultaneous event of cutting concession prices by 50 percent is treated as a change in the price of a related good that is a complement and purchased along with a movie ticket. With cheaper concession prices, moviegoers have 50 percent more available to spend on movie tickets.[11] This event alone would lead to an increase in market demand, resulting in an increase in the market equilibrium price and quantity of a movie ticket.

The result of the two events is identical to the illustration in Panel A of Figure 3.9—the new equilibrium quantity will be higher, but more information as to how much the market supply and market demand for movie tickets has increased by is needed in order to make a final determination of what the new equilibrium market price for a movie ticket would be. In this case the change in the equilibrium price of a movie ticket is non-determinant.

Example #2: A hurricane in the Gulf of Mexico suspends oil production from sea-based platforms for an unspecified period of time. Twenty-five percent of oil produced in the Gulf of Mexico serves the US market as an input in the refinement process to produce gasoline. News of the production suspension causes buyers in the market to expect gasoline shortages and higher gasoline prices. What can be expected to happen to the equilibrium and market price and equilibrium quantity of gasoline using the supply and demand model?

[11] Whether moviegoers will spend the savings of 50 percent on additional tickets depends on the strength of the goods as compliments. This can be determined by an examination of the change in cross-price elasticity of movie tickets and concession items.

The first event (suspension of oil production for an undetermined amount of time) will be reflected as decrease in the overall market supply of oil, causing the input price of oil to rise and the market supply of gasoline to decrease, leading to a higher market equilibrium price of gasoline and lower equilibrium quantity of gasoline. The second event affects the expectation of the future price of gasoline in the buying market.

An expectation of a future higher price of gasoline—compounded by an expected shortage from the supply disruption of oil (a critical input in the production of gasoline)—results in an expected increase in the market demand for gasoline. More buyers will enter the market today to purchase more gas to get ahead of the expected gasoline shortage and the higher expected price of gasoline. As such, the increase in market demand for gasoline, from an expected increase in the future price of gasoline and more buyers entering the marketplace to secure gasoline, would lead to a higher equilibrium market price for gas and a higher equilibrium quantity demanded.

The outcome of the simultaneous two events confirms the market equilibrium price of gasoline will be higher. But, without knowing more information about the overall decrease in the market supply of gasoline and the overall increase in market demand in market demand for gasoline, the overall change in the equilibrium quantity for gasoline will be non-determinant: higher, lower, or unchanged.[12]

3.5 CONCLUSION: THE SUPPLY AND DEMAND MODEL AND THE MACROECONOMIC ENVIRONMENT

The coverage of the supply and demand model in this chapter provides one of the first basic tools of economic analysis. The assumptions of the model are quite unrealistic:

1. *Assumes a perfectly competitive marketplace where all buyers and sellers are price takers. In the real world, marketplaces are imperfectly competitive, firms are price setters, and the majority of consumers are price takers.*
2. *Market prices are fully flexible to adjust to changes in supply and demand conditions in order for the market to reach a new equilibrium level. In the short run, prices are not as flexible and are what economists call "sticky" as a result of "sticky" wages.*
3. *The model neglects market structure issues such as the pricing power of influential firms and influential buyers, market obstructions preventing buyers and sellers from exploiting all gains from exchange, rigidity in market prices, market regulation affecting the cost of buyer and seller participation, and so on. As well, the model assumes that markets operate efficiently and on 100 percent perfect information.*

Even when more realistic market assumption are applied, the context of the market supply and demand model provides a useful guide of what can be expected as future result; providing all events extinguish in effect and all other possible market events are held constant.

Changes in equilibrium prices and quantities happen over time and will be subject to further changes as any market event unfolds, setting off a possible chain reaction of events across other markets (i.e., the butterfly effect). This means the market adjustments to equilibrium are ongoing and trending to higher or lower equilibrium levels in prices and quantities but never reaching a new final state of equilibrium. The model is not intended to be a 100 percent predictive tool of what is expected to be observed, but a useful predictive guide between the short run and the long run (future), holding all other exogenous factors and unidentifiable ones constant.

If micro markets are always in motion, then so is the broader national economic picture that is being shaped by it. Changes in the non-price determinants of market supply and demand will be useful in the application of the

[12] Panel B in Figure 3.11.

supply and demand model at the aggregate level of the economy.[13] The utility of examining the market supply and demand outcomes for a single product and all products in their respective micro markets will shape the broader macro picture in terms of important macroeconomic measurements being followed.

The next chapter will consider how the output supplied in micro markets and expended on by participants on the buying side shape the broader economic components influencing the final market value of output and income—GDP—and other important macroeconomic measurements economists track. The following brief case study covering the global copper market during the 1997-1998 Asian Financial Crisis illustrates how the global market supply and global market demand for copper responded to the region macroeconomic contraction; impacting global copper prices during this period.

CASE STUDY: APPLICATION OF SUPPLY AND DEMAND ANALYSIS: BEHAVIOR OF COPPER FUTURES (1997-1998 ASIAN FINANCIAL CRISIS)[14]

Prior to the 1997–1998 Asian Financial Crisis, a large share of global copper consumption was held by China and other Southeast Asian economies as a production input in these countries' telecommunication and semiconductor industries. In response to a regional financial crisis, the macroeconomic performance of the economies of the region contracted and contributed to a cut in the region's share of global copper imports for consumption into these industries.

The contraction in domestic and trade credit resulted in Malaysia and Indonesia cutting their consumption of copper by 8 percent, with China's import share of copper remaining anemic for this period. With the exception of China, as the financial meltdown and responding economic contraction contributed to a period of "Asian deflation," regional demand of global copper for consumption weakened to a level that drove copper prices from a high of $1.23 per pound to $0.82 per pound. With expectations that regional risk and macro performance would worsen before getting better, copper future contracts fell nearly 40 percent for this period, with an expectation that copper prices would have to bottom out at around $0.68 per pound before buying opportunities would rise again.

Contributing further to this overall decline in copper future prices, previous copper mine expansion out of the United States and western Europe was expected to contribute to an unanticipated buildup of copper inventories going unsold for 1998–1999 as shown in Figure 3.10. As projects using copper in Asia began to dry up, copper inventories in the United States and Western Europe began to swell. With competitive devaluations spurning the Southeast Asian economies, China was left to make use of excess US Dollar holdings in its intervention to defend the US Dollar–Chinese Yuan exchange rate target. China's foreign exchange rate intervention using excess Dollar holdings spurned an opportunity to purchase copper from US and Western European firms which would have been a welcomed reprieve to help smooth out copper inventory buildup and declining copper prices.

In an attempt to curtail the decline in copper future prices, global copper production was cut by 30 percent, with the closing of a number of copper mines to meet lower production targets. However, the mines closed were small mines constituting a smaller share of global copper production. More of the larger mines profitable in scale at lower copper prices around $0.75 per pound remained operational. As a result, the attempt to curtail global copper production through mine closings to prevent unwanted additions of copper to already burgeoning copper inventories was unsuccessful. Weaker regional demand contributing to an overall slower growth in global demand for copper was outpaced by global copper production, resulting in the deflation of copper futures during this period. It would not be until 2002–2005 that copper would become "hot" again.

[13] Will be covered in the short-run and long-run aggregate demand and aggregate supply model in Chapter 7.

[14] Lucchetti, A. "Copper Limbo: Just How Low Can It Go?," *Wall Street Journal*, February 23, 1998.

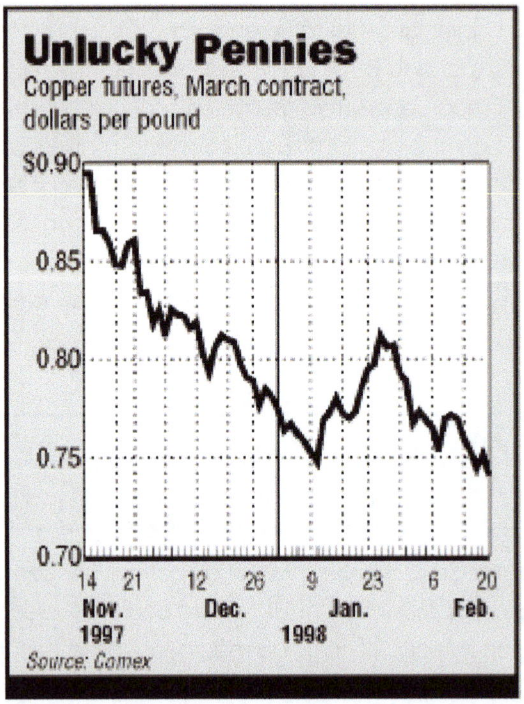

Figure 3.10. Performance in copper futures during the 1997–1998 Asian Financial Crisis. Copper futures had fallen to historic lows last seen in 1975. Copper futures fell by 40 percent during this 1997–1998 period in response to weakened demand for copper out of Asia and excess copper inventory buildup in the United States and western Europe from copper mining expansion.

QUESTIONS FOR CLASS DISCUSSION

1. Accessing the link below, read the following article, "Sheikhs v. Shale" from the *Economist* magazine on December 6, 2014. Apply and explain the concepts you and your classmates have learned about market forces and supply and demand analysis to explain why the "economics of oil have changed" and why some oil producers risk going bust if global oil prices fall too low.

   "The New Economies of Oil: Sheikhs v Shale," *Economist*, December 6, 2014, http://www.economist.com/news/leaders/21635472-economics-oil-have-changed-some-businesses-will-go-bust-market-will-be

2. Equilibrium in the marketplace is deemed to be efficient but may not always be equitable. Discuss among your classmates market examples where this would be the case, and discuss how policy makers, in an attempt to create a more equitable outcome, generate market distortions that reduce overall economic welfare to the constituents the policy was intended to help. Consider the policy and/or market control used and illustrate these welfare effects between buyers and sellers in a supply and demand model. Does the use of such policy and/or market control attempts that you and your classmates are discussing provide a better or poorer tool for rationing as opposed to the price mechanism?
3. Using supply and demand analysis, discuss the following statement: "If you think it is expensive now, wait till it is free."

IMAGE CREDITS

- Fig. 3.10: "Copper Limbo: How Just How Low Can It Go" (The Wall Street Journal, 02/28/1998). Copyright © 1998 by Dow Jones & Company, Inc.

CHAPTER 4

THE MACRO ECONOMY: PUTTING THE MACRO BUILDING BLOCKS TOGETHER

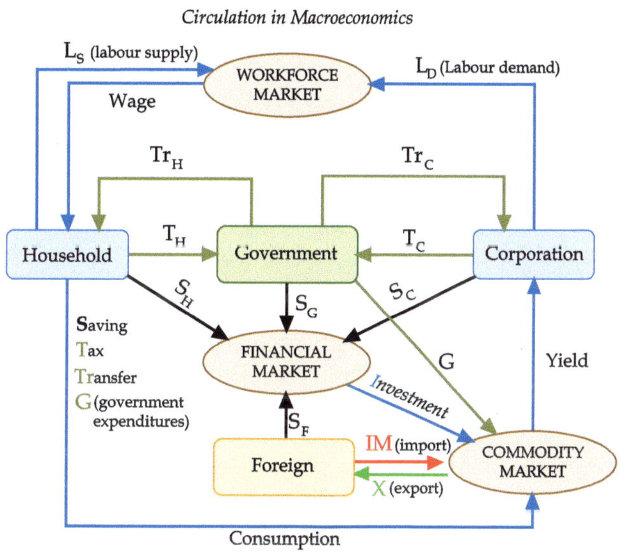

Figure 4.0. How do the micro building blocks shape the macro building blocks of the national economy?

4.0 OVERVIEW: PACKAGING THE MICRO INTO MACRO BUNDLES

This text has so far taken the approach of building a descriptive picture of the macro economy through an examination of the importance of micro markets as building blocks. Chapter 1 stipulates that the existence and interaction of market activity is developed on the availability of exploitable opportunities in environments of resource (product) scarcity. To best illustrate the exploitation of opportunities for market creation, Chapter 2 examined how the exploitability of differences in comparative advantages (opportunity costs) between actors creates incentives to produce and trade/exchange. This analysis was carried over into Chapter 3 using the application of a market supply and market demand framework. This framework is used to demonstrate how the exploitation of scarce opportunities in numerous micro markets shape the overall market value of output produced at a national level.

As a whole, the equilibrium (as well as non-equilibrium) outcomes across all market segments provide a final composition of the type and value of an economy's total output (income) level. In equilibrium, the gross market value of total output will equal total gross expenditures and will equal total gross national income payments. These gross payments will be in the form of gross earnings in wages, interest payments, rental payments on land and capital, and profits paid out in the form of dividends.

Each micro market will be important, since changes in market prices and changes in market output in each micro market will shape the measurable changes of broader economic performance domestically and globally. The measurable changes at the macro level can be scaled down and examined at different micro market levels. Each micro market, regardless of size, is having an overall influence on the composition of what an economy produces and the measurable performance in areas of employment, income, purchasing power, income distribution, the ability of the economy to translate its wealth base into income streams, and so on, from a nationwide level down to state, metro, and community levels.

The focus of Chapter 4 is to take the micro building blocks and aggregate them into a smaller number of critical but bigger building blocks—consumption spending, investment spending, government spending, and the trade balance (for an open economy). Changes in these aggregate expenditure components will be used to describe the economy's flow of income (Chapter 4) and loanable funds for investment spending in closed and open economies (Chapter 5).

In each building block there are numerous micro markets. These are very much like cells in a biological system, shaping a subsystem's role in the performance of the overall biological system. The type of economic system that manages the preference and coordination between private choice and public choice will affect resource and output allocation. The outcomes of these allocations will be reflected in the behavior of our critical building blocks and impact the size of the overall economy's workable market value.

As stated in Chapter 1, the systems-view approach will be used to describe the interaction of micro market activities shaping consumption spending, investment spending, government spending, and international trade to shape the profile of the "big picture" of a national economy. This systems-view approach will allow the user to examine the economic trade-offs aggregately made at the micro level and reflected at the macro level helping to shape the trade-offs of macro policy as visualized in Figure 4.0.

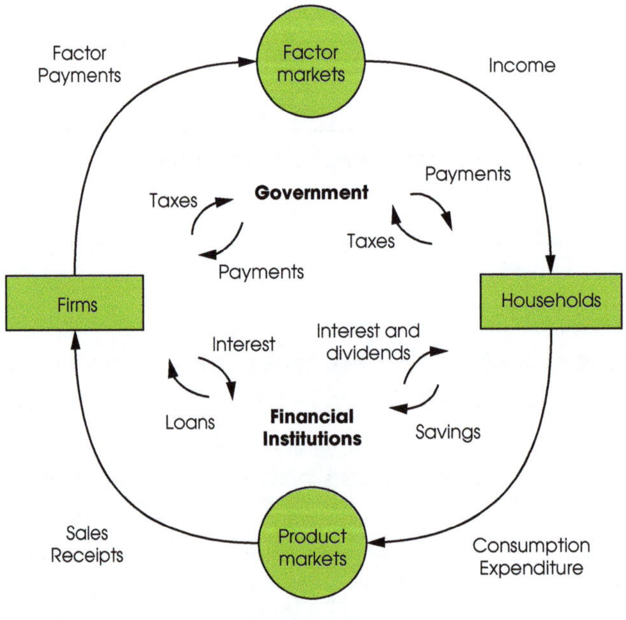

Figure 4.1a. CFI model for a closed economy with no output (income) leakages and injections from foreign trade and cross-border financial flows.

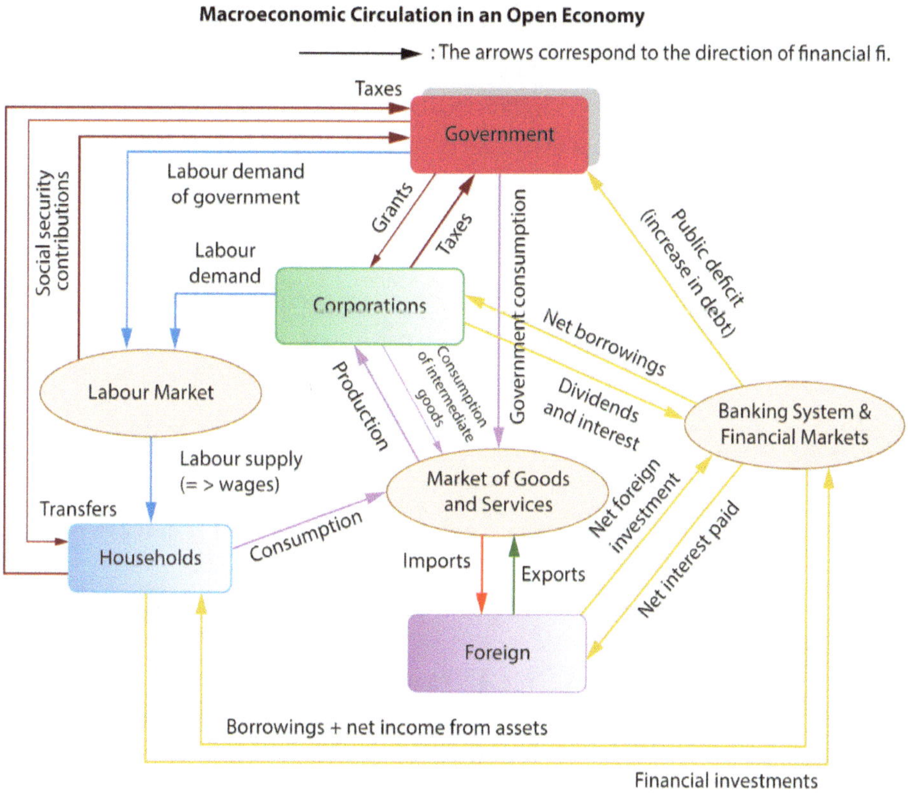

Figure 4.1b. An expanded CFI model for an open economy that accounts for openness to trade (exports and imports) and cross-border international financial flows. Notice in the illustration that leakages and injections of output (income) come in the form of trade countered with cross-border international financial flows recycling savings held abroad back through financial intermediaries making up the banking and capital markets of an economy.

4.1 THE CIRCULAR FLOW AGAIN (CLOSED AND OPEN ECONOMY): THE PLAYERS AND THE MARKETS

Any search on the Internet for detailed images of the circular flow of income provides an array of simplified to highly detailed interactions of the critical building blocks or economic aggregates—consumption spending, investment spending, government spending, and the trade balance—and the associated flows of income and loanable savings throughout the economy.

A review of a simplified circular flow of income, as shown in Figure 4.1a, for a closed economy shows that what is produced is expended on, and this would be equal to what is expected as an economy's chosen production point on its descriptive PPF without trade. When this model is opened up to the rest of the world as shown in Figure 4.1b, the total output in the global system will be equal to the total global expenditures on the output in the long run. A key difference between two models will be the treatment of the savings-investment identity covered in Chapter 5.

Breaking down the CFI model into its building blocks for a closed economy

Breaking down Figure 4.1a, the CFI model for a closed economy is made up of four important players and two broader markets. The economic players will be defined as households, firms, government, and financial institutions (or financial intermediaries). The markets will be defined as product markets—for the buying and selling of goods and services—and factor markets (aka resource markets)—for the purchase or lease of factors of production to be employed in the production of goods and services. The equilibrium (non-equilibrium) outcomes in both markets will be shaped by the changes in market supply and market demand in these organized markets.

Households

In Chapter 1, the CFI model was first introduced. A household was defined as any domicile made up of one or more group of persons that share income as a household. In most but not all cases, this will be families. Figure 4.2 shows the distribution and concentration of households by counties across the United States from 2007 to 2011.

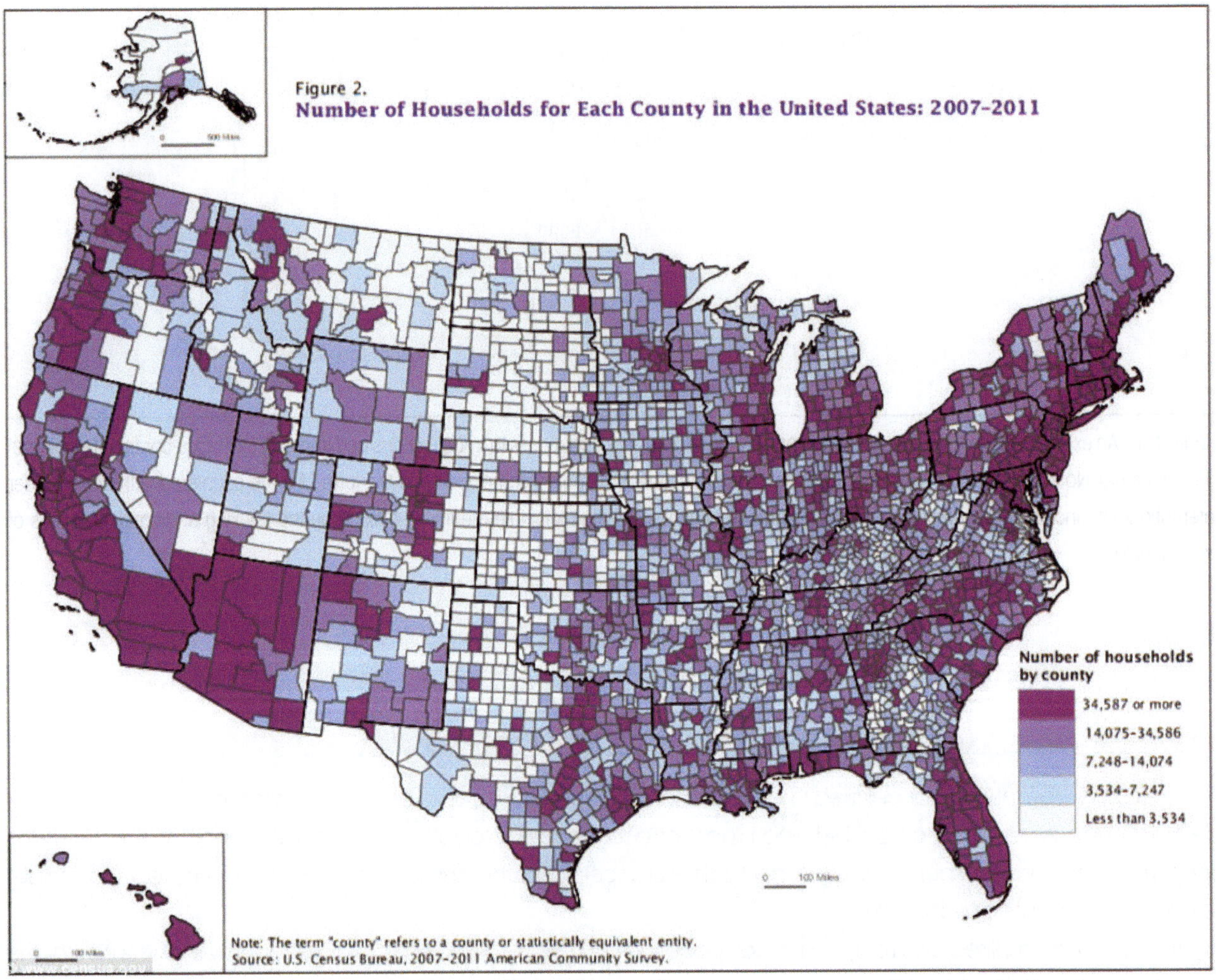

Figure 4.2. Number of households for each county in the U.S. 2007–2011.

Although the figure does not provide information as to the concentration of household size or degree of home ownership versus renting, it does suggest there should be an observed higher concentration of households by number in larger metropolitan areas as opposed to smaller metro areas and rural areas.

Areas on the map that represent higher concentration in number of households would suggest a higher degree of market activity by size in terms of participation by household members. This would suggest a larger variety of exploitable opportunities. Figure 4.2 in no way clearly shows what the market value of the activity would be. This would have to be ascertained with an examination of production activity on a state-by-state level.

For instance, counties in the Midwest—where a larger share of land space is used for farming activities—would show a small concentration of households by number. As well, it should be observed on the map a greater concentration of wealth and income creation in counties with larger household numbers. Would such higher household concentration be supportive of higher household median income?

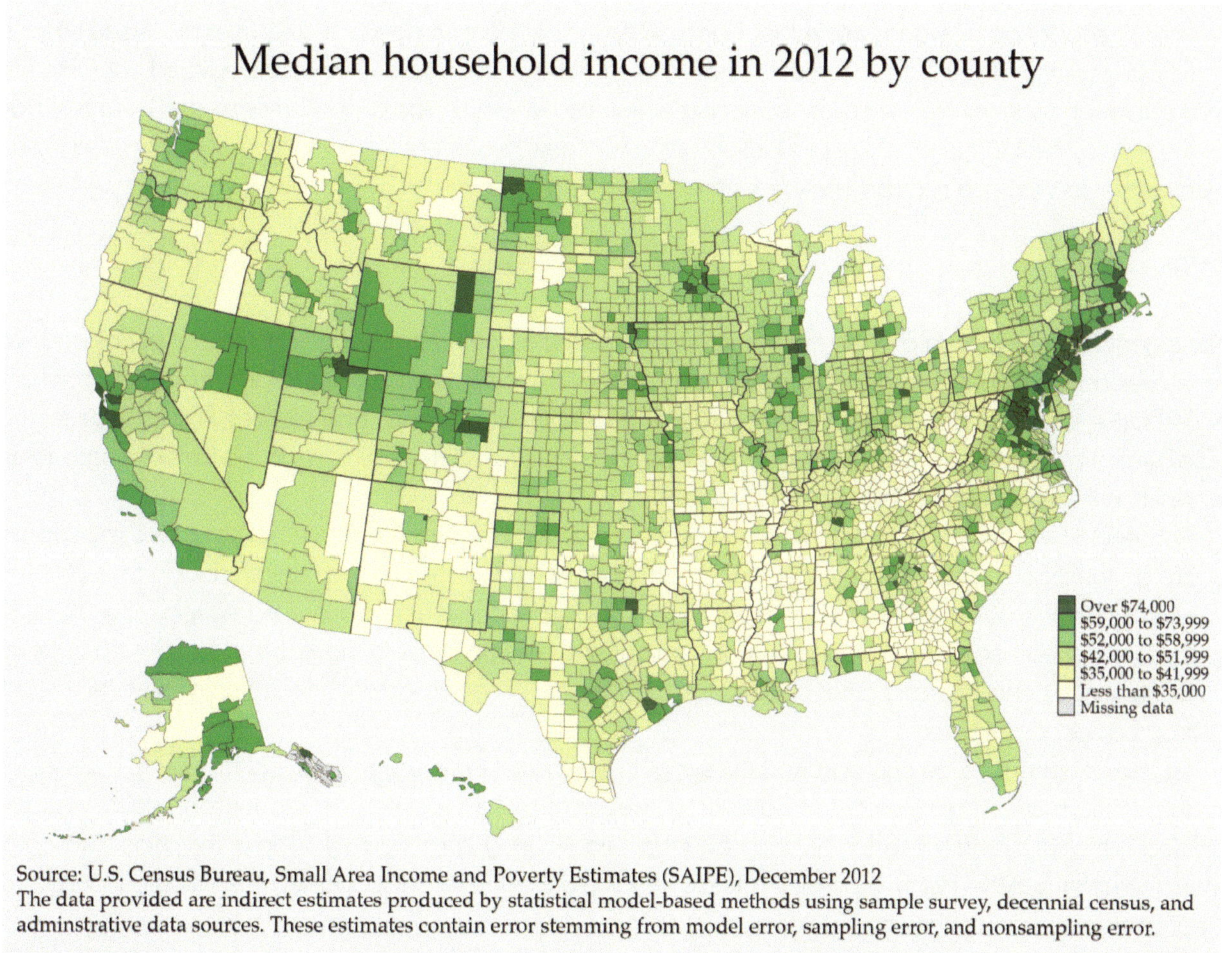

Figure 4.3. Median Household Income in 2012 by county.

Where Figure 4.2 shows the concentrated distribution of households nationwide by county, the figure would also imply counties with larger metropolitan areas should be complemented with larger concentrations of wealth supporting higher median income streams. However, Figure 4.3 provides a stark contrast to the expected observation from Figure 4.2, suggesting large household concentrations in counties does not necessarily translate into normalized income distribution.

What would be needed here is an examination of the type of economic activities in these counties that support a given level of median household income. Figure 4.3 suggests a heavier concentration of households in given areas does not immediately translate into higher median income values. Factors affecting this would be the stock and quality of human capital and physical capital, quality of infrastructure, geographical constraints, and the level of financial intermediaries able to translate savings into investment, and so on.

Unlike other parts of the United States, counties in the Midwest experience a smaller concentration of households in number but higher median household income. The discrepancy in the expected observation can be explained from wealth concentration in the hands of land ownership and farming activities supported by family farms (small to large) and commercialized farming operations.

In the circular income flow, it is important to examine the ability of the numerous marketplaces at the micro level to translate wealth held (Real and implicit) by households into income streams.[1] Households play an important role in the ownership and supply of the factors of production into the marketplace for employment by firms in exchange for income—wages, interest, rent, and profits—to be spent on goods and services produced by firms.

Of the income not spent, this income in the form of savings held by households will be recycled back into the market through financial intermediaries, supporting borrowing by households for consumption and by firms to pay for the employment of the factors of production along with new investment for production capacity (fixed investments), inventory replacement, and new residential housing starts.

Firms

Any organization employing privately the members of households for the production and sale of goods and services in exchange for payment will be treated as a firm. In the CFI model, firms employ the factors of production from households—land, labor, and capital—to be used by firms to produce goods and services. In exchange for the employment of their factors of production, firms will pay households income payments in the form of wages, rents, interest payments, and profits in the form of dividends.

Households will spend a share of these payments earned and received as a reflection of their ownership on claims on the income stream from the production of final goods and services they are producing through firms. The fraction that is not spent is saved and will be held with financial intermediaries to directly and/or indirectly finance new investment activities supporting new output and new additions to the wealth base to support future consumption expenditures and other borrowing endeavors (i.e., ongoing payment of committed wage, interest, rent, and dividend obligations).

Like households, firms are also borrowers of savings in the market to be used to make payments to households for the employment of their factors of production as well as to make investments in production capacity (plants and equipment), inventory investment, and new residential housing starts. Figure 4.4 shows the concentration of manufacturing activity—highly important in terms of value-added creation supporting the wealth and income creation process—across the Unites States as of 2010.

This figure helps shed light on evidence in Figure 4.3 of the impact of transformational activities (value added) has had on the distribution of median income levels nationwide. Areas of the United States reflecting a greater share of manufacturing activity are supportive of higher median household income values as shown in Figure 4.4.

Firms play an important role in the organization of market activities for households to participate in, not only as a source of employment but also in the wealth, income, and credit-creation process. Well-functioning financial markets, with mature financial intermediaries able to translate savings today and expected savings in the future into investment spending today, provide households and firms direct and indirect channels for the most optimal use of their savings. This is done in an attempt to bring expected growth in the future closer to the present.

[1] Chapter 5 will examine how certain factors—some already suggested above; including education, functionality of property rights, and infrastructure—play a crucial role in the type of expected wealth creation (following the concepts of specialization and comparative advantage) and income created in the hands of participating households supplying the factors of production.

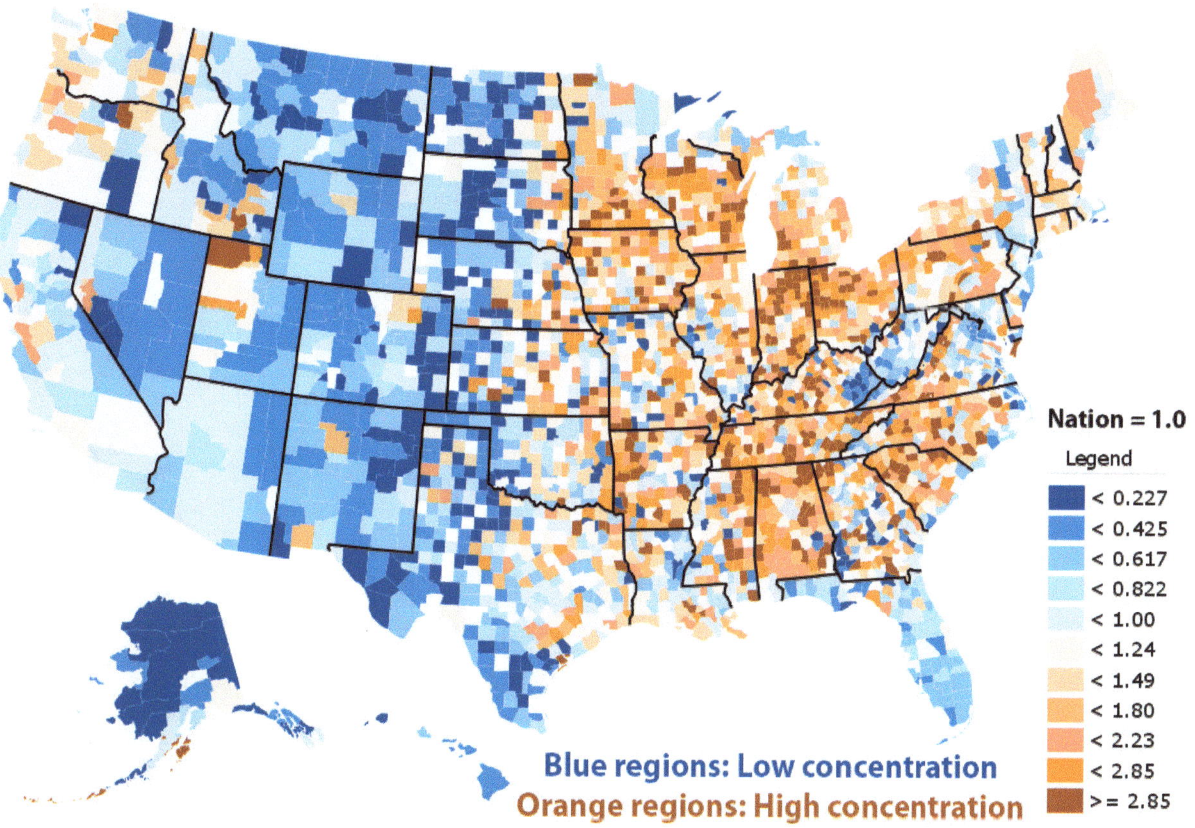

Figure 4.4. The Industrial Belt: Manufacturing Concentration by County, 2010.

Source: www.american.com.

Financial Institutions

Banks, pension funds, investment banks, insurance companies, and other financial intermediaries take in savings—a share of wages, interest payment, rent, and profits (dividends)—as payment for financial management and wealth-building activities offered. These monies are leveraged through the creation of loans, private securities, public securities, and other market security instruments to act as a mechanism to channel scarce savings to the most productive areas of the economy for the highest possible return.[2]

Government

The government is an interesting economic actor. Not only is government treated as a taxer and regulator of economic activity, it is also treated as a buyer of goods and services from the private market. Figure 4.5 shows the rate of change in all US federal outlays against the growth in US GDP. In Chapter 7 fiscal policy—changes in spending and taxation—will be examined to look at the overall contribution total government spending (federal, state, and local) has on GDP growth. The government spending multiplier and tax multiplier will be covered against the backdrop of the debt debate and its impact on Real growth. Figure 4.5 shows a breakdown of total government spending

[2] Chapter 5 will cover these activities with an examination of the savings and investment identity for a closed and open economy. Chapter 9 will explore the money-creation process through the use of fractional reserve banking and open market operations by a central bank.

among federal, state, and local outlays and their respective percentage shares of GDP from 1960 to 2010. Figure 4.6 also shows that state and local government expenditures combined on nondefense output is a large share of total government expenditures.

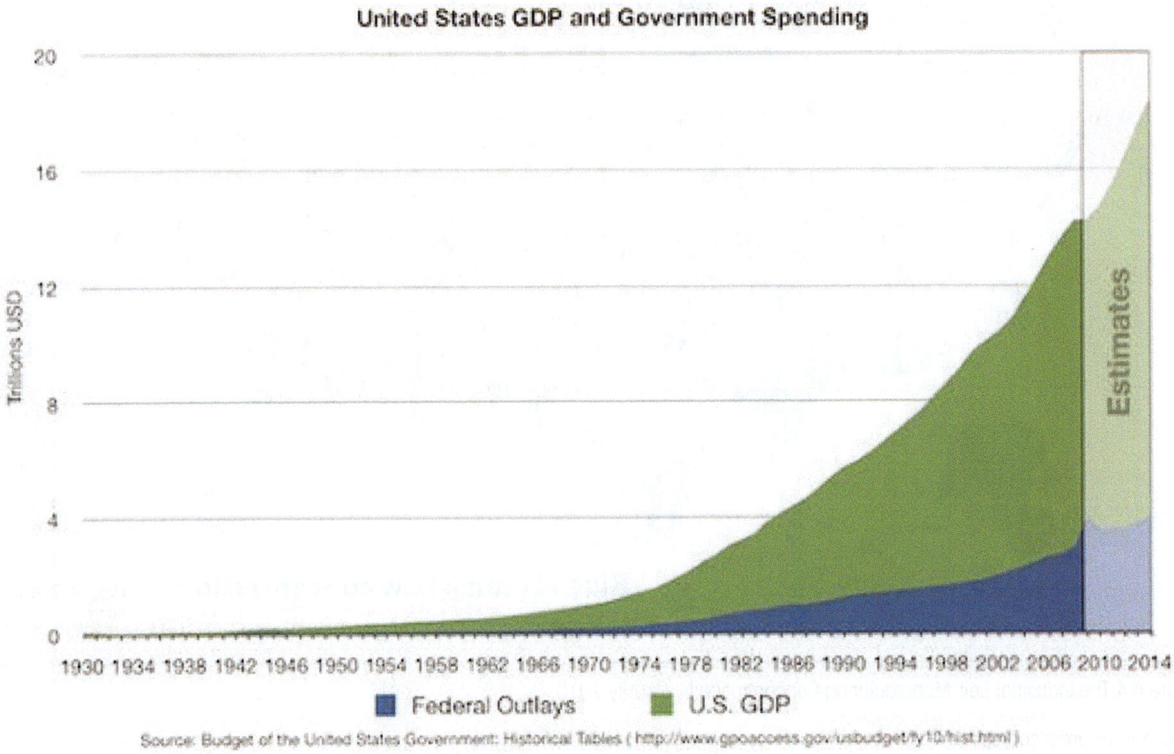

Figure 4.5. The path of federal spending outlays against the behavior of US GDP growth. The figure shows all spending outlays having an impact on multiplying GDP growth that is slower than what models covered in this text would expect. In an examination of the multiplier, this text will critique reasons why GDP growth has not kept pace with US federal spending.

4.2 THE COMPONENTS OF GDP AND ITS MEASUREMENT: THE NATIONAL EXPENDITURE APPROACH

A look at each actor's role in their respective market participation allows for the CFI model to be broken down into a number of spending aggregates, with each spending aggregate broken down further into different respective spending components. The summation of total spending among our spending aggregates will gives us the total market value of the economy's total output for a given period of time, called gross domestic product, or GDP. GDP is the market value of all final goods and services produced and expended on within a nation's borders, including net foreign expenditures for an open economy. Table 4.1 provides a breakdown of the aggregate spending components (in billions of US Dollars) for US GDP from 2012 to 2014.

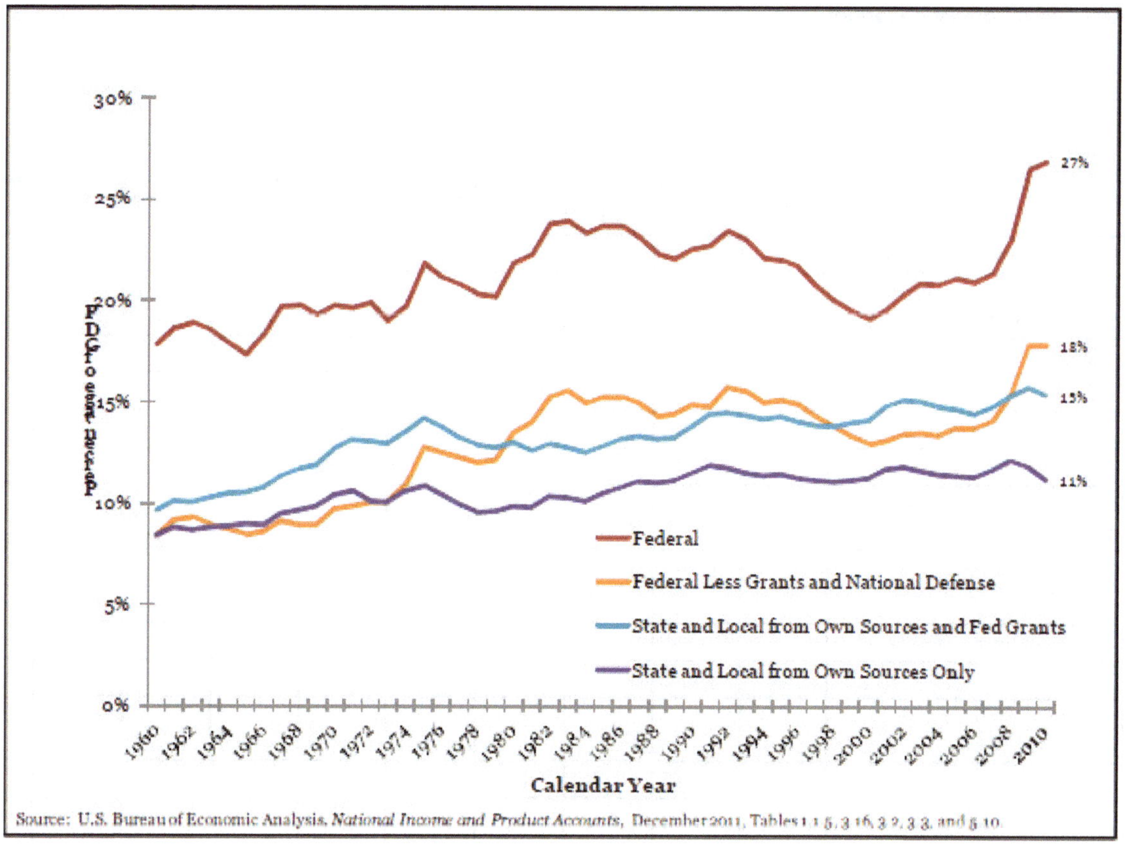

Figure 4.6. Government Expenditures by Level.

The formulaic identity of the national income expenditure approach

GDP for any given year (or period of time measured) can be expressed as the summation of total spending for the following economic aggregates: total consumption spending, total investment spending, total government spending, and the trade balance (exports minus imports). The expression is simplistic in its nature. Just sum up gross expenditures for each domestic spending component plus the trade balance (net exports = exports – imports) to get GDP. The national income identity can be expressed as:

$Y = C + I + G + (EX\text{-}IM)$

C = personal consumption spending on durable goods, nondurable good, and services

I = gross private investment spending on fixed investment (factories), nonresidential (structures, equipment, and intellectual property product), and residential (new housing starts)

G = government consumption expenditures on private goods and services produced by the marketplace (defense and nondefense), state and local consumption expenditures on private goods and services, and gross government investment

EX = exports of goods and services

IM = imports of goods and services produced in other countries

Table 4.1 Gross Domestic Product

[Billion of dollars] Seasonally adjusted at annual rates

Bureau of Economic Analysis

Last Revised on: August 28, 2014—Next Release Date September 26, 2014

		2012				2013				2014	
Line		**I**	**II**	**III**	**IV**	**I**	**II**	**III**	**IV**	**I**	**II**
1	**Gross domestic product**	15956.5	16094.7	16268.9	16332.5	16502.4	16619.2	16872.3	17078.3	17044	17311.3
2	**Personal consumption expenditures**	10959.7	11030.6	11119.8	11222.6	11351.1	11414.3	11518.7	11653.3	11728.5	11867.8
3	Goods	3709.6	3717.2	3751.9	3788.8	3832.2	3821	3865.3	3886.1	3890.6	3963.3
4	Durable goods	1177.3	1179.4	1195.4	1216.1	1237.8	1245.4	1252.4	1261.5	1262.3	1299.2
5	Nondurable goods	2532.3	2537.8	2556.5	2572.8	2594.4	2575.6	2612.9	2624.6	2628.4	2664.1
6	Services	7250.1	7313.3	7367.9	7433.8	7518.9	7593.2	7653.4	7767.2	7837.8	7904.5
7	**Gross private domestic investment**	2445.4	2489.3	2500.4	2481.5	2543.3	2594.6	2708.9	2745.2	2714.4	2834.2
8	Fixed investment	2364.3	2397.1	2424.7	2471	2499.1	2543.8	2598.1	2654.6	2674.3	2734.8
9	Nonresidential	1942	1968.8	1978.3	1998.7	2010.3	2026.9	2060.2	2118.7	2134.6	2184.6
10	Structures	437	452.5	452.2	445.9	435.4	448.5	463	481.7	487.9	500.7
11	Equipment	894.9	897.1	901.4	922.8	933.1	937	948.8	980	979.5	1007.3
12	Intellectual property products	610.1	619.2	624.7	630	641.8	641.4	648.4	657	667.2	676.6
13	Residential	422.3	428.3	446.4	472.3	488.9	516.9	538	535.9	539.7	550.2
14	Change in private inventories	81.1	92.2	75.7	10.4	44.2	50.8	110.7	90.5	40.1	99.4
15	**Net exports of goods and services**	–614.8	–588.5	–541.7	–528.2	–528	–532	–509.9	–462.9	–538	–551.8
16	Exports	2162.4	2192.5	2203.2	2218.5	2219.4	2236.4	2268.4	2324.6	2284.7	2340
17	Goods	1510.1	1530.7	1538.5	1529.2	1528.4	1543.2	1565.7	1614	1575.3	1622.1
18	Services	652.3	661.8	664.7	689.3	691	693.2	702.7	710.7	709.5	717.9
19	Imports	2777.1	2781.1	2745	2746.7	2747.4	2768.4	2778.3	2787.5	2822.7	2891.8
20	Goods	2327.2	2326.2	2287.7	2283.1	2288.6	2302.2	2308.6	2309.7	2341.5	2404.7
21	Services	449.9	454.9	457.3	463.6	458.8	466.3	469.7	477.8	481.2	487.1
22	**Government consumption expenditures and gross investment**	3166.2	3163.3	3190.5	3156.6	3135.9	3142.4	3154.7	3142.7	3139.1	3161.1
23	Federal	1291.4	1290	1314.3	1269.9	1241.9	1234.1	1233.9	1216.2	1208.1	1210.5
24	National defense	818.6	817.1	840.9	795.4	775.1	772.2	774.9	757.5	749.9	754.7
25	Nondefense	472.8	472.9	473.4	474.4	466.8	461.9	459	458.7	458.2	455.9
26	State and local	1874.8	1873.3	1876.2	1886.8	1894	1908.3	1920.7	1926.5	1931	1950.5

Table 4.1. Breakdown of the aggregate spending—consumption, investment, and government spending—for US GDP from 2012 to 2014 by quarter and year.

Source: Bureau of Economic Analysis.

For the second quarter of 2014, total personal consumption expenditures equaled $11,867.8 billion. Gross private investment spending was $2,834.2 billion. Gross government consumption expenditures and gross investment was $3,161.1 billion. Net exports were a –$551.8 billion, with exports in goods and services totaling $2,340 billion and imports of goods and services totaling $2,891.8 billion.

The summation of these aggregates will give US GDP for the second quarter of 2014 as shown in the first row and last column in Table 4.1. Table 4.2 provides the percentage share of GDP for each aggregate expenditure component. From this table, consumption expenditures constitute the lion share of the national market value; reinforcing the very important role consumers play in the circular flow of income model.

$Y = C + I + G + (EX\text{-}IM)$

Y = \$11,867.8 billion + \$2,834.2 billion + \$3,161.1 billion + (\$2340 billion – \$2891.8 billion)

Table 4.2 Percent Shares of Gross Domestic Product

[Percent]

Bureau of Economic Analysis

Last Revised on: August 28, 2014 – Next Release Date September 26, 2014

Line		2012				2013				2014	
		I	II	III	IV	I	II	III	IV	I	II
1	**Gross domestic product**	100	100	100	100	100	100	100	100	100	100
2	**Personal consumption expenditures**	68.7	68.5	68.3	68.7	68.8	68.7	68.3	68.2	68.8	68.6
3	Goods	23.2	23.1	23.1	23.2	23.2	23	22.9	22.8	22.8	22.9
4	Durable goods	7.4	7.3	7.3	7.4	7.5	7.5	7.4	7.4	7.4	7.5
5	Nondurable goods	15.9	15.8	15.7	15.8	15.7	15.5	15.5	15.4	15.4	15.4
6	Services	45.4	45.4	45.3	45.5	45.6	45.7	45.4	45.5	46	45.7
7	**Gross private domestic investment**	15.3	15.5	15.4	15.2	15.4	15.6	16.1	16.1	15.9	16.4
8	Fixed investment	14.8	14.9	14.9	15.1	15.1	15.3	15.4	15.5	15.7	15.8
9	Nonresidential	12.2	12.2	12.2	12.2	12.2	12.2	12.2	12.4	12.5	12.6
10	Structures	2.7	2.8	2.8	2.7	2.6	2.7	2.7	2.8	2.9	2.9
11	Equipment	5.6	5.6	5.5	5.7	5.7	5.6	5.6	5.7	5.7	5.8
12	Intellectual property products	3.8	3.8	3.8	3.9	3.9	3.9	3.8	3.8	3.9	3.9
13	Residential	2.6	2.7	2.7	2.9	3	3.1	3.2	3.1	3.2	3.2
14	Change in private inventories	0.5	0.6	0.5	0.1	0.3	0.3	0.7	0.5	0.2	0.6
15	**Net exports of goods and services**	–3.9	–3.7	–3.3	–3.2	–3.2	–3.2	–3	–2.7	–3.2	–3.2
16	Exports	13.6	13.6	13.5	13.6	13.4	13.5	13.4	13.6	13.4	13.5
17	Goods	9.5	9.5	9.5	9.4	9.3	9.3	9.3	9.5	9.2	9.4
18	Services	4.1	4.1	4.1	4.2	4.2	4.2	4.2	4.2	4.2	4.1
19	Imports	17.4	17.3	16.9	16.8	16.6	16.7	16.5	16.3	16.6	16.7
20	Goods	14.6	14.5	14.1	14	13.9	13.9	13.7	13.5	13.7	13.9
21	Services	2.8	2.8	2.8	2.8	2.8	2.8	2.8	2.8	2.8	2.8
22	**Government consumption expenditures and gross investment**	19.8	19.7	19.6	19.3	19	18.9	18.7	18.4	18.4	18.3
23	Federal	8.1	8	8.1	7.8	7.5	7.4	7.3	7.1	7.1	7
24	National defense	5.1	5.1	5.2	4.9	4.7	4.6	4.6	4.4	4.4	4.4
25	Nondefense	3	2.9	2.9	2.9	2.8	2.8	2.7	2.7	2.7	2.6
26	State and local	11.7	11.6	11.5	11.6	11.5	11.5	11.4	11.3	11.3	11.3

Table 4.2. Percentage share of the aggregate expenditure components of GDP quarterly for 2012–2014. The data shows that from year to year, personal consumption expenditures and gross private domestic investment constituted the largest shares of GDP. The most volatile component was changes in private inventories.

Source: Bureau of Economic Analysis.

$$Y = \$11{,}867.8 \text{ billion} + \$2{,}834.2 \text{ billion} + \$3{,}161.1 \text{ billion} + (-\$551.8 \text{ billion})$$

$$Y = \$17{,}311.3 \text{ billion}$$

What does GDP tell us and not tell us?

So, what does the final value of GDP communicate? What does $17,311.3 billion Really tell us? Answer: Only the Nominal market value of final output in the market supplied as a summation of the aggregate expenditures on the output.

As a value, GDP communicates the total gross value of output to be reflected as total gross income flows in our CFI model. The information is used as a barometer of a country's economic health and how well the country's economy is able translate its working wealth stock—used to produce output—into a flow of income streams to support transactions throughout the broader marketplace in the numerous arrays of micro markets that shape the national output (income) picture. The final value does not communicate enough information about changes in social statistics—literacy rates, educational attainment, technological innovation, mortality rates, longevity, environmental costs, income and wealth distribution, and so on—that would otherwise impact the overall growth rate of GDP and the economy's ability to translate wealth into working income flows. Beyond this overall simplified expenditure approach to calculating GDP, are there other approaches that may communicate a bit more information as to the composition of GDP, the role of firms in different stages of production to influence the final market value, and distribution of national income?

Other Measurements of Gross Domestic Product: Value-Added Approach and Factor Payments Approach

In the previous section, the expenditure approach provided a total sum of the national income in the economy equal to the observed gross expenditures on final output produced using gross personal consumption expenditures, gross private domestic investment expenditures, gross government consumption spending and government investment, and the running trade balance with the rest of the world.

The final calculated value of GDP (national income) using the national expenditure approach does not provide adequate information as to the contribution each economic sector provides for its share of the total value of national output (income). Nor does the approach present the distribution of income payments paid to the factors of production employed by firms for the production of final output and other goods and services produced.[3] And finally, the approach does not communicate the economic trade-offs made and associated consequences incurred across numerous micro markets in the final national market value.

Recall that GDP is the market value of all final output produced within a nation's borders for a given period of time supported by gross expenditures for the same period. Where the expenditure approach is only concerned with the value of the final goods and services produced using final quantities and prices, two other measurements—the value-added approach and the factor-payments approach—will be helpful in calculating GDP and examining the role that each stage of production and factors of production employed contribute to the final market value of output (total income).

Value-Added Approach

Table 4.3a provides a hypothetical example of the auto industry. The final output is one car produced by American Motors and sold in the marketplace for a final value of $21,500. Using the expenditure approach—using the final price of a car and current quantity of cars produced—GDP will be equal to:

$$GDP = (P_{car})(Q_{car}) = (\$21{,}500)(1) = \$21{,}500$$

[3] In the United States this important data is collected, tracked, and analyzed by the Bureau of Economic Analysis in the US Department of the Treasury.

	American Ore	American Steel	American Motors*	Total Income**
Value of Final Sales	$4,200.0	$9,000.0	$21,500.0	
Cost of Intermediate Goods	$0.0	$4,200.0	$9,000.0	
Factor Payments				
Wages	$2,000.0	$3,700.0	$10,000.0	$15,700.0
Interest Payments	$1,000.0	$600.0	$1,000.0	$2,600.0
Rent	$200.0	$300.0	$500.0	$1,000.0
Profits (dividends)	$1,000.0	$200.0	$1,000.0	$2,200.0
Total Firm Expenditures	$4,200.00	$9,000.00	$21,500.00	
Value Added Per Firms = Final Sales – Cost of Intermediate Goods	$4,200.00	$4,800.00	$12,500.00	$21,500.0

*The final output in the example above is the production of 1 car with a final sale value of $21,500
**The summation of the value added at each stage of production equals the summation of all factors payments made equaling the final market value of the 1 car produced
Source: "*Macroeconomics*", *3rd edition, Krugman and Wells (2012)*

Table 4.3a. Value Added Approach.

Source: Adapted from Macroeconomics, 3rd Edition, Krugman and Wells.

The production of a final car(s) and its value makes use of different stages of production involving other firms contributing to the final market value of the output. Considering the concept of specialization and comparative advantage, each firm in its designated stage of production is specializing in the production of some output—final good or intermediate good—that it holds a "suggested" comparative advantage in.

The production of output broken down according to a division of specializations will not only be efficient according to the concept of specialization and comparative advantage, but the division of specializations will also be value adding to the economy in the respective local markets the activities are taking place in. As such, these value-adding activities (which are transformational in nature) will shape the overall final market value in the national marketplace and the employment of factors of production supplied in respective micro markets. This means:

> *The production of a car in the example is integrated across micro markets of participating firms that will make up the overall auto industry. This integration of stages of production will affect the distribution of income across locality for the factors of production employed in making the final output and the intermediate output that will be transformed along the way into a car.*

For an activity to be considered value adding, there must a transformational process employed. This means the output produced by one firm will be purchased by another firm and transformed into a different type of useable output to be sold at a higher market value to another firm.[4] A portion of Table 4.3b is provided below to examine the value-added creation process across different stages of production and the final market value of output (total income).

[4] In Chapter 5, the role of investment (domestic and foreign) will be explored to support value-adding production activities that support growth in exploitable opportunities supporting broader industry development and growth in Real income per person locally and across borders.

	American Ore			American Steel			American Motors				
		% of Total Sales	*% of Value Added*		*% of Total Sales*	*% of Value Added*		*% of Total Sales*	*% of Value Added*	**Total Income**	*% of Total Income*
Value of Final Sales	$ 4,200.0			$ 9,000.0			$ 21,500.0				
Cost of Intermediate Goods	$ -	0%		$ 4,200.0	47%		$ 9,000.0	42%			
Factor Payments											
Wages	$ 2,000.0	48%	48%	$ 3,700.0	41%	77%	$ 10,000.0	47%	80%	$ 15,700.0	73%
Interest Payments	$ 1,000.0	24%	24%	$ 600.0	7%	13%	$ 1,000.0	5%	8%	$ 2,600.0	12%
Rent	$ 200.0	5%	5%	$ 300.0	3%	6%	$ 500.0	2%	4%	$ 1,000.0	5%
Profits (dividends)	$ 1,000.0	24%	24%	$ 200.00	2%	4%	$ 1,000.0	5%	8%	$ 2,200.0	10%
										$ 21,500.00	100%
Total Firm Expenditures	$ 4,200.00			$ 9,000.00			$ 21,500.00				
Value added per firms	$ 4,200.00			$ 4,800.00			$ 12,500.00				

*The final output in the example above is the production of 1 car with a final sale value of $21,500
**The summation of the value added at each stage of production equals the summation of all factors payments made equaling the final market value of the 1 car produced
Source: "Macroeconomics", 3rd edition, Krugman and Wells (2012)

Table 4.3b. Value Added Approach.

In Figure 4.3b the production of the one car is broken up into three different stages of production. The first stage of production is the production of the raw material (ore) produced by American Ore. The second stage of production is the production of steel by American Steel. The final stage of production is the production of the car by American Motors.

Production Stage Number One

In the first stage, American Ore employs factors of production and technology to extract/mine the raw material from its geographical source(s). In this stage, no intermediate goods are used to be transformed into ore. The final value of this ore produced is $4,200.00, and the entire ore inventory is sold to American Steel.[5] The economic value American Ore adds to the economy from its mining operation is:

Value added = Total firm sales – Cost of intermediate goods used = $4,200.00 – $0.00 = $4,200.00

If the market activity ended with just the mining and extraction of ore, the economy's GDP would be the market value of American Ore's sales ($4,200.00), and this would also be equal to the sum of payments (expenditures) made to the factors of production employed in the mining and extraction of ore.

[5] Any inventory of output unsold will be repurchased by firms and treated as inventory investment to be sold at the beginning of a future period.

Production Stage Number Two

The total output of America Ore (the supply) is sold to American Steel (the demand) equal to its market value or sale.[6] In the second production stage, American Steel takes this ore and making use of employed factors of production and technology, American Steel transforms the ore into steel equal to a market value of $9000.00. This market value (sale) is equal to the cost of the ore purchased and the payments made to the factors of production.

American Steel's transformation of ore into steel, having a higher market value and more valuable use by another firm along the supply chain, adds additional economic value to the economy in its marketplace. The economic value American Steel adds to the economy from this transformation process of taking the value of an intermediate good (ore) and transforming it into a different good with a higher market value and more valuable use is:

Value added = Total firm sales – Cost of intermediate goods used = $9,000.00 – $4,200.00 = $4,800.00

If the production and market process ended with the production of steel, then the GDP of the economy would just be equal to the final market value of the steel produced by American Steel. Since all the market value of the ore produced is accounted for in the production of steel, we do not count the value of the ore output produced, as this would be double counting.

American Steel is producing this steel, which is being demanded by American Motors to be used to produce a car. American Steel sells its entire inventory of steel to American Motors for $9000.00, equal to the cost of the ore it purchased plus the payments it made to its factors of production employed.

Final Production Stage

In the final stage of production, American Motors will take this steel as an intermediate good and transform it into a car. It will then sell the car for $21,500.00. The value of the car sale will be equal to the cost of the steel (the intermediate good) purchased and the sum of payments made to the factors or production employed to transform the steel into a car. This transformation process in the final production stage adds economic value to the local marketplace and the economy of:

Value added = Total firm sales – Cost of intermediate goods used = $21,500.00- $9,000.00 = $12,500.00

Since this is the final stage of production and the final good is a car, final GDP for the economy in this hypothetical example is $21,500. Why is just the final market value of the car counted toward GDP, and the market value of the ore and steel produced not included?

Just like our ore-to-steel example, this is because all intermediate goods produced have been transformed along different stages of production and accounted for in the final market value of the car. The market value of the car already accounts for the additional economic value added from the production and transformation of ore and steel at different production stages.

Since there is no ore and steel left over (no excess inventory held at the end of any production stage), those amounts do not get counted into GDP as inventory investment. Had the approach accounted not just for the final

---

[6] To keep this hypothetical example simple, all firms in the example are considered perfectly competitive and will sell their respective output equal to the expenditures (costs) to make it. All firms in this example are considered to be price takers. Transaction costs (including taxes and other fees applied at the time of sale) between them are assumed to be zero, and there is zero markup at the time of sale to exclude monopoly power and the incidence of double marginalization of cost(s).

value of the car, but also the market value of the ore and steel produced, then the final GDP value would have been inflated through double accounting.

Some additional comments on the value-added approach

Taking the summation of the value added at each stage of production will be equal to the market value of the total output (income) as shown in Table 4.3a and 4.3b:

GDP = Summation of value added at each stage of production = \$4,200.00 + \$4,800.00 + \$12,500.00 = \$21,500.00

Using the value-added approach in this example shows the percentage share of the final market value each firm is responsible for in their respective stage of production. American Ore contributes 19.53 percent to the final value of the car produced in the economy, American Steel contributes 22.33 percent to the final value of car produced in the economy, and American Motors contributes the remaining 58.14 percent of the final market value. This means each firm's contribution to the final market value of a car (the final output) will be equal to the share of GDP each firm is responsible for in output and income creation.

So how would GDP be different overall had American Motors only needed half of the market value of steel to produce the same car it will sell for \$21,500? In this case the remaining half of the steel not sold to American Motors would be purchased back by American Steel. This will be treated as inventory investment. This inventory would be held aside for sale at a future date to American Motors for its production and sale of another car. How would this now be reflected in our national income identity?

If we assume that the car produced is sold and consumed in the same time period, then total consumption expenditures, C, would equal \$21,500. With only half the market value of steel used, this would leave American Steel with an inventory balance of steel of \$4,500. This market value amount will be treated as inventory investment and will be counted toward total investment expenditures for the same period. Keeping the analysis simple, let's for the time being consider the role of government as a buyer of goods and services as being absent in the marketplace such that G = 0. Then our national income identity will be:

$$Y = C + I$$

$$Y = \$21{,}500 + \$4{,}500 = \$26{,}000$$

As result of American Motors using less steel to produce the same market value of the car, GDP has increased by \$4,500 Dollars. All of this increase comes from the increase in inventory investment by American Steel. In addition, American Motor's ability to use half the market value of steel to produce the same car has resulted in the firm's increase in total value added to the economy to \$17,000 and increasing the firm's share of the final market value to 79.07 percent.[7] Table 4.3c shows the new value added by each firm for this scenario and how the sum of the total value added at each stage of production sums to a new total national income amount of \$26,000.

The value-added measurement approach and accompanying analytical exercise shows that an economy allowing for a division of production specializations along comparative advantage lines supports larger national output (income) values when such activities are value adding through transformation processes. In international trade there follows a similar discourse.

> *The trade of intermediate goods as a reflection of outsourcing and offshoring will be value adding to the economies that participate; enlarging their overall GDP potential and Real GDP per person.*

---

7 Value added by American Motors = Total sales – Cost of intermediate goods = \$21,500 – \$4,500 = \$17,000

	American Ore	American Steel	American Motors	Total Income
Value of Final Sales	$4,200	$9,000	$21,500	
Cost of Intermediate Goods	$0	$4,200	$4,500	
Value Added per Firm	$4,200	$4,800	$17,000	$26,000

Table 4.3c

This helps explain why in a global economy countries are competing for foreign direct investment in order to add new value-adding activities to their respective economies for both industry development and economic growth purposes to capture and retain new product/resource scarcity exploitable opportunities.

Figure 4.7 shows a breakdown of the percentage change in contribution of Real value added to US Real GDP by quarter from 2012 to 2014 for each sector.

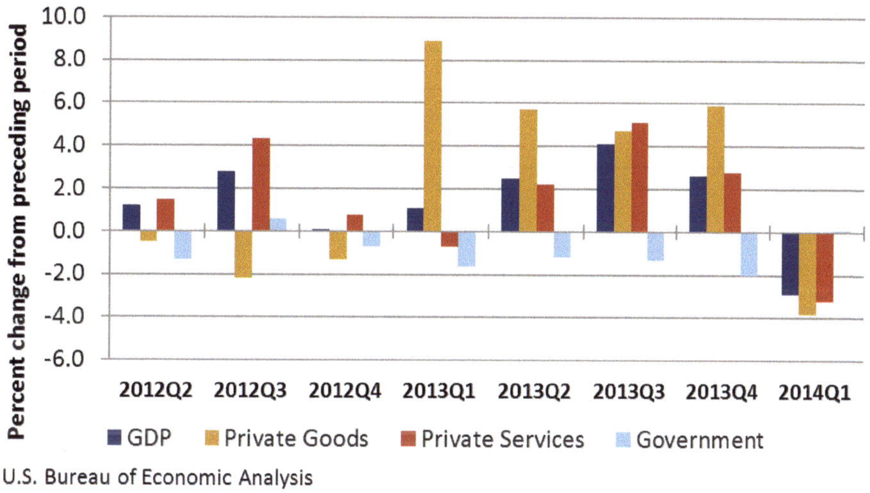

Figure 4.7. Real GDP and Real Value Added by Sector.

The figure shows that private goods followed by services add the most value added to the economy with government making no significant value-added (transformational-process) contribution. This is because the government is a buyer of goods and services, a taxer, and a regulator—not a producer of goods and services in the marketplace. *As a regulator, the government provides and supports the regulatory environment firms will engage in to conduct value-adding activities that will be beneficial for the growth of the economy's tax base. In addition, the public services the government provides at the federal, state, and local level will provide a value-added component that the private sector is able to exploit as a workable base to drive new value-added creation.*

Factor Payments Approach

If the economic system of a country encourages production specialization along the lines of comparative advantage, such activities will help incentivize a healthy division of factors used. This division of factors, otherwise known generally as the "division of labor," helps allocate factors to their most productive uses. This exploitation of productivity difference among factors allows an opportunity for each factor to capture its specialized share of the market value of the output it is responsible for producing. Transforming low-value (low-tech) intermediate goods into high-value (high-tech) final goods should have demonstrative effects on wealth and income disparities and a country's tax base.

As shown earlier in the chapter, areas of the US economy exhibiting a higher concentration of manufacturing (transformational processes that are value adding) also exhibited higher median income levels. The final portion of Table 4.4 examines a final GDP measurement approach: the factor payments approach.[8]

	American Ore	American Steel	American Motors	Total Income
Value of Final Sales	$ 4,200.0	$ 9,000.0	$ 21,500.0	
Cost of Intermediate Goods	$ 0.0	$ 4,200.0	$ 9,000.0	
Factor Payments				
Wages	$ 2,000.0	$ 3,700.0	$ 10,000.0	$ 15,700.0
Interest Payments	$ 1,000.0	$ 600.0	$ 1,000.0	$ 2,600.0
Rent	$ 200.0	$ 300.0	$ 500.0	$ 1,000.0
Profits (dividends)	$ 1,000.0	$ 200.0	$ 1,000.0	$ 2,200.0
				$ 21,500.0
Total Firm Expenditures	$ 4,200.00	$ 9,000.00	$ 21,500.00	

Table 4.4

Returning to the initial conditions of the working example in Table 4.3a, at each stage of production, each firm employs factors as inputs in the production of an intermediate good, the transformational process of an intermediate good into another intermediate good, or final good. At each stage of production these factors are employed and paid according to the share of the market value of the output they are responsible for creating. In Table 4.4 the firm's total sales are equal to the cost of their intermediate goods used plus factor payments. These factor payments are paid in the form of:

Wages: Paid to labor units employed according to the respective market value of the output labor is responsible for producing. Wages can be paid on an hourly basis or contracted amount for specific labor services rendered (i.e., salaries and other compensation schemes).

Interest payments: Paid on borrowed funds used for the purchase of production assets. These borrowed funds maybe in the form of structured borrowing (mixed use of lines of credit, loans, and other lending products from banking institutions) and/or bonds (an IOU) sold by the firm in financial markets to borrow directly from savers wishing to hold savings in an instrument (security) earning higher yield than may otherwise be earned on savings instruments offered in the banking system.

The owner of the bond is paid a fixed stream of interest payments (claim on income earned off the production asset and/or other collateral) during the holding period up to the time of maturity of the instrument where the face value (principle) of the bond is redeemed. The holder of the bond may sell the instrument in the market for a capital gain/loss prior to the maturity date.

Rent: Paid to owners of capital (i.e., other physical production assets, including business structures) that is leased as opposed to being owned. The rental income should be a reflection of capital's contribution to the total value of output produced.

[8] To keep the analysis of the hypothetical auto industry simple using the factors-payment approach, factor payments (income) are taxed at a zero rate. All income payment earned are fully disposable.

Profits: Paid in the form of dividends to owners of the company according to stock ownership (equity) held in the firm. Unlike a bond, which is a financial stake in the firm through a claim on the firm's sales (income) in the form of interest payments, a stock is an equity stake in the firm in terms of external ownership as a dividend claim on the firm's profits after taxes. Stocks can be sold at any time for a capital gain/loss. Not all stocks pay a dividend.

According to the CFI model for an open and closed economy, the total market value of output supplied should be equal to the total sum all expenditures made on the demanded output and equal to the total sum of all income earned (wages, interest, rent, and profit [dividends]) and used for those expenditures. Looking at Figure 4.9c, a summation of all wages, interest payments, rent, and profits paid out across all stages of production will equal the market value of the output (income) or GDP.

GDP = Summation of all factor payments made = wages + interest + rent + profit

GDP = $15,700 + $2,600 + $1,000 + $2,200 = $21,500

Additional comments on the factors-payments approach

From the variables in the summation above, there is not one factor earning payments large enough to purchase a car!! How then can this be reconciled with the CFI model?

Recall from the model again that all output produced is equal to the total flow of income. The model does not suggest or imply that income equality is a necessary precursor for equilibrium to prevail between the output and expenditure sides of the market. Referencing Figure 4.2 and 4.3 for both closed and open economies, the presence of financial institutions drives the recycling process of savings into loanable funds that can be used for all consumption, investment, government, and trade expenditures driving the transactions rings of the CFI model.

Applying the CFI model from Table 4.4, the factor payments earned as wages, interest, rent, and profit will find their way into depository financial institutions. Through fractional reserve banking (covered in Chapter 8), these deposits will be transformed into a loan lent to a borrower for the consumption of the car in the example. This also means the money on deposit in the banking system will also be used to directly and indirectly finance the production of new cars and the continued employment factors of production to produce them in our hypothetical example.

The CFI model and income distribution

As previously stated, income equality is not a precursor to the overall function of the CFI model. How the income flows and where the income ends up is irrelevant to the "feelings" of the marketplace.

As shown in Table 4.5 for the hypothetical example, labor constitutes the factor of production capturing the largest share of total sales and value added at each stage of production with 73 percent of total income (GDP) captured.[9] Data presented earlier in the chapters confirms this would be an ongoing expected observation in the US marketplace, as households in the United States outnumber firms and personal consumption expenditures accounted for a little more than 68 percent of GDP for all quarters since 2012 as shown in Table 4.2.[10] Yet firms as corporate entities capture the largest share of total sales (market value). Since total sales = total expenditures = total income, firms play an important role in employing members of households for employed access to a resource base

[9] From the CFI model, households supply factor markets with the factors of production to be employed by firms in exchange for payments made in the form of wages, interest, rent, and profits. In the hypothetical example, wages paid to households represented the largest share of the factor-payment type made. Interest payments, rent, and profits are also remitted back to households via claims that household members hold on those income streams.

[10] According to the US Census Bureau, from 2008 to 2012 there were 115,226,802 households with an average of 2.61 persons per household, and 27,092,908 firms as of 2007.

and market base to drive the creation of market value and income streams. This allows households to capture a larger share of national income through a single entity than they otherwise could on their own.

	American Ore			**American Steel**			**American Motors**				
		% of Total Sales	*% of Value Added*		*% of Total Sales*	*% of Value Added*		*% of Total Sales*	*% of Value Added*	**Total Income**	*% of Total Income*
Value of Final Sales	$ 4,200.00			$ 9,000.00			$ 21,500.00				
Cost of Intermediate Goods	$ –	0%		$ 4,200.00	47%		$ 9,000.00	42%			
Factor Payments											
Wages	$ 2,000.00	48%	48%	$ 3,700.00	41%	77%	$ 10,000.00	47%	80%	$ 15,700.00	73%
Interest Payments	$ 1,000.00	24%	24%	$ 600.00	7%	13%	$ 1,000.00	5%	8%	$ 2,600.00	12%
Rent	$ 200.00	5%	5%	$ 300.00	3%	6%	$ 500.00	2%	4%	$ 1,000.00	5%
Profits (dividends)	$ 1,000.00	24%	24%	$ 200.00	2%	4%	$ 1,000.00	5%	8%	$ 2,200.00	10%
										$ 21,500.00	100%
Total Firm Expenditures	$ 4,200.00			$ 9,000.00			$ 21,500.00				
Value Added Per Firms	$ 4,200.00			$ 4,800.00			$ 12,500.00				

	American Ore			**American Steel**			**American Motors**				
		% of Total Sales	*% of Value Added*		*% of Total Sales*	*% of Value Added*		*% of Total Sales*	*% of Value Added*	**Total Income**	*% of Total Income*
Value of Final Sales	$ 4,200.00			$ 9,000.00			$ 21,500.00				
Cost of Intermediate Goods	$ –	0%		$ 4,200.00	47%		$ 9,000.00	42%			
Factor Payments											
Wages	$ 2,000.00	48%	48%	$ 3,700.00	41%	77%	$ 10,000.00	47%	80%	$ 15,700.00	73%
Interest Payments	$ 1,000.00	24%	24%	$ 600.00	7%	13%	$ 1,000.00	5%	8%	$ 2,600.00	12%
Rent	$ 200.00	5%	5%	$ 300.00	3%	6%	$ 500.00	2%	4%	$ 1,000.00	5%
Profits (dividends)	$ 1,000.00	24%	24%	$ 200.00	2%	4%	$ 1,000.00	5%	8%	$ 2,200.00	10%
										$ 21,500.00	100%
Total Firm Expenditures	$ 4,200.00			$ 9,00.00			$ 21,500.00				
Value Added Per Firms	$ 4,200.00			$ 4,800.00			$ 12,500.00				

Table 4.5a-b

4.3 NOMINAL VS. REAL GDP AND THE CONSUMER PRICE INDEX

Up to this point in the chapter, the examination of GDP has been on Nominal GDP (NGDP). Recalling the national income expenditure approach, Nominal GDP is the final market value of goods and services produced within a nation's borders. This final market value, for any period of time, is derived using current period final prices and current period final quantities.

Using this approach provides the Nominal market value of final output for any current period. For simplicity, defining a period of time as a year, then Nominal GDP for any economy in a current year producing final goods $Q_i = 1,2, \ldots .n$, and sold at final prices $P_i = 1,2 \ldots n$, can be expressed as:

$$NGDP_{cy} = (P_1^{cy})(Q_1^{cy}) + (P_2^{cy})(Q_2^{cy}) + \ldots \ldots \ldots \ldots \ldots (P_n^{cy})(Q_n^{cy})$$

The identity shows for the current year, if all prices increase (or decrease) holding all quantities constant NGDP will increase (or decrease). And for the current year, if all quantities increase (or decrease), holding all prices constant, then NGDP will increase (or decrease).

In the market supply and market demand model for an observed micro market, deviations from market equilibrium in the short run, followed by the long-run equilibrium price and quantity adjustments, contribute to the overall change in the final market value in the observed micro market and that of the broader national market's Nominal GDP performance.

Just tracking changes in the growth rate of Nominal GDP does not provide indication of whether overall economic welfare has changed in terms of purchasing power to raise the standard of living per person. In terms of the NGDP identity, if the prices of goods rise faster than the rise in quantities of those goods produced, NGDP has increased but purchasing power of the economy's output has been eroded. In this case, the growth in Nominal GDP is all inflation. Figure 4.8 examines the impact of hyperinflation on a country's exchange rate for Germany (1921–1924), Yugoslavia (1990–1993), and Zimbabwe (2005–2008).

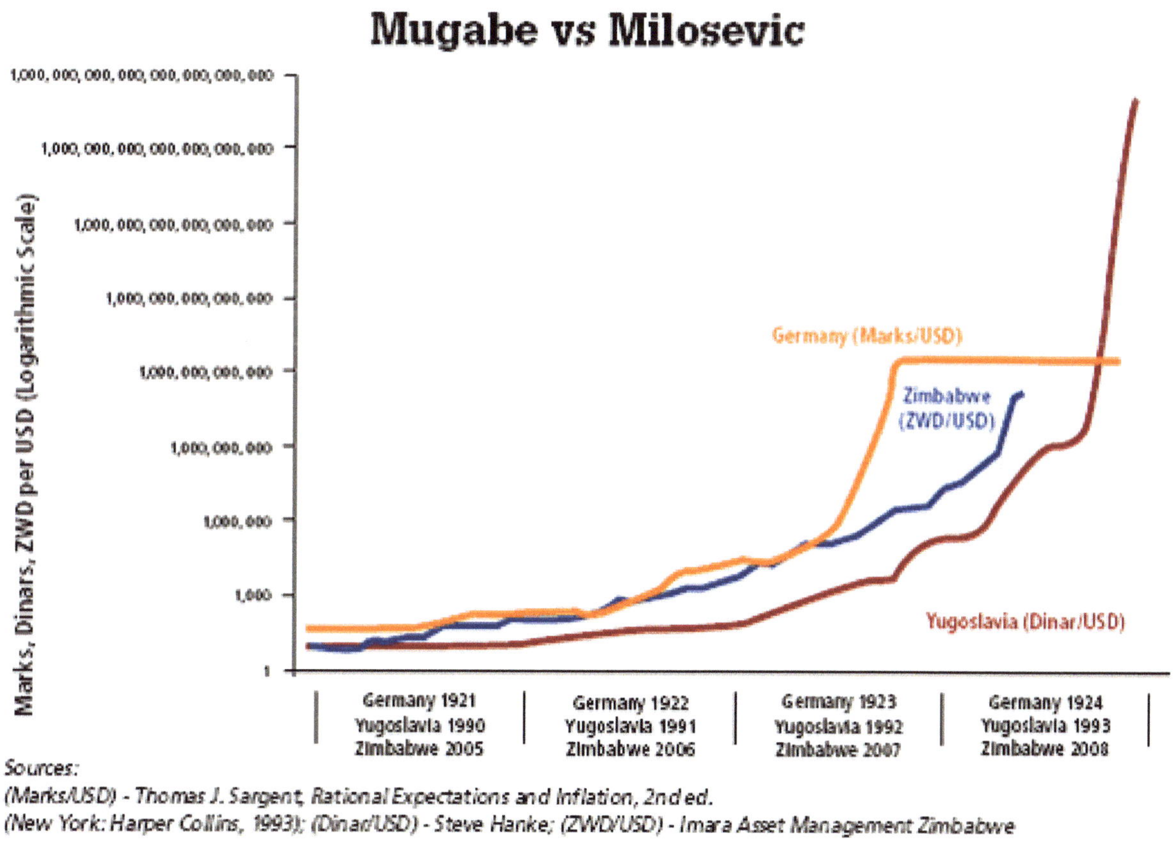

Figure 4.8. Impact of hyperinflation on a country's exchange rate for Germany (1921–1924), Yugoslavia (1990–1993), and Zimbabwe (2005–2008).

In all three cases, hyperinflation deteriorated each country's current exchange rate against the Dollar and destroyed Real economic opportunities with it. Following the peak of Zimbabwe's hyperinflation in 2008, the economy entered a period of Dollarization. Without the Dollarization of its economy, coupled with a price boom in oil, agriculture and other commodities priced in Dollars from 2008 to 2012, Zimbabwe's expected GDP growth would have remained at negative growth rates.

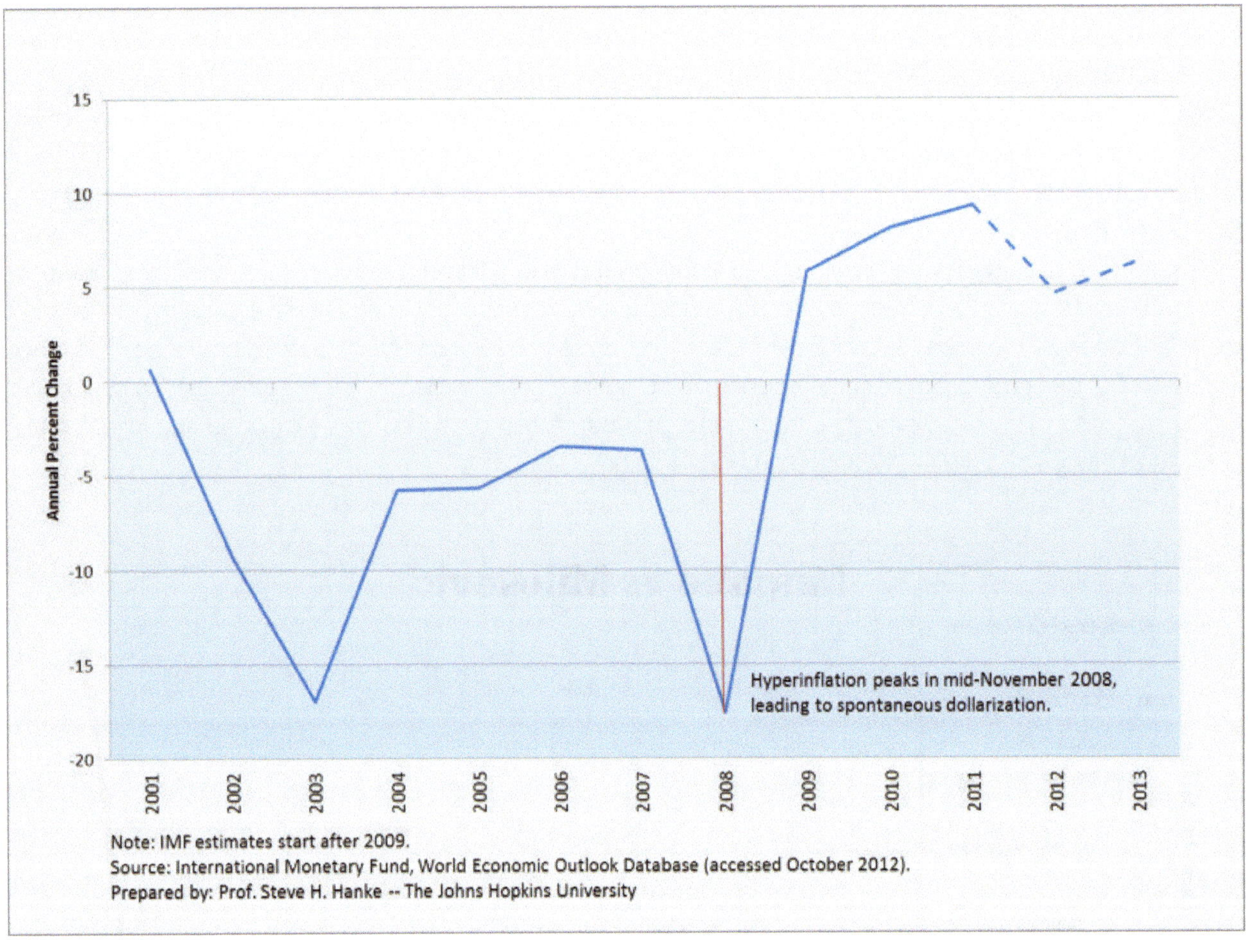

Figure 4.9. Zimbabwe's GDP Growth Rate.

As Figures 4.8 and 4.9 show, it is important to discuss GDP as a "Real" value as opposed to a "Nominal" value influenced by changes in market prices. Calculating and using Real GDP and Real GDP growth rates becomes a much better barometer of economic performance than Nominal GDP growth when accounting for an inflation bias. Unlike changes in Nominal GDP accounting for both changes in prices and changes in quantities, Real GDP discounts the value of Nominal GDP created by inflation from period to period and focuses on changes in quantities from period to period only in the measurement.

Calculating Real GDP

To calculate Real GDP requires prices in a period of time to which all real values of output past and future periods will be anchored. In the calculation of Real GDP (RGDP) for any chosen period, base year prices and current period quantities will be used. For simplicity, defining a period of time as a year, then Real GDP for any economy in a current year producing final goods $Q_i = 1,2, \ldots .n$, will be valued at base year prices $P_i = 1,2 \ldots n$, can be expressed as:

$$RGDP_{cy} = (P_1^{BY})(Q_1^{CY}) + (P_2^{BY})(Q_2^{CY}) + \ldots \ldots (P_n^{BY})(Q_n^{CY})$$

Table 4.6 looks at the example of the TOM economy again from Chapter 2, but now the TOM economy is a much larger national economy producing yards of cloth and bushels of wheat. The figure provides hypothetical final prices in Dollars and final output totals for Year 1 and Year 2. Using the data provided, Nominal GDP is calculated for both years, and Real GDP is calculated for both years.

The Economy of TOM						
	Year 1=Base Year		Year 2		Growth Rate	
	Price	Quantity	Price	Quantity	Price	Quantity
Yards of Cloth	$2.00	50,000	$2.50	65,000	25.00%	30.00%
Bushels of Wheat	$3.25	125,000	$3.30	133,000	1.54%	6.40%
Nominal GDP	$506,250.00		$601,400.00		18.80%	
Real GDP	$506,250.00		$562,250.00		11.06%	

Table 4.6

Because Year 1 is the base year, Real GDP for Year 1 will equal Nominal GDP for Year 1. Conclusively, the data show that the Nominal growth in GDP from Year 1 to Year 2 (18.80 percent) was driven by 25 percent inflation in the price of yards of cloth and the corresponding 30 percent increase in output. Despite the year-to-year Nominal growth, accounting for inflation by using Year 1 prices for yards of cloth and bushels of wheat and holding these prices constant across both years, Real GDP grew 11.06 percent from Year 1 to Year 2. Because of inflation, for years following the base year, Nominal GDP will be higher than Real GDP. This confirms what we know about the time value of money: A Dollar today is worth more in buying power in the present than in the future.[11] So, what if there is deflation instead of inflation?

During the Great Depression, the overall price level in the economy deflated and contracted by some 30 percent and was coupled with a contraction of national output and a rise in unemployment by similar amounts. Figure 4.10 puts the Great Recession of 2007–2009 in perspective with the Great Depression in the 1930s.

Deflation over time has the consequence of making the value of output and income more expensive in real terms. This is why unemployment rises during deflationary cycles, because the real wage = (Nominal wage/price level) rises, making it more expensive in real terms for firms to retain the use of labor at agreed-upon wage rates. As such, every real Dollar of income in the economy becomes more valuable to hold than to expend. This act of saving more expensive Dollars in real terms created a negative consequence on consumption and investment spending, leading to contracted Nominal growth during this period.

4.4 THE PRICE INDEX AND THE INFLATION RATE

In the economy of TOM, the rate of inflation in the price of yards of cloth was 25 percent in one year, and the rate of inflation in the price per bushel of wheat was 1.54 percent. But overall, how much more expensive is the output basket from Year 1 to Year 2?

[11] Present value of a single future value amount is a discounted value: $PV = FV/(1 + i)^n$.

Putting the Recession in Perspective
In terms of economic output and jobs lost, this recession pales in comparison with the Great Depression.

The Charts show the course of the recession that started in December 2007 and of the Great Depression of August 1929 through March 1933. The lines show how much higher or lower each indicator was in the months before or after the recession started, measured as a percentage of the level of that indicator at the start of the recession.

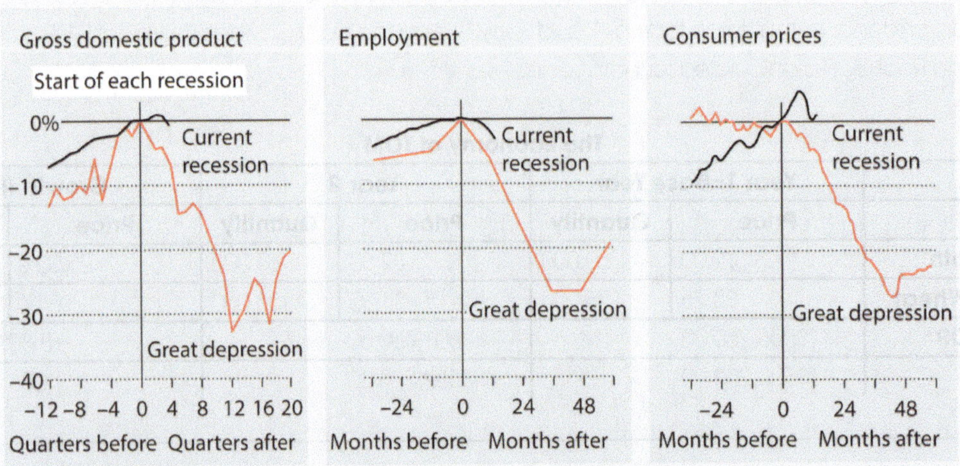

Notes: GDP is measured at a seasonally adjusted annual rate in constant (1939 and 2000); employment levels are for nonagricultural jobs; 1920s–30s figures are annual and exclude the military; price data are consumer price indexes.

Sources: National Bureau of Economic Research Macrohistory Database (Depression-era GDP and employment); Commerce Department (current GDP); Labor Department (current employment and all price data)

Figure 4.10. GDP is measured at a seasonally adjusted annual rate in constant (1939 and 2000); employment levels are for nonagricultural jobs; 1920s-30s figures are annual and exclude the military; price data are consumer price indexes.

To make this determination, the percentage change in the calculated price indexes for both years is needed, and this information will be used to calculate the rate of inflation in the overall price level in the economy of TOM from Year 1 to Year 2.

Inflation: It's both "bad" and "good"

First, what is inflation, and what makes it so "bad"? Inflation is described as an overall rising trend in the measured price level at the national, regional, state, and local level. The price level is a weighted measurement in which prices of goods and services serve as weights for the corresponding quantities produced. Inflation is "bad" in the sense that it erodes purchasing power. This is why growth in Real GDP is preferably tracked to Nominal GDP. If total output is considered to be total income for the economy, any inflation in prices driving the increase in NGDP growth—outpacing growth in physical output supplied—will be evident in slower growth in Real GDP and slower growth in Real purchasing power per person.

Also, not all inflation is "bad." Inflation can be a positive indicator of good growth in the economy that is demand driven, and the demand side inflation can be tempered by positive supply side responses and macro policy intervention. Expectations of higher future prices gets consumers to go out and demand more today, bidding up the equilibrium quantities to be supplied at higher prices. This benefits sellers able to supply greater quantities at higher prices in the form or higher sales revenue per unit.[12]

[12] Whether or not profits earned by sellers will be overall higher depends on any inflation in the price of inputs used increasing total costs of production.

Investors anticipating rising interest rates from expected increases in inflation will borrow more at today's interest rates to invest in different projects that are expected to produce returns greater than the financing costs and rate of inflation.[13] On the debtor side, inflation is beneficial, since the repayment of debts over time is done with less-valuable Dollars. Whether this eases the debt finance burden on borrowers depends on the growth rate in Real income having been adjusted for inflation.

And finally, on the hiring side—if inflation is demand driven and driving higher sales revenue per unit against slower rises in costs of production—hiring of labor can increase as inflation lowers the Real wage (Nominal wage adjust for inflation) paid by firms.

When the market experiences a rise in the price level (inflation), this does not mean all prices for goods and services are rising. It can be verified that prices of those goods and services—representing an influential share of total GDP—are rising faster relative to changes in the price of other goods, and this is causing the aggregate price level to rise. If the aggregate price level is rising nationally, does this mean that the price level in all regions, states, and cities is rising?

The answer is ambiguous. The rise in the national inflation rate (demand or supply side driven) may just be driven out of a few industries in certain states, with the remaining states seeing some to very little increases in inflation filtering into their markets. This depends on the integration of market segments across borders and the mobility of activity across borders bringing in inflationary pressures as well as shifting inflation out from cross-border transactions.

Also, it is possible the anticipated inflation expected in goods and services from a growing economy is only showing up in financial securities and physical assets such as housing and financial securities held in portfolios. This today has been more the result of US monetary policy quantitative easing. Either way the inflation rate of an economy is an important economic indicator to follow that will communicate the trend in Real growth and affect the allocation of resources and spending through our expenditure aggregates. As a result, changes in inflation across micro markets will impact the final composition of what an economy produces, along with its final Nominal and Real market values.

Looking at the inflation rate in the TOM economy example

Back to the economy of TOM, from Year 1 to Year 2 there is evidence of inflation in the prices of yards of cloth and bushels of wheat, and this is complemented with increases in the growth in quantities of output supplied at higher price levels for both goods.

Using a calculated price index for each year, the percentage change in the price indexes for both years will give the inflation rate over the two-year period. Keep in mind that in a two-good model, there are only two goods buyers can substitute between in terms of relative price changes, and therefore the inflation rate will be much higher as opposed to an economy with a larger variety of goods serving as substitutes to buyers seeking to evade inflationary effects.

An expanded model of n-amount of goods of differing varieties will provide strong substitution effects within the output composition, and this will help soften the general rise in the inflation from year to year. More opportunities to exploit with a larger variety of goods in the output mix to substitute among will allow for a better distribution of economic welfare—wealth and interest rate effects—from inflation.

Calculating a price index

To calculate a price index, a base period must be chosen. In this case the base period for the economy of TOM will be Year 1. The calculation of a price index for any current year (period) is as follows:

[13] The Fisher equation provides what the Real interest rate paid/earned on the use of funds is when expected inflation is accounted for: $r = i - \pi^e$. Any increase in expected inflation over a period for constant interest rate lowers the Real interest rate paid on funds by borrowers and earned by lenders.

PI_{cy} = [*Market value of basket of goods (output) for the current year/Market value of basket of goods (output) for the base year*] × 100

Unlike the calculation of Real GDP, where market prices from period to period are constant to a base period and quantities from period to period vary, in the calculation of a price index, quantities from period to period are constant to a base period, and market prices are allowed to vary. This means in the numerator and denominator of the calculation, base year quantities of goods (output) will be used, and the market value of the basket of goods (output) in the numerator and denominator will be determined by that current period's prices. For example, the calculated price indexes for Year 1 (base year) and Year 2 are:

$$PI_{Y1} = [((P_{Y1}{}^{Cl})(Q_{Y1}{}^{Cl}) + (P_{Y1}{}^{W})(Q_{Y1}{}^{W}))/((P_{Y1}{}^{Cl})(Q_{Y1}{}^{Cl}) + (P_{Y1}{}^{W})(Q_{Y1}{}^{W}))] \times 100 = (\$506{,}250/\$506{,}250) \times 100 = 100$$

$$PI_{Y2} = [((P_{Y2}{}^{Cl})(Q_{Y1}{}^{CL}) + (P_{Y2}{}^{W})(Q_{Y1}{}^{W}))/((P_{Y1}{}^{Cl})(Q_{Y1}{}^{Cl}) + (P_{Y1}{}^{W})(Q_{Y1}))] \times 100 = [\$537{,}500/\$506{,}250] \times 100 = 106.17$$

From the results, for any year (period of time—including month and quarter) chosen as the base period, the calculated price index for the period will be 100. This is because for the chosen base period, Nominal GDP equals Real GDP. So the Year 1 calculated price index is equal to 100. For Year 2 the calculated price index uses Year 1 quantities in both the numerator and denominator, but Year 2 prices in the numerator and Year 1 prices in the denominator to calculate the market values to be used.

As a result, our calculated price index for Year 2 is equal to 106.17. Taking the percentage change in the price indexes between Year 1 and Year 2 shows a rate of inflation of 6.17 percent. What this says is if the same quantities in the output mix produced in Year 1 were to be purchased in Year 2 at Year 2 prices, the same basket of output would be 6.17 percent more expensive. Table 4.7 provides a final summary of macro measurements covered for the economy of TOM.

		The Economy of TOM						
	Year 1=Base Year		**Year 2**		**Growth Rate**		**Price Index**	**Inflation Rate**
	Price	***Quantity***	***Price***	***Quantity***	***Price***	***Quantity***		
Yards of Cloth	$2.00	50,000	$2.50	65,000	25.00%	30.00%	100	—
Bushels of Wheat	$3.25	125,000	$3.30	133,000	1.54%	6.40%	106.17	6.17%
Nominal GDP	$506,250.00		$601,400.00		18.80%			
Real GDP	$506,250.00		$562,250.00		11.06%			

Table 4.7

This approach in using calculated price indexes for two or more periods and calculating the percentage change in the indexes from year to year gives the user an idea of what inflation is currently and expected to trend at over time using historical observation. The changes in the index numbers alone do not communicate if the rate of inflation is demand side driven or supply side driven. More detailed analysis will need to be done to make this determination.

At a consumer level and investor level, this information is useful to gauge an anticipated change in the expected value of future earnings (direct and indirect) that will affect the allocation of spending and investment today and into the future. Consumers will want to know, based on inflation trending today, what to expect in future purchasing power and future interest rates they can save/invest at.

Investors will want to know, based on returns today adjusted for inflation, what projects to invest into today or in the future that will earn rates of return greater than anticipated inflation. As well, social insurance payments coming out of unemployment compensation schemes, Social Security, Medicare, and Medicaid may be indexed or adjusted for inflation to allow those persons' welfare to remain unchanged.

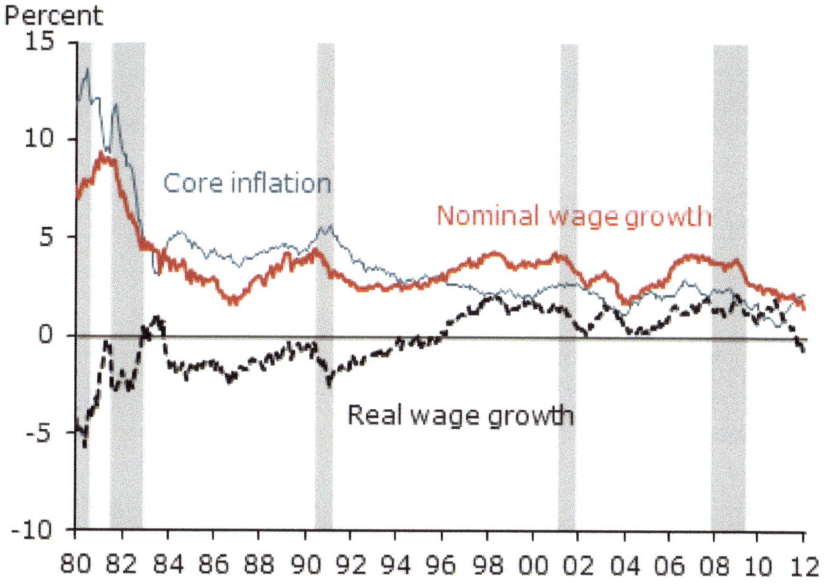

Figure 4.11. U.S. core inflation, nominal wage growth and real wage growth.

Source: Federal Reserve Bank of San Francisco, www.frbsf.org.

Figure 4.11 provides data on the trends in core inflation in goods and services against trends in growth in Nominal and Real wages from 1980 to 2012. During the economic recession period of 1981 to 1983, core inflation and Nominal wage growth fell as higher interest rates in the late 1970s were used to contract the economy to bring inflation down. As core inflation fell during this period, Real wages (Nominal wages adjusted for inflation) grew, causing a rise in unemployment during this period.

Over much of the 1990s and into the early 2000s, lower interest rates stimulated an investment recovery driven by information technology, having positive supply side effects on production and lower transaction costs and growth in residential housing starts. During this period core inflation trended toward a flatter level of growth and the gap between Nominal wage and Real wage growth began to close. The closing of this gap came from positive supply side shocks (technology and productivity driven) to the economy that drove a recovery in Nominal and Real wage growth.

The leveling off of core inflation over this period was thought to be the "death of inflation," with monetary expansion being successful in driving credit expansion for consumption and investment expansion with little risk for rising core inflation. However, during this same period, the inflation that was anticipated to show up in core inflation had shown up in inflated asset and financial securities prices as evident in the financial markets "busts" resulting from an overinvestment in new dot-com companies and information technology (2001–2002) and residential housing (2007–2009).

4.5 CONCLUSION: FINDING THE ELUSIVE ELIXIR TO GROW REAL GDP

In the end it's all about growth. Not Nominal growth BUT Real growth, driven by real exploitable opportunities translated into a lifting of economic boats at all levels of the economy. Even small marginal gains in the poorest of areas provide unique opportunities to exploit and add more to an environment trying to escape the grasp of resource and opportunity scarcity.

As stated in this chapter, an economy's ability to add value to marketplaces through transformational activities is crucial to the encouragement of a division of production specialization along the lines of comparative advantage. Existing and new value-adding activities that transform low-value goods into high-value ones will not just enlarge Nominal and Real total income but also shape the economy's growth path and distribution of income streams among the factors of production responsible for creating more of the market value.

Whether an economy has the means or will be able to attract the means to do this will be covered in the next chapter. The pursuit of an elixir that will drive a sustainable long-run growth path reaching the lowest rungs of an economy and narrowing income and wealth divides is the holy grail of economics.

What factors more prevalent in an economy are more responsible for economic growth? What makes an economy poor, and for what reason will poverty remain persistent? How powerful a force are human incentives in determining a growth path and reasons for a why an economic take-off may or may not occur with the best designed macro policy approaches? If the pace of globalization is integrating world economies into what appears to be a smaller space, then why are growth rates among regions and the respective economies diverging as opposed to converging? What are the limits of current theory and application stressing demand-driven investment, and is there now an opening to consider supply side approaches?

Chapter 5, which looks at economic growth and development, can be designed into a course all its own. A savings and investment growth model taught even at the intermediate level will be considered along with the limits of the approach against the Realities that developed and developing economies face.

If all resources are scarce, then each economy started off with an unbalanced mix of advantages and disadvantages that was going to determine the economy's exploitable future. If it is about driving new capital creation and employing people with capital, can an economy sustain itself off machines? If technology and innovation play a star role in raising productivity and income per person, then why do they also displace resources?

The questions posed are designed to encourage critical thinking and introduce a healthy critique of traditionally taught development approaches supported by the theory of their parent growth models. In the end it is all about growth while minimizing the trade-offs between efficiency and equity in a cost-shifting globalized world.

CASE STUDY: CAN GDP TELLS US ANYTHING ABOUT OVERALL LIFE SATISFACTION?

In this chapter, we covered three distinctive ways for calculating GDP:

1. *Sum all of the gross expenditures: consumption spending, investment spending, government spending, and net foreign spending on domestic goods and services.*
2. *Sum all of the value added to the economy at different stages of production.*
3. *Sum all the gross earnings made in the form of wages, interest payments, rent, and profits.*

For all its uses, GDP is an imperfect measurement that can be quite misleading as a barometer of human welfare. Of the three distinctive approaches covered in this chapter, each measurement told a different story of where income comes from and where it goes. For practical purposes, the measurements of GDP are used to tell us how the economy is evolving over time. Real GDP per person is used the most as a barometer of individual standard of living, suggesting that higher Real GDP per person translates into a higher standard of living and a higher level of happiness.

This can be quite misleading. For instance, expenditures on market activities that add to total water, air, and land pollution will show up in GDP numbers. Yet these market activities may not add to an improvement in standard of living. How so? If such activities add to total pollution and correlate with an increase in infant mortality rates, respiratory diseases, waterborne illnesses, reduced life expectancy, and so on, then how can one say higher GDP per person from such expenditures has raised standard of living if human health risks have increased?

Although GDP over time (Nominal or inflation adjusted) will change, does this necessarily correlate with changes in average life satisfaction rates? If we just look at Real income per person as a barometer of standard living, we are only considering the Real market value of physical goods available to each person, not the types of goods available per person.

Not everyone in the market will have equal access to the per capita amount in the market supposedly available to them. Are such goods available low-value goods or high-value goods? To what degree do the goods themselves help lower the opportunity cost of a person's choices, allowing them to create and accomplish more within their economic constraints?

This makes sense as one can observe how more innovative products in the marketplace have altered the opportunity costs of human choices in terms of time and place in a way that has helped raise social welfare, income mobility, and improved market access. One only need to look at the products in their own home and consider how such products have contributed to their overall productivity in and outside the home. What would economic welfare be like without cars, computers, cell phones, television, kitchen appliances, and so on? This is not to say that such products have not had an offsetting social and economic consequence, but one cannot say for sure how much different average life satisfaction would have been without them.

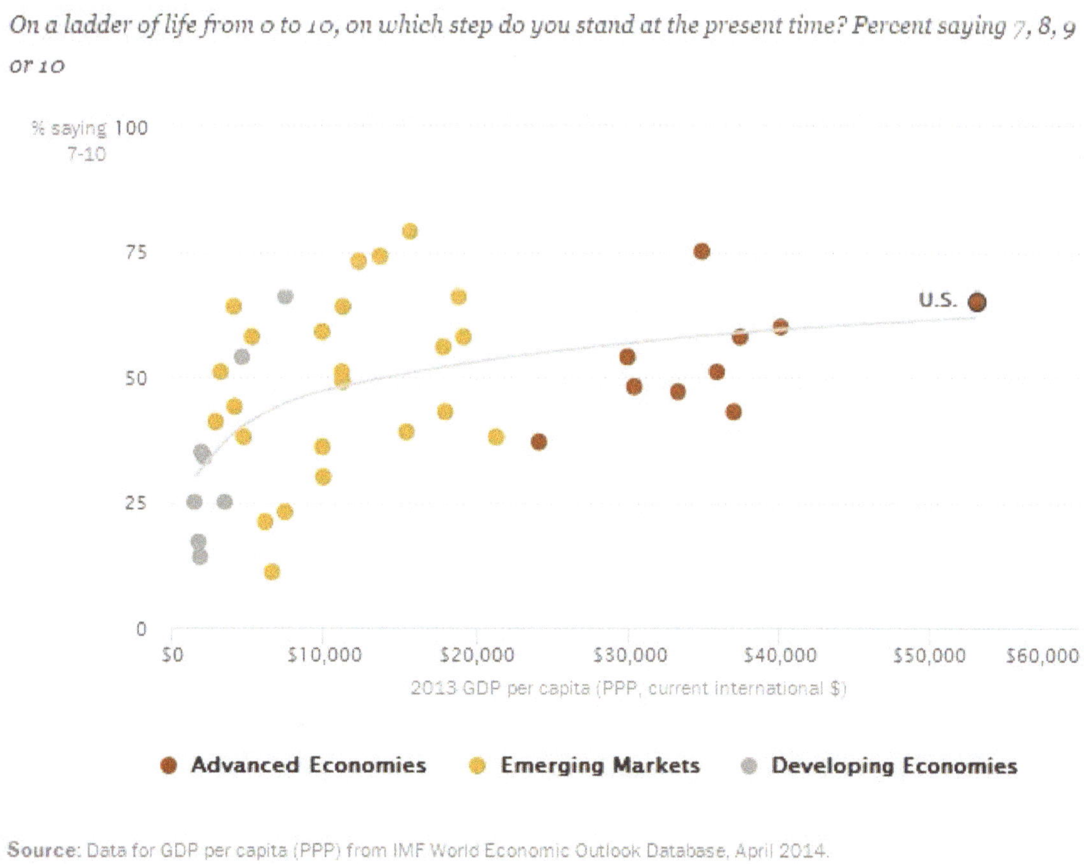

Figure 4.12. GDP per Capital and Life Satisfaction: On Average, Life Satisfaction Higher in Richer Nations, Up to a Point.

On par, growth in GDP per capita correlates with a higher average life satisfaction rate. But, as Figure 4.13 shows, the correlation is not grounds for strong causality. Excluding those countries that lie at or near the regression line, there are a number of countries showing a higher mean life satisfaction rate at lower GDP per capita and some showing a lower mean life satisfaction rate at higher GDP per capita. So why the disparity?

Keep in mind that each economy takes a different approach to how choices will be managed privately and publicly for the greater good of the marketplace, the state, and society. Other factors helping explain a weaker GDP per capita correlation with mean life satisfaction would include (to name just a few): cultural attitudes toward wealth creation and distribution of income, climate, geographic location, level of political and economic freedoms, life expectancy, access to and strength of public services, and levels of water, air, and land pollution.

In all, Figure 4.13 does suggest that for some but not all countries, as an economy gets richer, money may matter less. And, because each economy is inherently different, it would be haphazard to think any economy can successfully replicate what makes a country happier. Without efficient proxies to go by, gross happiness is just difficult to measure. Although imperfect, the distinctive measurement approaches covered in the chapter will still be used to give us a "good old" GDP number to gauge how an economy's standard of living is evolving in terms of income.

QUESTIONS FOR CLASS DISCUSSION

1. Parallels are often drawn between the Great Depression of the 1930s and the Great Recession of 2007–2009. However, these two very important events in the history of the US economy are quite different.

   In students groups, compare and contrast the quantitative changes in the economic spending aggregates of consumption spending, investment spending, government spending, and net exports for these events. Then discuss economic reasons for any similarity and dissimilarity in the behavior of the economic aggregate between these two market events; along with the policy approaches to address the events and the respective policy outcomes on Nominal GDP and Real GDP.
2. As a class, discuss the role that value-added production activities play in an economy's development and distribution of income. Next, using the article "The Third Industrial Revolution" (*Economist*, April 21, 2012), explain how the digitization of manufacturing will impact the future of offshoring; the distribution of national income in developed, less-developed, and emerging economies; the pattern of global trade; and global economic security.
3. During Ronald Reagan's first term in office, the Federal Reserve increased interest rates in order to dis-inflate the economy from the high inflation of the mid and late 1970s, and did so at the cost of sacrificing economic growth. The increase in domestic interest rates resulted in a decrease in investment spending, contraction in growth and national income, and a rise in the unemployment rate.
4. But as the world's largest debtor nation, bringing inflation down was seen as vital to sustaining the Dollar's position in global financial markets and addressing the emerging problems of long-term unemployment brought on by higher domestic inflation that risked becoming more permanent.

   Using what you have learned about inflation and Real growth from this chapter (along with outside research), explain and discuss the short-run trade-offs of the US policy approach to bringing inflation down in the late 1970s.

   Finally, had the policy approach to dis-inflate the economy been unsuccessful, discuss how different the US Dollar position and US debt position in global markets would be today and how different the relationships with foreign economic counterparts would have been at the trade, investment, and international security level.

IMAGE CREDITS

- Fig. 4.0: http://commons.wikimedia.org/wiki/File:Circulation_in_macroeconomics.svg. Copyright in the Public Domain.
- Fig. 4.1a: Copyright © Le0t (CC BY-SA 3.0) at http://commons.wikimedia.org/wiki/File:Circular_flow_of_income.png.
- Fig. 4.2: U.S. Census Bureau. Copyright in the Public Domain.
- Fig. 4.3: U.S. Census Bureau. Copyright in the Public Domain.
- Fig. 4.4: "The Industrial Belt," www.american.com. Copyright © 2010 by American Enterprise Institute.
- Fig. 4.5: Budget of the United States Government. Copyright in the Public Domain.
- Fig. 4.6: U.S. Bureau of Economic Analysis; National Income and Product Acounts, December 2011, Tables 1.15, 3.16, 3.2, 3.3, and 5.10www.brookings.edu. Copyright in the Public Domain.
- Tbl. 4.1: U.S. Bureau of Economic Analysis. Copyright in the Public Domain.
- Tbl. 4.2: U.S. Bureau of Economic Analysis. Copyright in the Public Domain.
- Tbl. 4.3a: Paul Krugman, Macroeconomics. Copyright © 2012 by Worth Publishers.
- Tbl. 4.3b: Paul Krugman, Macroeconomics. Copyright © 2012 by Worth Publishers.
- Tbl. 4.3c: Paul Krugman, Macroeconomics. Copyright © 2012 by Worth Publishers.
- Table 4.4: Paul Krugman, Macroeconomics. Copyright © 2012 by Worth Publishers.
- Table 4.5a &b: Paul Krugman, Macroeconomics. Copyright © 2012 by Worth Publishers.
- Fig. 4.7: U.S. Bureau of Economic Analysis. Copyright in the Public Domain.
- Fig. 4.8: Thomas Sargent, "Mugabe vs Milosevic," www.cato.org.
- Fig. 4.9: Dr. Steve Hanke, John's Hopkins University, IMF World Economic Outlook Database.
- Fig. 4.10: National Bureau of Economics Research, Commerce Department, Labor Department, The Economist Magazine. Copyright © 2009 by The Economist Newspaper Limited. Reprinted with permission.
- Fig. 4.11: Federal Reserve Bank of San Francisco, www.frbsf.org.
- Fig. 4.12: IMF World Economic Outlook Database, 2014; www.fruittreeblog.com.

CHAPTER 5

ECONOMIC GROWTH: CAN AN ECONOMY ALTER ITS DESTINY WITH JUST INVESTMENT?

Figure 5.0. What a difference thirteen years can make! The illustration shows the results of Dubai's transformation of oil wealth into domestic investment, translating into added economic capacity for larger economic potential.

5.0 OVERVIEW

In Chapter 4 the concept of growth in total income was introduced through the different measurements of GDP. As output/income expands and contracts from changes in the economic spending aggregates, the resulting changes in the availability of opportunities and their exploitability will affect the behavior of other economic measurements. These measurements include the growth in income per person, the distribution of income among the factors of production, changes in the aggregate price level (inflation rates), and the rate of unemployment.

The most important for an economic system is an economic path of long-run growth sustaining a real rise in income per person that reaches all levels of the economy. An important question to consider is to what degree economic growth is an outcome of "best" macro policy practices or a natural phenomenon of an outcome of human incentives exploiting resource constraints with a mixed bag of advantages and disadvantages at the starting line.

Just as the genetic traits of human biology provide a disposition of what potential human capabilities will be (outside of environmental influences), even the poorest of economies have a long-run growth picture dependent on the economic base the economy is starting from.

If human beings born with genetic attributes making some humans grow in height at rates above, equal to, or below an average rate, then is the long-run growth course of a country's economy already predetermined from the starting point of its resource and technological base? In what way can an economy alter the "stars" that defines its "destiny"? What qualitative factors can be altered or even exploited from fixed physical factors so that an economy is growing somewhat sustainably above its long-run trend?

In this chapter, a healthy critique will be given to the Solow growth model that has been the paradigm that more modern economic growth models have been benchmarked against. Economic and noneconomic reasons will be offered to provide best explanations for why certain economies have been consistently "richer" and others consistently "poorer."

Before proceeding to future chapters, this chapter on growth should encourage a healthy critique of macro policy (fiscal and monetary) attempts to drive and alter a course of short-run economic growth away from a predetermined long-run trend. If it is true that consequences of economic activities naturally regress to a long-run trend, then much of the development approaches in raising the economic welfare of less-developed economies have been just short-run panaceas.

5.1 THE BUSINESS CYCLE, UNEMPLOYMENT, AND REAL GDP PER CAPITA

According to Figure 5.1, a system in motion is deviating about a natural rate and trending toward a new level(s) of equilibrium along its growth path. As covered in Chapter 3, supply and demand analysis illustrated how changes in overall market demand and market supply created disequilibrium in the form of market shortage/surpluses in the short run, followed by a long-run adjustment to new equilibrium prices and corresponding equilibrium quantities. This means the changes in the equilibrium outcomes across all micro markets are changing the behavior of a business cycle over the short run.

Looking at the business cycle in the figure, a rising trend in the business cycle above the economy's long-run trend is treated as an economic expansion. During economic expansions, consumption spending and domestic investment spending should be higher. Government spending at all levels may also be higher and trade deficits may also be wider, as the import of savings from abroad as loanable funds is used to support credit creation for use in consumption and domestic investment spending.

During this period of economic expansion, GDP in the economy expands, and the unemployment rate in the economy should be lower, supported by a higher growth rate in real income per person—provided core inflation in goods and services is fairly constant or rising at a rate slower than the growth in physical output. This may not be the case for this expected trend in real GDP per person if economic expansion is nominal in nature and driven by inflation.[1]

[1] From 1997 to 2007, Venezuela experienced nominal growth of 27 percent each year, outpacing the nominal growth of the United States and China. Over this same period, growth in real income remained flat, indicating the nominal growth in the economy was driven by higher inflation.

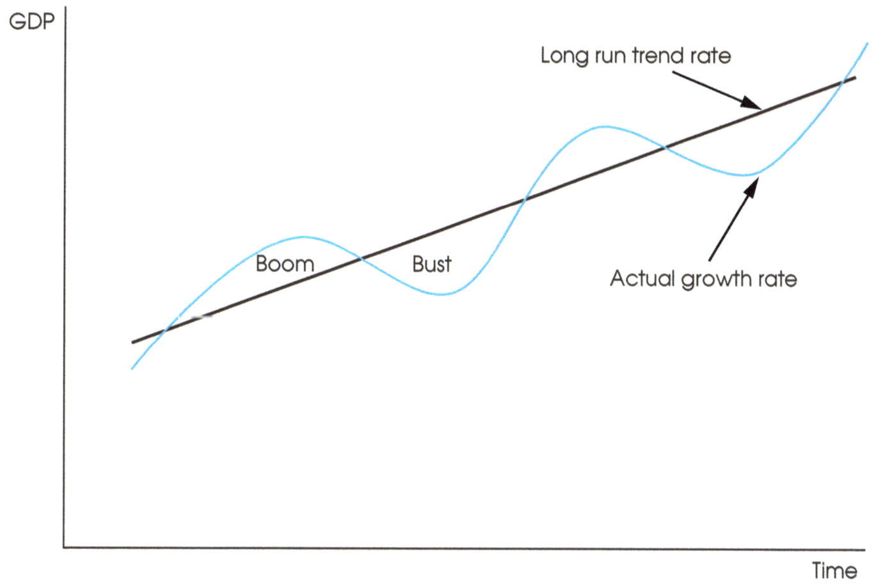

Figure 5.1. This figure illustrates the behavior of a business cycle over short-run periods. It suggests that in the long run, all short-run deviations in the business cycle will trend toward a predetermined natural rate of growth. As such, the economy will be susceptible to boom—and bust—cycles over short-run periods that make up the long run, provided the long-run potential growth of an economy remains unchanged.

Conversely, during periods of economic downturn, GDP contracts, leading to higher unemployment and slower growth in real income per person. Typically, this period of contraction is considered recessionary if it is two consecutive quarters of contracted growth.[2] However, real GDP per person may be higher during this period if the contraction in the economy is coupled with a deflation in the overall price level. This would make real factor payments more expensive to pay and lead to higher unemployment of resources. The opposite occurs during periods of economic expansion when a steady rise in inflation makes factor payments cheaper in real terms to pay supporting more employment of resources.

Finally, as shown in the business cycle, economic expansion hits a limit and the economy peaks and goes through a correction process as it trends closer to a normalized long-run growth trend, provided the economy is not experiencing any negative demand or supply shocks. However, overshooting may occur, depending on the multiplier effects from changes in aggregate economic spending components moving the economy below its long-run trend until eventually bottoming out (hitting a trough), and there is an eventually recovery. These multiplier effects will be covered in more detail in Chapters 6 and 7.

The peaks and valleys of a business cycle are of interest to economists who are examining a number of questions in regard to business cycle behavior. What is causing the economy to peak out or bottom out? What role did changes in expectations of consumers, firms, investors, and the rest of the world play? Had the economy hit a capacity limit causing the economy to peak out, or did economic participants find new innovative ways to make use of idle capacity to spur an economic recovery? What is going on privately in the market that would best explain a turning point in the economy (i.e., housing bust or housing recovery, innovation that is productivity enhancing or

[2] Using this definition may be quite restrictive. An economy may experience positive growth in one quarter, followed by a quarter of negative growth, followed by another quarter of positive growth. Economist will look to the use of leading as well as lagging indicators to make a better determination of whether the economy has entered a recessionary period. For example, during periods of economic recovery, unemployment may rise as discouraged workers reenter the workforce, adding to the total number of unemployed workers looking for work.

creating resource displacement, and so on)? How responsible are macro policies for driving the correction as well as accompanying boom and bust cycles that tend to make up the behavior business cycle over the long run? What causes a boom? What causes a bust?[3]

Types of Unemployment and the Calculation of the Unemployment Rate

The unemployment rate in the economy is the percentage of total number of qualified workers who are unemployed and actively seeking a job as a percentage of the labor force. The labor force is the sum of total workers who are employed and total workers unemployed and actively seeking work.[4] A simple calculation of the official unemployment rates and types of unemployment are as follows:

Unemployment rate = (Total # of workers unemployed/Labor force) x 100

Total unemployed: 20 million

Total employed: 100 million

Unemployment rate = (Total # of workers unemployed/Labor force) x 100

= [20 million)/(100 million)] x 100 = 20%

Unemployment that varies according to season of the year: For example, during holiday shopping seasons, unemployment should be much lower and will tend to rise after the season, provided the work opportunities are temporary. Of interest to economists and policy makers will be the share of temporary employment opportunities that become more permanent.

Unemployment that varies over the course of the business cycle: During periods of economic expansion, prices and sales revenue tend to rise, supporting more employment; and during periods of economic contraction, prices and sales revenue tend to be much lower, supporting less employment of resources. During economic expansions and economic contractions, there will job creation as well as job loss.

Unemployment that is structural and underemployment: Unemployment that is structural in nature is in the form of the skill set of the labor available in the economy that is mismatched with needs of firms in the marketplace. A case for this can be explained by the fact that innovation at the production level makes certain skills in the marketplace obsolete.[5]

Unemployment of this nature tends to translate into higher levels of underemployment, in which skilled workers take employment opportunities making little to no use of their specialized skills, causing a loss in value-added potential to the economy. When the level of underemployment is not taken into account, the reported unemployment

[3] In Chapter 6, these short-run fluctuations in the business cycle will be examined in terms of the evolution output gaps—inflationary and recessionary—and how the economy as a system unhindered on its own may self-correct, explaining the peaks and valleys in the business cycle over time.

[4] A qualified worker is anyone above age eighteen who makes up the adult population. Not accounted for in the labor force are military personnel and institutionalized persons (i.e., inmates in a prison system or patients or in mental health facilities), high school students (employed and unemployed), and college students not actively employed and not seeking work. To be counted as unemployed, the person must be documented and actively seeking work. Not included in the total number of unemployed are workers who are marginally attached and discouraged workers who have exited the labor force and are no longer looking for employment.

[5] According to Paul Christensen's *The Innovators Dilemma* (1997), such technological progress may be considered as "disruptive innovation". In this case, newly adopted production technologies create a disintermediation between physical capital and labor shifting labor resources into the services sector of the economy. The results of disintermediated production processes may show up in a slower growth in real GDP per capita, suggesting that the pace of innovation from disintermediation is not beneficial to everyone. The negative externalities from disintermediation may be more noticeable in informational economies, where services represent a larger share of total output and income creation. Although there is a rise in the unemployment of resources from disintermediation, disintermediation may also create reemployment of unemployed resources in a specialized way.

in the economy will be understated as shown in Figure 5.2. Persistent structural unemployment of resources can cause long-run employment rates to be higher and more difficult for macro policy makers to address. Persistent underemployment, in which persons hold on to such jobs longer than need be, will impact median income growth rates.

Frictional unemployment: This type of unemployment is in the form of resources separating voluntarily/involuntary from business opportunities to later be employed in alternative or new opportunities. The time it takes for a single individual to find a new opportunity that matched well with his or her skill set is important. Websites such as LinkedIn help speed up the process of matching the skills of unemployed workers with existing or new opportunities in the marketplace demanding their skills, making the process less frictional. Often this type of unemployment is more predominate during expansionary periods of the business cycle. Over the course of any changes in the business cycle, economists will track the rate at which labor separates from opportunities and the rate they find new opportunities.

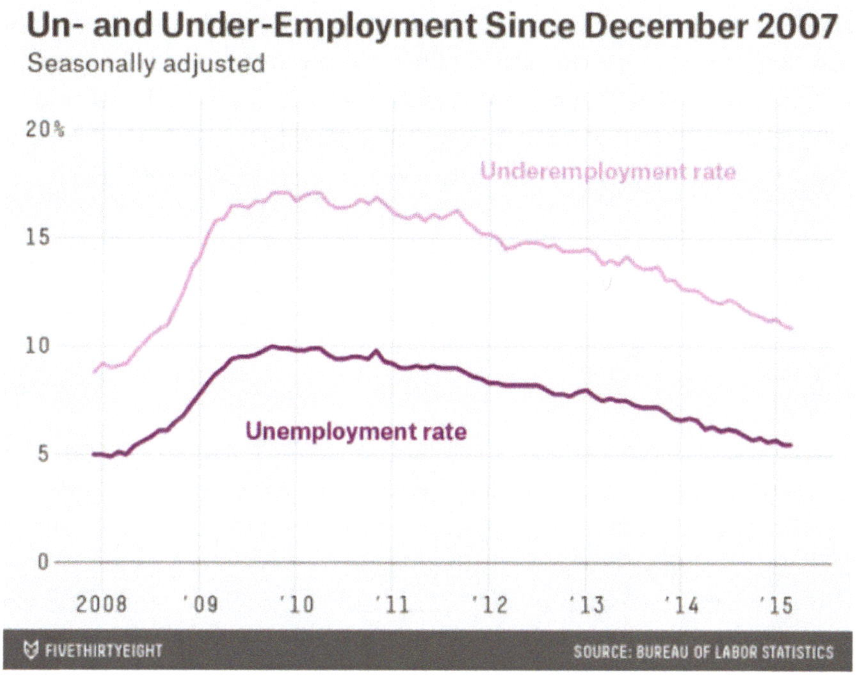

Figure 5.2. Accounting for the share of the employed labor force that is underemployed, the official rate of unemployment for 2008–2015 should be higher.

Real GDP per Capita

Real income per capita (per person) will be the economy's real GDP divided by the population and is used as an important barometer of the economy's standard of living. Growth in the economy that translates into a rise in real GDP per capita will be important in order to consider how much of the growth in the economy has helped close income and wealth gaps with and without macro policy assistance.

If the entire real economic pie was divided by the population, this would provide an idea of an ideal share of output/income each person should be able to feasibly capture. However, national income streams come in many forms—wages, interest, rent, and profits in the form of dividends. These income stream shares (differentiated further and taxed differently) will accrue to those factors of production in the economy more responsible for the growth in output and market value; right down to the micro level. The equation for calculating real GDP per capita for any current year (period) is as follows:

$$\textit{Real GDP per capita}_{cy} = \textit{Real GDP}_{cy} / \textit{Total population}_{cy}$$

Real GDP per capita is influenced not only by the inflation-adjusted value of nominal GDP but also by the size of the population and concentrated share of the market value of the type of output produced. Countries with larger populations relative to economic size will have lower real GDP per capita numbers, suggesting lower standards of living per person. This would be the case for a country like China, with the world's second-largest economy and one of the world's largest population bases. In 2013 China GDP was $17.02 trillion, with a population of 1.367 billion people. GDP per capita for China for the same year was $11,200 per person.[6]

Figure 5.3 shows GDP per capita (adjusted for purchase power parity) for the top twenty-five countries in 2011; China does not make the list, due to the population bias in the calculated statistic. In the figure, Qatar has the largest income per capita (around $99,000 per person), but this result is very much biased by concentration of the economy around oil production and very high per barrel prices experienced in 2011.[7] If the population included the total number of expatriate workers that make up the economy's labor force, income per capita would be much lower.

5.2 THE PRODUCTION FUNCTION, SAVINGS, AND INVESTMENT

Section 5.1 stresses economic growth in the form of real GDP per capita that raises standard of living in the form or purchasing power. This increase in buying power can be evident in the improved composition of goods in households. Figure 5.4 shows how the standard of living in the economy has improved from 1905 to 2005 through a larger percentage of households improving their material ownership of a number of products.

For instance, in 1905 less than 10 percent of all households in the United States had electricity, less than 20 percent had a cooking range and a telephone, and less than 2 percent had an automobile. With a large share of US households in 1905 not being connected through a public utility infrastructure, there would be limited exploitable opportunities available to households and businesses. This means most of the economic activity took place during daylight hours only; whereas one hundred years later, 100 percent of homes and businesses had electricity, allowing for economic activity to run twenty-four hours a day, seven days a week.

The figure also suggests it takes time for innovation and growth to reach all levels of the economy. The pace at which this takes place is a factor of the growth of a middle class benefiting from improved availability and affordability of products that were also productivity enhancing to households (i.e., the automobile, the cooking range, dishwasher, washing machine, cell phones, computer, Internet, and so on).

[6] *CIA World Factbook 2015.*

[7] According to the *CIA World Factbook 2015*, Qatar had a native population of 2,194,817 persons and economy with oil and natural gas exports accounting for 92 percent of all export earnings.

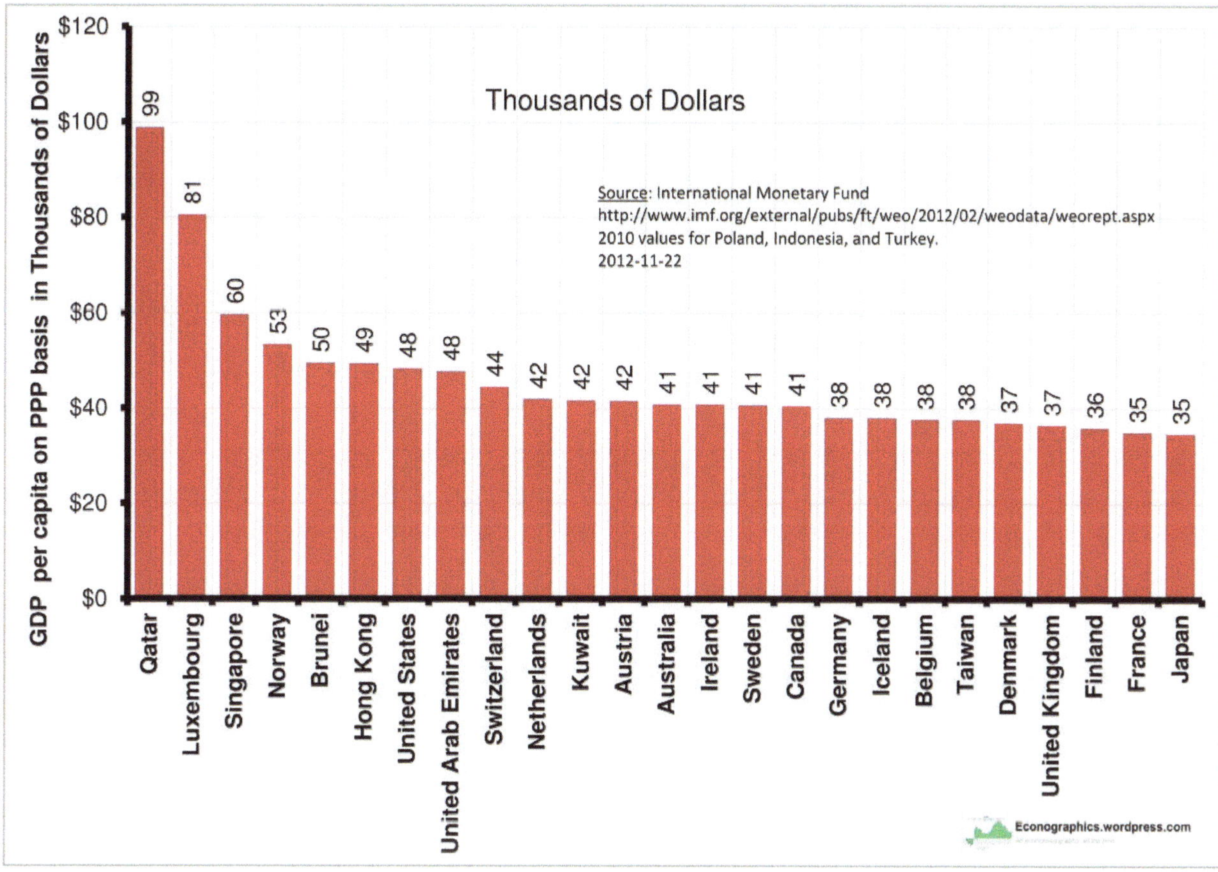

Figure 5.3. GDP per Capital Adjusted for Purchasing Power Parity. Top 25 Countries, 2011.

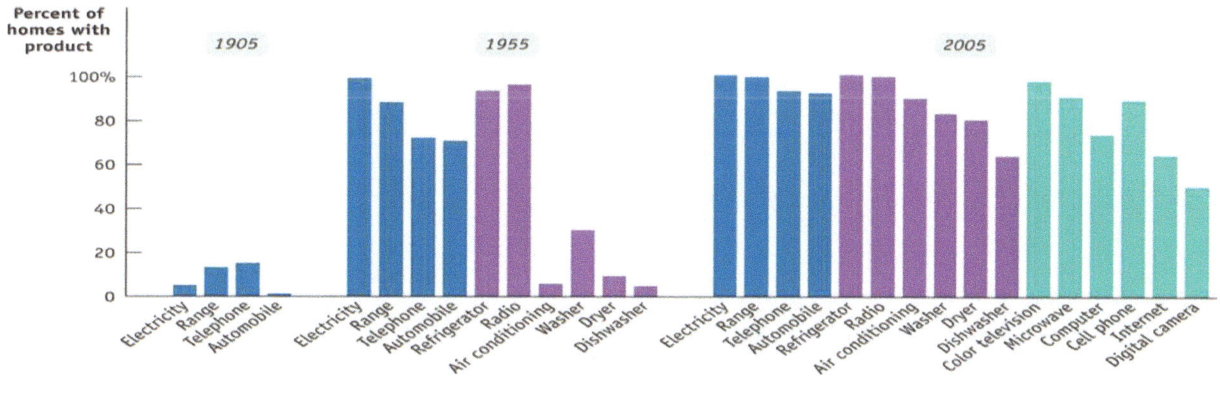

Figure 5.4

Source: Adapted from Krugman, P., and R. Wells. 2012. *Macroeconomics.* 3rd ed. New York: Worth.

This means growth in the size of a middle class was made possible from the growth in real GDP per capita driven by industries adopting new value-adding production methods. Firms employing strong divisions of production specializations with groupings of labor and capital inputs exploited strong internal economies of scales to deliver volume to the market at lower prices and average costs. Complementing this was a boom in housing production and home ownership during the early post—World War II years, increasing the wealth base of middle- to higher-income groups and supporting economies of scale in large public utility infrastructures (water and electricity), as well as enlarging retail channels and supporting volume production to deliver more products at lower prices.

Higher volume in output and lower core inflation—driven by the exploitation of opportunities to address scarcity—resulted in strong real GDP growth per capita. Accounting for a number of historical market and economic events, Figure 5.5 shows the short-run behavior in the growth rate in real GDP per capita (measured in 2005 Dollars) over its long-run trend from 1871 to 2009.[8] Despite the cyclical ups and down, correlating Figure 5.5 with Figure 5.4 shows standard of living has improved, with growth in real output per capita over the long term. This is provided that the employment of the factors of production are able to capture a competitive share of the growth from exploitable opportunities, improving the composition of goods in their households.

So, what is driving growth, and is the economy growing along a predetermined growth path or just exploiting a mixed bag of ever changing advantages in the short-run to alter the long-run direction of the economy? To what degree do past market lags from events influence the behavior of the current business cycle and the economy's long-run course?

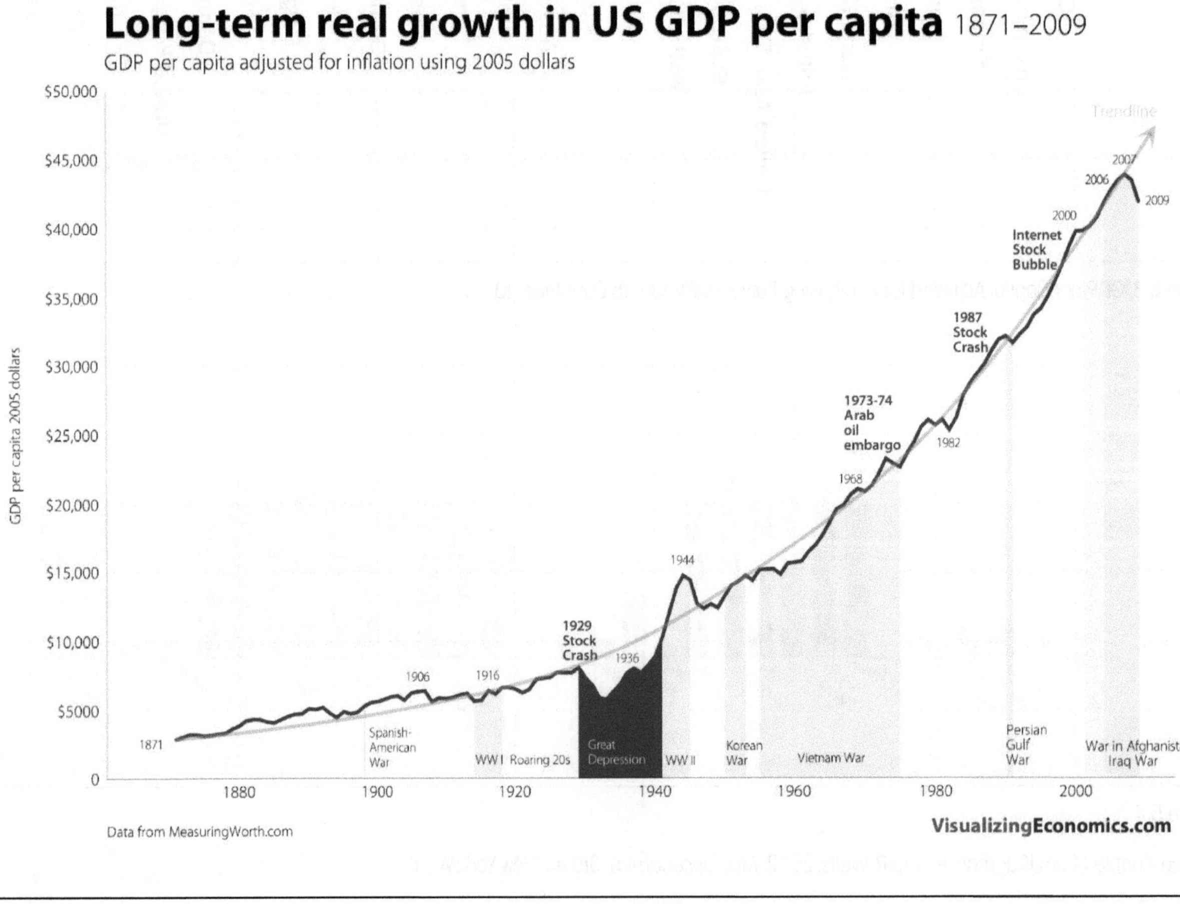

Figure 5.5

[8] The decline in real GDP per capita for 2007-2009 was the result of the Great Recession, driven by a market bust in residential housing coupled with the negative supply shock from inflated global energy and commodity prices.

Production Function and Marginal Productivity of Capital and Labor

In order to maximize the highest growth rate potential in per capita income, the thought process is labor must be employed with capital in order to produce more output than it would otherwise on its own. This will allow labor to claim a greater share of the income from the production stream and incorporated value-adding processes. It suggests for an economy, domestic investment spending in capital per worker is needed to raise output (income) per worker. And the technology in the capital investments coupled with human capital (the skill sets of labor) help raise the productivity of each worker employed with such capital investments. With capital investments employed with labor, this should support a stronger division of production specialization to support the growth of value-adding activities.

At the macro level, the total output produced will be represented in the employment of capital and labor together using some technology set.[9] At the micro level of the firm, these resources are also employed together in different shares, making the output produced either labor intensive or capital intensive. A useful approximation of an aggregate production for an economy is the Cobb-Douglas production function.[10] The production function takes the form of:

(Equ. 1.0) $Y = AK^{\alpha}L^{1-\alpha}$

In the expression, the value of α represents a value between 0 and 1 such that: α will represent capital's (K) share of output (Y) it is responsible for producing, 1-α will represent labor's (L) share of output (Y) it is responsible for producing, and A will represent the technology level in the economy. Therefore, according to the function, the distributional share of total income across capital and labor will be allocated to the respective shares of total output the factors are responsible for producing. This will also mean that the sum of gross factors payments—wages and rent—paid to labor and the owners of capital according to their contribution to total output will sum to the gross value of output produced.

Taking the first derivative of the production function respect to capital and then to labor derives the marginal product functions of the factors: the marginal product of capital and the marginal product of labor.[11]

(Equ.2.0) $MPK = (\alpha)AK^{\alpha-1}L^{1-\alpha}$

(Equ.3.0) $MPL = (1-\alpha)AK^{\alpha}L^{\alpha}$

Equation 2.0 and 3.0 show as the stock of physical capital increases at a rate greater than the increase in the stock of labor and employing the additional increases in the physical stock of capital with labor, the marginal productivity of capital diminishes and the marginal productivity of labor rises. This is because as the capital stock grows faster than the growth in the labor stock, then each unit of labor will have more available of capital to work with exclusively.[12]

[9] The aggregate production function only considers the employment of labor and capital together (intermediation) in different input amounts. Across micro markets, capital and labor will be responsible for different shares of total output. Some production processes will be labor intensive (using more labor inputs for every capital input), and some production processes will be capital intensive (using more capital inputs for every labor input). An aggregation of all micro production processes will look at total output produced and consider of the total output produced the capital and labors' responsible production shares as an aggregation.

[10] Over the long run, the production function exhibit constant returns to scale to show over the long run (taking the log of the behavior of national income paid to labor and capital) remains fairly constant. This is due to the diminishing returns to the resources as the capital-to-labor ratio in the economy changes over time with changes to the quantity.

[11] The marginal product of capital and marginal product of labor describe the additional contribution to total output when one more unit of capital and labor are employed. The wage rate paid to labor will be equal to the value of the additional contribution labor makes to total output produced that will be sold in the marketplace, w = MPL x P. The rental raise paid to owners of capital will be equal to the value of the additional contribution capital makes to total output produced that will be sold in the marketplace, r = MPK x P. Any intensive increase in the use of one factor more than another will result in the diminishment of the factor's productivity lowering the factor payment to be earned to that factor.

[12] This theoretical application explains why countries attempt to control the inflow of immigrated labor in their economies.

However, when there is not enough labor available to be fully employed with every unit of capital this causes an underutilization of capital and lowers the productivity of all capital. As a result, earnings to labor will rise with the increase in labor's productivity and earning to capital will decline with the decrease in its marginal productivity.

Payments made to capital (a rental rate, r) and labor (a wage rate, w) will be equal to the value of the factor's marginal productive contribution. According to equations 4.0 and 5.0, holding the price of output constant, a rise in the marginal productivity of a factor will raise the factor payment paid to the factor. Declines in productivity of a factor will lead to lowers earnings for that factor.

(4.0) $w = MPL \times P$; where $MPL \times P$ is the market value of labor's marginal contribution to total output to be sold at the output's price level

(5.0) $r = MPK \times P$, where $MPK \times P$ is the market value of capital's marginal contribution to total output to be sold at the output's price level

Conversely, as the stock of labor increases at a rate greater than the increase in the stock capital, the marginal productivity of capital will rise as more labor is available to work with every unit of capital, causing the earnings to capital owners to rise as shown in equation 2.0. As well, with more labor employed with fewer units of capital, each unit of labor will have smaller share of capital to work with resulting in a smaller share of output captured causing a decline in the overall productivity of labor and a decline in earnings to labor as shown in equation 3.0.

The goal of any economy is to produce a level of output that represents a maximum production outcome. In order to maximize the production of total output (income) the employment of capital and labor will take place up to the point where the real wage paid to labor and the real rental rate paid to capital is equal to their respective marginal products for the last unit employed. Rewriting equations 4.0 and 5.0 provides the following:

(Equ.6.0) $MPL = w/p$

(Equ.7.0) $MPK = r/p$

Such that the total income created in the economy (as reflected in the maximized level of output produced) will be:

(Equ.8.0) Total Income = MPL (L) + MPK (K); where MPL(L) = total labor income paid in the form of real wages and MPK(K) = total capital income paid in the form of real rental rates.

Equations 6.0 and 7.0 show rises in the productivity of labor and capital result in proportional increases in real compensation economy wide in equation 8.0. This is conditional to technological progress raising the productivity of both factors. Without this condition, productivity slowdowns will bring on an onset of diminishing returns lowering real earnings for both factors. Figure 5.6 illustrates real total compensation trends with the growth rate in productivity over the long run,[13] provided little or no technological regression takes place. With some deviations in the figure, the deviations are reconciled in Figure 5.7 as impacts of changes in the business cycle—economic expansions and recessions—that have helped or not helped keep the growth in real earnings in par with the growth in productivity.

13 Over a long-run time period, all factors of production are treated as variable, resulting in factor prices paid being fully flexible. In the short run, contractual arrangements for the use of factors of production keep factor prices such as wages and rents fixed for some period of time. Outside of fluctuations in the business cycle, this helps explain periods in which the growth in real earnings did not keep pace of the growth in productivity.

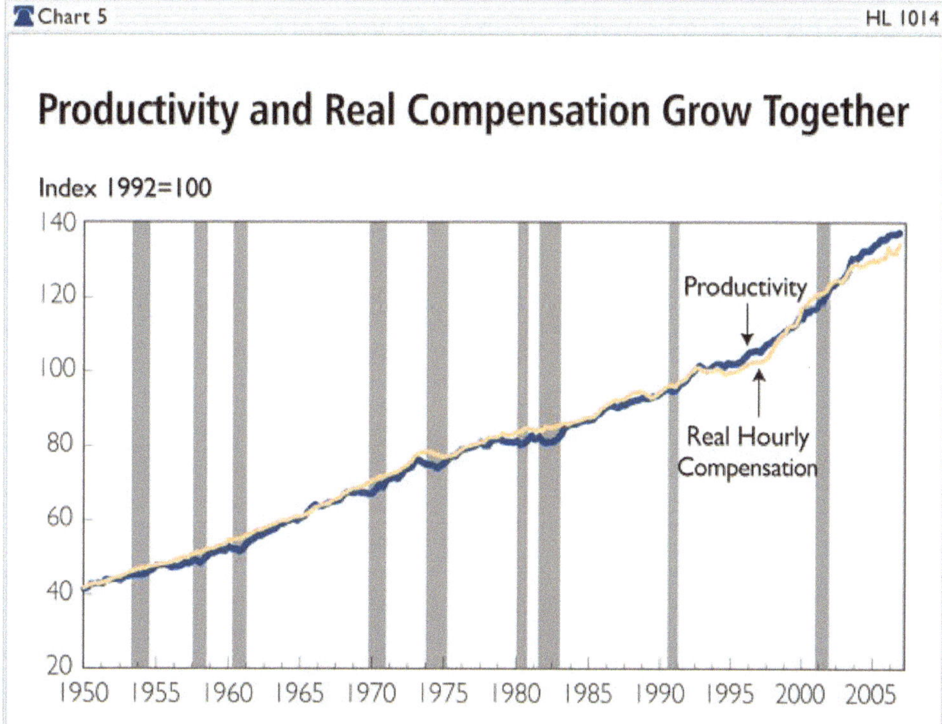

Note: These data cover all persons (including supervisors and proprietors) in the nonfarm business sector. The real hourly compensation is compensation deflated by the price index for nonfarm output. Shaded areas denote recessions.

Source: Bureau of Labor Statistics.

Figure 5.6

Raising Income per Worker through Capital Investment per Worker

Increases in an economy's capital stock relative to the stock of labor will raise the marginal productivity of labor (equation 3.0) and the real wages paid to labor (equation 6.0). However, this is offset by a decrease in the marginal product of capital in the short-run lowering real rental rates paid to the owners of capital keeping the potential total income in the economy unchanged and also real GDP per capital unchanged, as inferred from equation 8.0. In order for total income in the economy to increase, the productivity of all factors must increase, as shown in equation 8.0, in order for real GDP per capita to increase. This also means that such technological progress should be complementary to the skills and quality of the labor and capital components already employed.

If labor is the predominant factor of production supplied by households, the thought process is that by increasing the amount of investment in capital per worker, the output/income per worker will increase as well. And if factors of production are to be paid total compensation according to the real value of their market contribution, then real income per capita should increase, provided the labor force represents a significant share of the total population.

Since of interest here is the growth in output per worker, taking the aggregate production function and dividing both sides by L yields our production function expressed in per worker terms.

(Equ.9.0) $Y/L = (AK^{\alpha}L^{1-\alpha})/L = A(K/L)^{\alpha}$

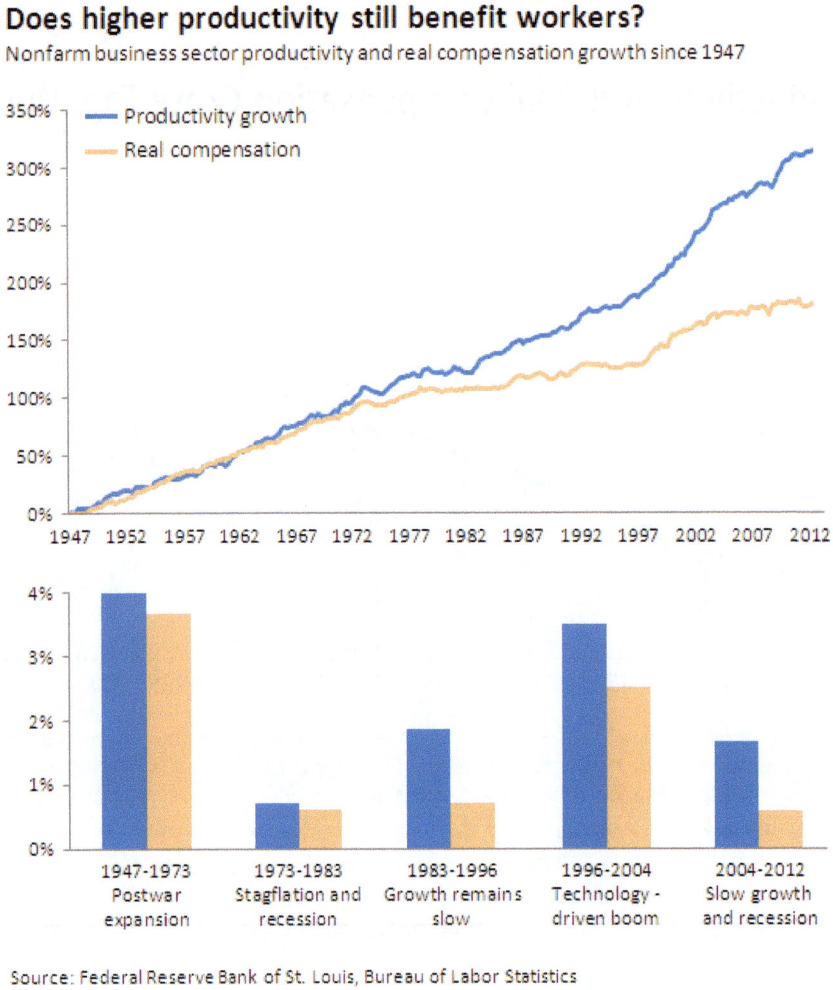

Figure 5.7

In order maximize the highest attainable growth in income per labor unit from capital investments per worker, the labor stock in an economy will be treated as a constant; not even allowing for additions to the labor stock via immigration. As a result, the production function will be subject to the diminishing returns to capital. Denoting $Y/L = y$, $K/L = k$, and the technology level of the economy, $A = 1$, the production function in per worker terms and the corresponding MPK (marginal product of capital) function is:

(Equ.10.0) $y = k^{\alpha}$

(Equ.11.0) $MPK = \alpha k^{\alpha-1}$

Figure 5.8 shows the behavior of the corresponding per worker production as capital investments per worker are increased over a constant endowment of labor. The figure shows that as capital investments per worker (K/L) increases, increases in output per worker (Y/L) rise at a declining rate due to the subjection of diminishing returns to capital.

The shape of the production function, $y = k^{\alpha} = f(k)$, is described by the changing slope of the curve, which is the MPK, approaching a value equal to 0 before becoming negative when further additional capital inputs employed take away from total output per worker.

This graph also suggests that without any changes in technology raising the MPK of capital per unit of labor—resulting in an upward shift of the production function per worker at every level of capital investment per worker, K/L—there is a maximum amount to which the growth in output per worker will rise.

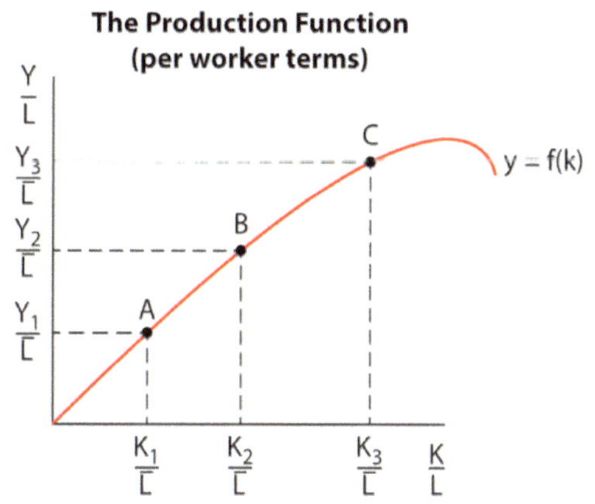

Figure 5.8. As capital investments per worker increase, output/income per worker increase at a declining rate subject to the diminishing returns of capital when the endowment of labor is held constant.

In an economy experiencing diminishing returns to capital per worker, Figure 5.8 begs the question as to how much capital investment per worker should take place in order to maximize the highest attainable growth in income per worker within existing production and technology constraints.

According to the Robert Solow Growth Model an economy with a given savings rate should tend toward steady state of capital invested per worker that will attain the highest possible level of income per worker for a given technology environment. This migration of the economy over time to a steady state of capital per worker is described in the model's steady state of motion of capital equation for an economy without population growth and without growth in a share of the labor force that is becoming more effective.[14]

$$\Delta k - sf(k) - \delta k \; [where\ I - sy - sf(k)]$$

This equation for the evolution capital shows that at a given rate of depreciation, δ, of the economy's capital stock, the economy must translate its share of output per worker saved,

sf(k) = *sy*, into investment per worker, i, in the form of enough additions to the capital stock, Δk, needed to replace the share of the economy's capital stock that is wearing out.

In the long run, as the growth rate in the capital stock equals zero, Δk = 0, the economy will have reached its long-run level of capital investment per worker, k* = K/L, to attain the highest attainable level of output per worker,

---

[14] Nobel laureate economist Robert Solow, in his expanded economic growth model for a closed economy, transforming savings into capital investment per worker accounted for population growth, n, and the growth rate of the effectiveness of the labor force, g, augmented by improved technology and human capital investments, $\Delta k = sf(k) - (\delta + n + g)k$. This was sound, provided after covering the rate of depreciation of the capital stock there was enough savings to turn into capital investments to cover the growth rate in the population making up the labor force and covering the growth rate in the labor force becoming more effective. His final conclusion would show at the Golden Rule level of capital, where consumption was maximized, MPK − δ = n + g, an increase in the productivity of capital would increase the growth rate in output, n + g, and the growth rate in output driven by population growth and growth rate in the effectiveness of the labor force would widen the margin between MPK − δ, attracting an inflow savings to cover the investment gap. Source: Solow, Robert M. *A Contribution to Theory of Economic Growth. The Quarterly Journal of Economics*, Vol. 70, No. 1. (Feb., 1956), pp. 65–94.

$y^* = Y/L$, for a given level of technology used (Figure 5.10). Using the equation of motion of capital and setting $\Delta k = 0$, the stead state level of investment in capital per worker, k^*, for a closed economy can be found.

$sf(k^*) = \delta k^*$ [where $f(k^*) = (k^*)^\alpha$]

$s(k^*)^\alpha = \delta k^*$

$s/\delta = k^*/(k^*)^\alpha$

$s/\delta = k^*\ (k^*)^\alpha$

$s/\delta = (k^*)^{1-\alpha}$

$(s/\delta)^{1/1-\alpha} = [(k^*)^{1-\alpha}]^{1/1-\alpha}$

$(s/\delta)^{1/1-\alpha} = k^*$

Solving for the Long-Run Steady State of Capital for a Closed Economy

Suppose a per-worker production function for a closed economy is $y = k^{.5}$. The economy has a savings rate, $s = .30$, and its stock capital depreciates at a constant rate of $\delta = .10$. What is this closed economy's long-run steady state of capital and output per worker in the steady state?

Answer: Applying the information in the problem above, the equation of motion of capital will be $\Delta k = s(k^*)^\alpha - \delta k = .3(k^{.5}) - .10k$. Setting $\Delta k = 0$, and solving for $k^* = (s/\delta)^{1/1-\alpha}$ yields $k^* = (.30/.10)^{1/1-.5} = 9$. Substituting $k^* = 9$ back into the per worker production function, $y = k^{.5} = (9)^{.5} = 3$ for the output per worker, Y/L in the steady state.

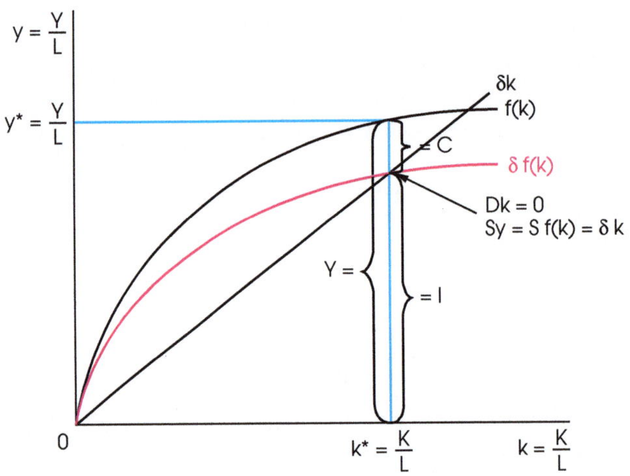

Figure 5.9. The steady state of capital per worker.

So how much time does it take for an economy to get to its steady state of capital to obtain its highest attainable level of output per worker within its production and technology constraints?

The answer is: an infinite amount of time. As shown in Figure 5.9, starting with any initial level of k, $0 < k < k^*$, in an environment of diminishing returns to capital, there is an infinite amount of values to cover between k and k^* as the growth rate in capital, Δk, over time approaches zero.

Because of the nature of the diminishment returns to capital, each additional unit of capital invested per workers increases output per worker at a declining rate a described in the nature of the per worker production function, $y = k^\alpha$. This would also suggest over the long run that the initial capital, labor, and technological base an economy starts from would yield a predetermined long-run growth path for the economy provided the quality of the resources and technology remained unchanged.

Since the future course of a system is based on its performance today, the long-run path of a system can be altered by changes in the in the quality of the factors that make up its base, along with technological innovation. Just as the descriptive picture of a typical business cycle presented at the start of this chapter suggests, an economy is trending above and below but always along and toward its long-run growth trend, then Figure 5.9 suggests without any changes to the quality of resources and level of technology, the economy would trend toward a constant growth rate approaching its steady state of capital for a given savings rate and given level of productivity in the economy.

If it will take an infinite amount of time to reach a steady state of capital for any economy—no matter how developed—and starting from an initial base, then innovation in technology raises productivity of intermediated factors of production and will raise income per capita and standard of living. This is sound, provided the level of investment in an economy at some savings rate maximizes consumption for the highest attainable standard of living level.

As shown in equation 8.0, raising the marginal productivity of labor and capital through changes in the technology set as defined by the increase in the value of A> 1 in the production function will raise total factor productivity and increase returns in output per worker for each capital investment per worker. This is provided such innovation in technology does not create disintermediation of tasks between capital and labor; it must create a stronger intermediation to exploit deeper economies of scale to add more volume in the market to be made available per person at lower prices.

Figure 5.10 shows how an increase in total factor productivity raises output per worker at each level of k = K/L. Figure 5.11 shows for a given savings rate, changes in technological progress raise total factor productivity and will allow the economy to reach a higher level of output per worker for every level of capital investment per worker.

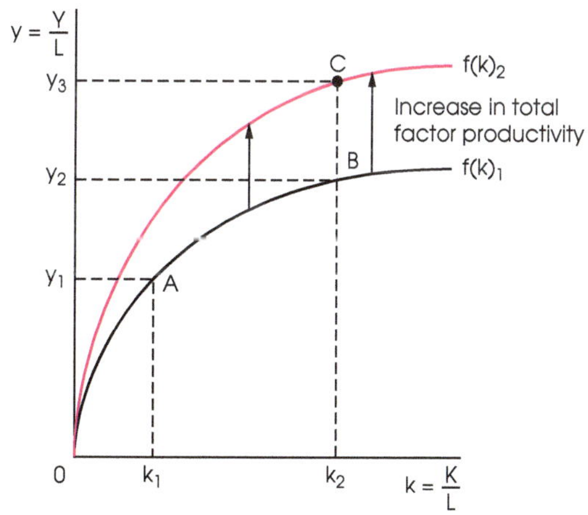

Figure 5.10. Technological progress raises total factor productivity and output per worker.

Increases in capital investments per worker with a fixed level of technology will be represented as a movement along the production function from point A to B for $y = f(k)_1$. Improvements in the marketplace efficiency and/or improvements to how capital and labor are organized and employed together that raise total factor productivity will be represented as an upward shift of the production from $y = f(k)_1$ to $y = f(k)_2$. This will raise the level output per worker for each level of capital invested per worker.

Figure 5.11 illustrates that at a given level of technology, economies that save more will be able to invest more and achieve a higher steady state of capital as noted in the movement of the economy from k_1^* and k_2^*. If higher savings rates are translated into higher investment rates in capital per worker, then without technological progress, output per worker will grow from y_1* to y_2*. However, once the economy's growth rate in its capital stock converges closer to the economy's new higher steady state of capital, the growth rate in output per worker will also converge to a zero growth, due to the diminishment returns to capital as described in the production function.

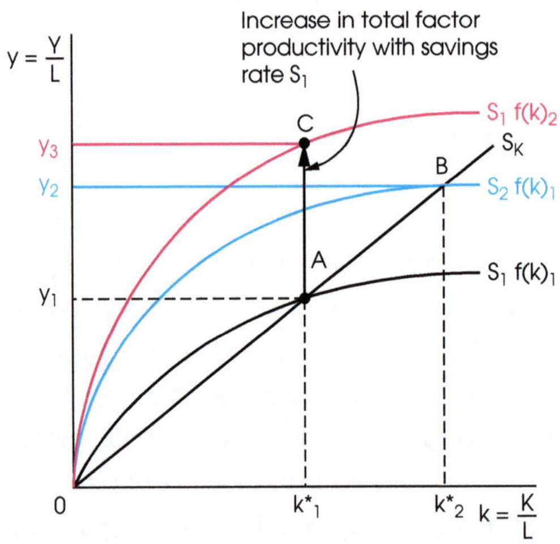

Figure 5.11. Increases in total factor productivity raise income per worker in the steady state.

As noted by Nobel laureate economist Robert Solow in his famous work introducing this model, an economy over the long run cannot just sustain itself off the accumulation of machinery; it is technological progress (improvements in total factor productivity) that will increase income per worker over time. As shown in the figure, at point A with k^*_1, without technological progress the growth rate in output per worker is zero, but with technological progress the growth rate in output per worker rises from y_1* to y_3* to point C. And since economic growth is a long-run concept, the focus on technological innovation that raises income growth per person at any level of capital investment per worker is more paramount.

The Savings and Investment Identity

So far, the theoretical example considers the growth in output per worker driven by an economy's ability to translate savings into capital investments per worker. To keep the thought process simple, for the time being, the assumption is that all available savings held in the economy are held in cash, financial instruments, and other assets that are highly liquid, and the economy has a unique ability in the use of healthy financial intermediation to extract savings in in most liquid form and allocate all savings (which are scarce) to their most productive use.

Revisiting the national income identity for a closed economy from Chapter 4, the total output supplied must be equal to the total gross expenditures on the output in equilibrium.

(Equ. 12.0) $Y = C + I + G$

The level of domestic investment spending in the economy will be expressed as:

(Equ. 13.0) $I Y - C - G$

National savings in a closed economy will be the sum of private savings among households and firms plus the public savings treated as the government's budget balance that can either be a budget surplus or a budget deficit.[15]

$$S = \textit{Private savings} + \textit{Public savings}$$

$$(\textit{Equ. 14.0})\ S = (Y + TR - C - T) + (T - TR - G)$$

In the national savings identity for a closed economy, private savings is the output (income) left over less consumption spending and taxes paid. Public savings is treated as the government's budget balance.

If $T - TR > G$, then the government is running a budget surplus, and if $T - TR < G$, then the government is running a budget deficit.[16] It is important here to differentiate transfer payments from government spending. Transfer payments are not government spending but a redistribution of taxes or borrowed funds to pay out in the form or benefits, which will be income received but not earned.

Such transfer payments come in the form payments paid out to participants in social insurance schemes such as Social Security, Medicare, and Medicaid in the United States or other similar redistribution schemes in other countries. Government spending on the other hand is the direct purchase of goods and services produced in the private sector and transformed into administered public goods in the economy, such as national defense, public education, public health care, and public transportation infrastructure (i.e., the US interstate highway system).

Equation 14.0 of the national savings identity for a closed economy can also be simplified further to:

$$(\textit{Equ. 15.0})\ S = Y - C - G$$

Taking equations 13.0 and 15.0 together shows for a closed economy, total domestic investment spending will equal total national savings. This case will also hold for any disequilibrium in the economy for which total output supplied exceeds total output demanded, such that any output unsold will be purchased back by firms as inventory investment and used as a beginning inventory balance to be sold in the next period.[17]

Equations 13.0 and 15.0 also show any net decrease in consumption and government spending will raise the national stock of savings and the corresponding national stock of investment spending for a closed economy. However, the investment side of the market takes its cues of where to invest in the economy from where consumption and government expenditures are taking place. If consumption and government expenditures in the economy have experienced a net decrease, would this not reduce liquidity in the economy creating a buildup of excess savings that does not get invested as the identity calls for?

[15] In Chapter 7, coverage of fiscal policy will consider the impact of running budget surpluses and budget deficits on the growth in equilibrium GDP.

[16] In the national savings identity, the level of private savings is affected by the amount of transfer payments received and lump sum total taxes paid. The level of lump sum taxes received and transfer payments paid out will affect the level of public savings. As shown in equation 14.0, changes to the level of taxes and transfer payments in the identity will have a neutral effect on overall national savings.

[17] This will be evident in an economic environment in which the level of total output produced is greater than the sum all total expenditures. In this case, firms in the economy would experience an unplanned accumulation of inventories, which will be equal to the level of excess savings above the equilibrium level in the marketplace. For firms experiencing an unplanned buildup of inventor balances, this inventory unsold will be purchased back by firm in the form of inventory investment such that in equilibrium, I = S.

To reconcile this, as the net decrease in consumption and government expenditures increases the level of national savings in the economy for investments, the market will allocate any excess savings in the form of inventory unsold as inventory purchased back by firms in the form of inventory investment.

(Equ. 13.0) $I = Y - C - G$

(Equ. 15.0) $S = Y - C - G$

(Equ. 16.0) $I = S$

Applying the savings and investment identity for a closed economy, the following example shows the level of domestic investment that will occur for different calculated values of private savings and public savings.

Example: Suppose for a closed economy, GDP = Y = \$400 million, transfer payments = TR = \$15 million, consumption spending = C = \$200 million, taxes = T = \$30 million, and government expenditures on final goods and services = G = \$100 million. What is private savings? What is public savings? What is national savings? What will be the level of domestic investment spending for the closed economy?

Answer:

Private savings = $(Y + TR - C - T)$ = \$400 million + \$15 million – \$200 million – \$30 million = \$185 million

Public savings = $(T\text{-}TR\text{-}G)$ = \$30 million – \$15 million – \$100 million = –\$85 million

National savings = Private Savings + Public Savings = \$185 million + (-\$85 million) = \$100 million

Investment spending = $Y - C - G$ = \$400 million – \$200 million – \$100 million = \$100 million

Allocating Savings to Investment: The Hypothetical Loanable Funds Market

In the above example, because the economy is closed, the budget deficit of –\$85 million has to be financed with government borrowing from the private savings pool made up of households and firms. This is accomplished by the government selling bonds (IOUs) in the market as a financial instrument used to borrow savings from households and firms at rates of interest competitive to other alternative instruments of different characteristics in terms of yield, liquidity, risk, and tax treatment. In the example, the budget deficit is financed with a share of domestic private savings. This crowds out private investment spending equal to the size of the deficit in the government budget balance of –\$85 million. What will be the consequence of this crowding effect on the economy?

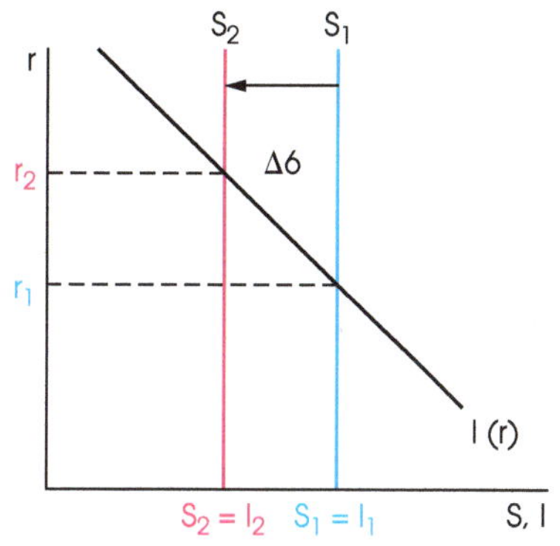

Figure 5.12. A hypothetical loanable funds market.

Treating savings as loanable funds and the investment spending as the demand for loanable funds, Figure 5.12 shows as the budget deficit widens from an increase in government spending above a planned level, the stock of national savings is decreased, which shifts the supply of savings curve from S_1 to S_2 and an accompanying rise in the equilibrium interest rate from r_1 to r_2.[18]

In the figure, the quantity of investment demanded is shown to be a function of the interest rate, such that the quantity of investment demanded changes inversely to the change in the market interest rate.[19] Crowding out of private investment takes place as projects that were earning rates of return greater than r_1 and less than r_2 are no longer invested in using borrowed funds (savings) from the marketplaces.

As the quantity of investment spending decreases at the higher interest rate, the national expenditure identity for GDP shows total output should decrease by the decrease in investment spending.[20] But what if the quantity of savings supplied in the economy is a function of the interest rate just like the quantity of investment? What if the holder of savings (stored in the most liquid form or stored in asset to be sold to acquire savings to lend) is allowed to allocate savings according to the highest interest rate paid? Would an increase in government spending still leading a crowding out of investment?

Treating the savings and investment market as a loanable funds market, where savings is supplied at different interest rates to be borrowed for consumption, investment, and government use for the highest value to be created and returned, the supply curve of savings (supply of loanable funds) will be upward sloping to designate that the holder of savings will supply a greater quantity of savings at higher rates of interest. The demand curve for loanable funds will be downward sloping to designate the inverse relationship between the interest rate and the quantity borrowed.

---

[18] According to the aggregate production function for the economy expressed in Cobb-Douglas form, the total potential level of output (income) supplied is $Y = AK^{\alpha}L^{1-\alpha}$ and is a function of the combined employment of capital (K) and labor (L) using a given level of technology A. Since level of savings for a closed economy is $S = Y - C - G$, the net amount output (income) left over after consumption and government expenditures, in Figure 5.13, the savings curve will be treated as vertical to show that the potential level of savings in an a closed economy is predetermined by the full exploitation of the resources base in the provided aggregate production function. Therefore, for a closed economy, the level of domestic investment spending will be equal to the level of output saved at a given savings rate, s, such that $I = S(Y)$.

[19] Follows the inverse relationship between price and quantity demanded as described in the law of demand.

[20] $Y = C + I(r) + G$ shows that a crowding out of investment spending, I(r), will lower GDP when the interest rate increases from a crowding out of the national savings stock due to financing a larger government budget gap. However, in the above section, the crowding out of investment spending came from an increase in the budget deficit of a rise in government spending, G, which according the national income identity would increase GDP. To reconcile how much crowding out may take place requires an examination of spending multipliers that will be presented in Chapter 6. According to the government spending multiplier, GDP, Y will grow by a multiplied amount over time from an increase in government spending, G—$\Delta Y = \Delta G[1/(1 - MPC)]$—provided certain assumptions of the multiplier and favorable market conditions hold. The growth in Y over time would add to the growth in private savings over time ($\Delta Y + TR - C - T$), supporting lower interest rates in the future due to an expanded national savings stock holding all other factors constant.

As shown in Figure 5.13, an increase in the budget deficit from an increase in government spending will increase the market demand for loanable funds. This will raise the equilibrium interest rate in the market as the government sells bonds in the market to borrow scarce private savings at higher rates of interest. In response to the higher rate of interest, the holder of savings will supply a quantity of savings at the higher equilibrium rate of interest; provided the savings instrument is more highly liquid and secure.

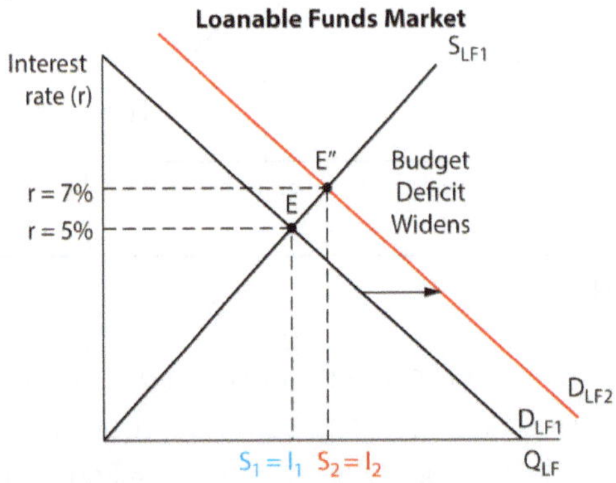

Figure 5.13. shows as the demand for loanable funds (savings) increases from an increase in government borrowing, the quantity of loanable funds supplied (savings) will increase as the equilibrium interest rate rises. Projects now earning a rate of return of equal to and greater than 7% will be funded. The increase in the government's demand for loanable funds has led to higher interest rates crowding investment projects earning rates of return less than 7%.

Because of the rise in the equilibrium interest rate, investors who are borrowing savings to invest will borrow savings at higher rates of interest and invest in those projects earning rates of return greater than the new equilibrium interest rate ($r_2 = 7\%$). As a result of the increase in the demand for loanable funds, investment projects earning rates of return greater than 5 percent but less than 7 percent will be crowded out. This is despite fact that the increase in the demand for loanable funds raises the equilibrium level of investment in the closed economy, from $S_1 = I_1$ to $S_2 = I_2$. This is allows the market to focus on the use of funds for projects earning higher rates of return.

In a closed economy, without trade, the productivity and technological constraints on resources put a limit on the maximum amount of output (income) that can be created without innovation or attainment of additional resources. This also puts a maximum limit on the capacity of the economy and the maximum amount of savings that an economy would yield in the market. At some point, as the economy approaches the full employment of resources to produce a desired maximum amount of output at full capacity, the supply curve of savings in Figure 5.13 would be become completely vertical.

Applying the Savings and Investment Identity for an Open Economy

To reduce the potential crowding out of private investment spending from increases in government borrowing, an economy that is open to the rest of the world in trade would run trade deficits to offset. The running of trade deficits is an attempt to externally borrow excess savings held abroad to finance domestic investment and government spending expenditures exceeding the supply of available private savings.[21] Recall from Chapter 4 the national income identity for an open economy.

---

21 This open economy model presumes the country's economy as a share of global GDP is very substantial, the share of global account balances are settled in the country's currency unit, and the country's currency holds a premium global reserve currency position. The United States utilizes the running of trade deficits to externally finance a share of the domestic budget gaps with foreign borrowing as well as for the economy

$Y = C + I + G + (EX - IM)$

Rewriting the expression to get investment spending, gives the investment identity for an open economy to be national savings (Y – C – G) plus capital inflows (IM – EX)

$I = Y - C - G + (IM - EX)$

$I = S + (IM - EX)$

$I - S = IM - EX$

The expression suggests economies investing more than they save domestically finance the higher level of domestic investment spending through the running of a trade deficit (importing more than exporting). This will externally finance the domestic investment spending and savings gap with borrowing of savings held by the rest of the world.

The following example reworks the previous savings and investment example for a closed economy, but now as an open economy running a trade deficit.

Example: Suppose for a closed economy, GDP = Y = \$400 million, transfer payments = TR = \$15 million, consumption spending = C = \$200 million, taxes = T = \$30 million, government expenditures on final goods and services = G = \$100 million, imports = IM = \$100 million, and exports = EX = \$15 million. What is private savings? What is public savings? What is national savings? What are capital inflows? What will be the level of domestic investment spending for the closed economy?

Answer:

$Y = C + I + G + (EX - IM)$

$I = Y - C - G + (IM - EX)$

Private savings = (Y + TR – C – T) = \$400 million + \$15 million – \$200 million – \$30 million = \$185 million

Public savings = (T-TR-G) = \$30 million – \$15 million – \$100 million = –\$85 million

National savings = Private Savings + Public Savings = \$185 million + (-\$85 million) = \$100 million

Capital inflows = Imports – Exports = \$100 million – \$15 million = \$85 million

Investment spending = Y – C – G + CI = \$400 million – \$200 million – \$100 million + 85 million = \$185 million

As a closed economy, the public savings deficit (budget deficit) of –\$85 million reduces net private savings to \$100 million supporting domestic investment spending of only \$100 million. As an open economy, the public savings deficit (government budget deficit) is externally financed by importing savings from the rest of the world in the form of capital

to compete for global savings abroad held in US Dollars to be reinvested back into the economy for portfolio and physical investment. Small and emerging economies that are part of a fixed exchange rate with the Dollar are able to run trade surpluses with the United States, and these trade surpluses are recycled back into the United States to finance the trade deficit, budget deficit, and available private sector capital investments. As part of the arrangement to defend an agreed-upon currency/USD exchange rate, these countries are required to hold U.S. Treasuries on reserve in their banking systems to back their respective domestic money supplies. As a result, this creates a foreign market to sell U.S. Treasuries into keeping the value of U.S. government debt instruments high and highly liquid. Finally, it supports a strong Dollar position relative to other currencies globally, attracting foreign investment in private and public Dollar securities. The inflow of Dollars, coming in the form of capital inflows, helps temper the rise of interest rates during economic expansion and fiscal expansion when government borrowing is higher.

inflows equal to $85 million via a trade deficit with the global economy. The use of the trade deficit as a source of external financing has eliminated the crowding out effect a budget deficit has on domestic private investment expenditures.

As shown in Figure 5.14, the increase in demand for loanable funds to finance the budget deficit does not create a crowding of domestic investment spending when a trade deficit externally borrows foreign savings. These foreign savings borrowed are added to the total national savings stock to support the desired level of domestic investment spending. In the problem, the private savings balance of $185 million is exclusively available to support $185 million in domestic investment spending.

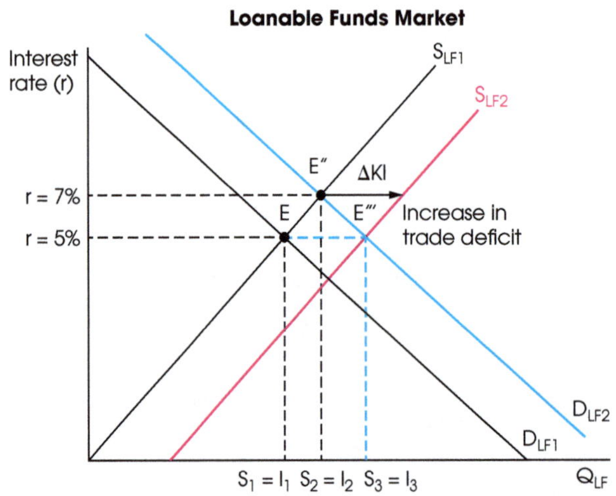

Figure 5.14. An increase in capital inflows from a running a trade deficit equal to the increase in government borrowing to finance the budget deficit helps keep interest rates unchanged to reduce the crowding-out effect. The capital inflows from abroad added to the economy's total saving stock leads to a higher equilibrium of domestic investment spending than would otherwise materialize in a closed economy.

However, external claims on the economy's future total income produced have increased by the amount of the trade deficit used to externally finance the budget gap. Going forward, the economy would needs to have a growth in the wealth base (and tax base) to produce a return on income streams used from it greater than the equilibrium interest rate of 5 percent, as shown in Figure 5.15.

5.3 CONCLUSION: IT TAKES MORE THAN THE INVESTMENT OF SAVINGS TO SUPPORT ECONOMIC GROWTH

According to the Solow growth model for a closed economy, economies saving more should have higher domestic levels of investment spending per worker and along the way realize an increase in the growth rate of output worker. This suggests poorer economies that are deficient in savings and capital would offer higher interests (with stronger incentives to save) and higher rates of return on capital to translate such savings accumulated at higher rates into more capital per worker to increase output/income per worker over time.

As a result, the savings and investment gaps in these economies would close and economic growth rates of these economies would converge closer to the growth rates of richer world economies. But the predictions of the model are difficult to reconcile with the economic observations seen in countries at different development levels around the world.[22] Figure 5.15 provides regional GDP growth rates from 1970 to 2015, expressed in 1998 US Dollars derived from the CIA's long-term growth model.

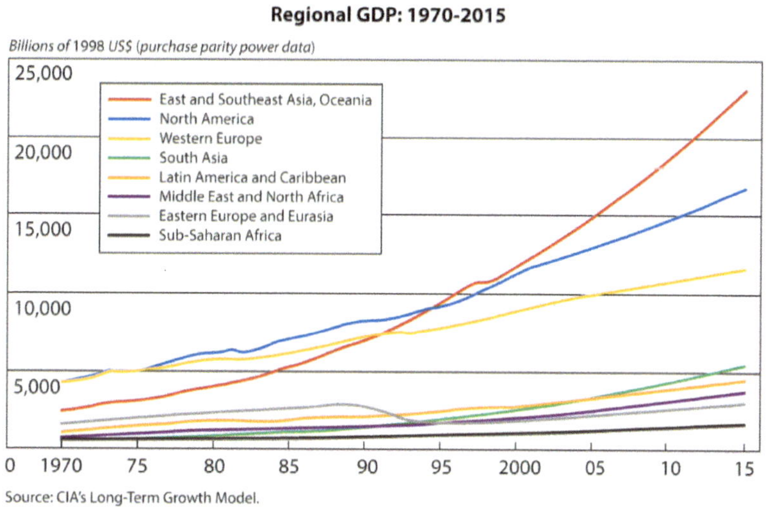

Figure 5.15

The output of the model shows from 1970 to 2015, every region experienced different rates of economic growth. Outside of sub-Saharan Africa, the regions of Latin America and the Caribbean, Middle East and North Africa, and eastern Europe and Eurasia experienced a slight acceleration of regional GDP growth around 1995; following a normalized long-run growth trend starting from their respective economic bases in 1970.

Reconciling the output of the CIA's long-term growth model with the Solow growth model, a few off-the-top questions come to the forefront. First, can it be adequately said this accelerated rate of regional growth was completely driven by the accumulation of capital per worker as the Solow model suggests? Second, which economies in these respective regions were more responsible for their overall region's GDP growth? Third, how does openness to trade for these economies with countries inside their region and outside their region account for a share of their region's growth rate imported or exported through trade channels?[23] Finally, are there noneconomic determinants—political, cultural, historical, geographical, and so on—which would have some explanatory power for the behavior of regional GDP growth over this period?

Figure 5.16 also points out a slight convergence of growth rates among these regions the model would predict, but the figure also shows a divergence in growth rates between these regions and the rest of the world. This is contrary to the predictions of the Solow growth model predicting a long-run convergence of economic growth rates between richer and poorer regions over longer time horizons. So what in the economies of these regions is

[22] A criticism of the growth model presented is that capital and labor in the economy are treated as homogenous. The model does not account for quality differences in the capital stock and labor stock that would impact the amount and type of capital investment per worker. Such capital investments per worker will often be specific to the quality and skill type of the worker. The model also assumes that any innovation in the economy is not disruptive to current employment levels and would broadly raise all welfare at all levels of the economy through an increase in total factor productivity. Unfortunately, not all innovation benefits everyone and will reach all levels of the economy in terms of purchasing power through better product availability or raising the effectiveness of all factors of production.

[23] The Solow growth model treats economies in the model as closed economies to the world: no trade and no cross-border financial flows. This model can sufficiently examine the role domestic capital investments per worker has in raising output/income per worker over time.

lacking or perhaps impeding a faster growth rate to converge closer over time to the growth rates of established richer economies?

The majority of economists agree the market presence of the following (not an exhaustive list) in terms of strength and maturity would best support an improved economic growth path for an economy:

- *Mature and healthy financial intermediaries able to translate savings held in different forms into domestic investment spending along with provided security to savers and investors.*
- *Educational systems that produce skills according to the type of capital investments needed and to be made that will make use of such skills. Educational type and quality in the early years of primary schooling will shape the type of education offered at higher levels supporting human capital investments and matching with current and new capital investments.*
- *A market system supporting entrepreneurial endeavors that are value adding to the economy.*
- *Stable and reliable public and private infrastructures. For example, without adequate transportation infrastructure, it is more difficult for output produced to reach the marketplace. Poor public infrastructure detracts from business development and value-added creation.*
- *Stable political systems with well-functioning court systems to enforce laws made. Without this higher levels of political rent-seeking and corruption are invited.*
- *Clearly defined and enforceable property rights.*

Even for economies with more of the above present, this suggests policy approaches to addressing the quality and improved conditions of the above would be influential in altering the course of an economy's long-run growth path. The question remains a difficult one to answer: Is long-run growth of an economy a phenomenon determined by its starting economic base? Are deviations from long-run growth best explained by exogenous domestic and global events or shifts in economic policy which will trend the economy above or below the long-run trend (Figure 5.16)?

The next chapter will lay the groundwork through which the efficacy of macro policy approaches—fiscal and monetary—can be theoretically evaluated in the context of a short-run and long-run growth using an aggregate demand and aggregate supply model. Can demand side–driven policies alter the long-run potential of an economy, or are supply side–driven policies better suited to do the job? Within the context of the systems-view approach and CFI model, this will invite an important debated question: Does demand drive supply, or does supply drive demand?

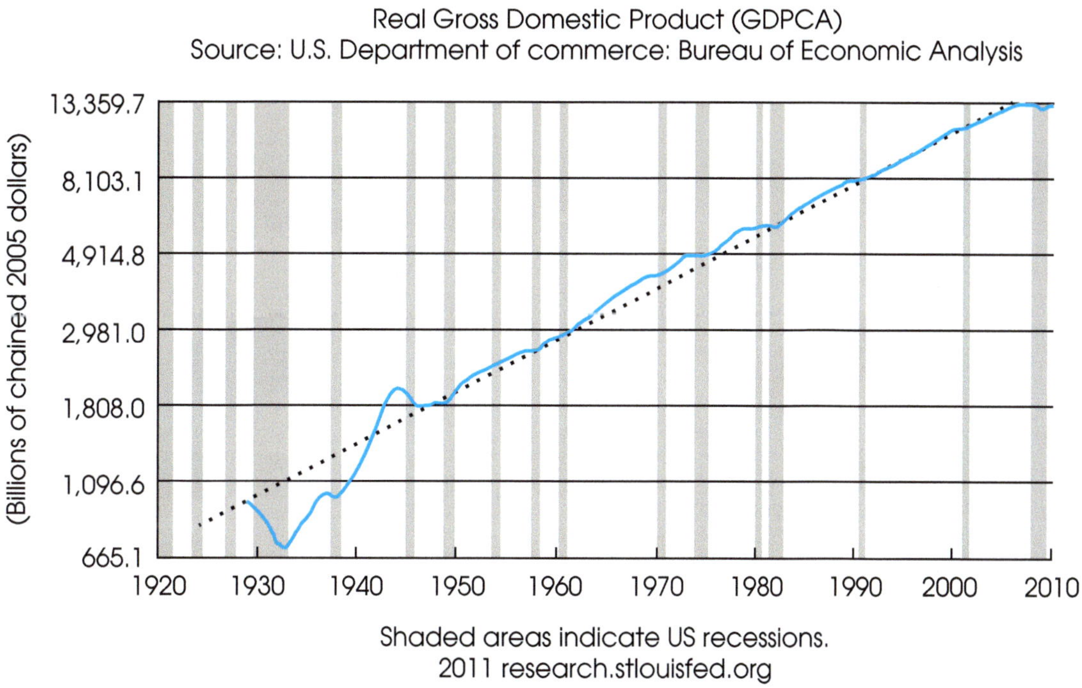

Figure 5.16[24]

Source: Economist, "GDP Growth: Long-Term Growth Policy Fatalism," July 11, 2011.

CASE STUDY: AFRICA AN AWAKENING MANUFACTURING GIANT: "CAN CHEETAHS BEAT TIGERS"? (*ECONOMIST*, FEBRUARY 8, 2014)[25]

The Solow growth model argues for an economy to escape the shackles of poverty, all is needed is the accumulation and employment of capital with workers. The history of developed economies has shown that the value-added creation from transformational processes from manufacturing has been quite instrumental in raising wealth and market value, income per worker, and living standards from goods and services produced from it.

Of course, an economy cannot be sustainable on services alone, as something tangible has to be produced to be serviced. But as mature economies continue a transition from manufacturing to service driven markets, it will reinforce the ongoing migration of manufacturing gateways to emerging economies.

This transitional shift by mature economies away from transformational activities to transactional ones provides a unique opportunity for the African continent to be the manufacturing gateway for more mature economies (Figure 5.17). For instance, China has relocated some low-level to mid-level manufacturing investments to different African economies. The World Bank has been suggesting Asian manufacturing may continue to migrate to Africa,

[24] The graph entertains the idea that the Great Depression and World War II were essentially sizable economic shocks—market driven and a result of macro policy shifts—deviating the economy from its long run average growth average. Between the years 1947 and 2007, the economy did not deviate much from its long run growth average. Using a logarithmic scale, economic "bumps" such as the Great Depression and World War II will make the scale of data look quite smooth over time over this time frame. To the extent that US macro policy can alter along run growth path, infers that in the post New-Deal era, long run growth has trended at a normalized rate but deviations in the growth trend since the late 1970 may be accounted for in macro policy shifts. Source: GDP Growth: "Long-Term Growth Policy Fatalism." *Economist* (2011).

[25] *Economist*, "Manufacturing in Africa: 'An Awakening Giant,'" February 8, 2014.

provided African labor productivity continues to rise and infrastructure improves, which will help lower the average cost of manufacturing.

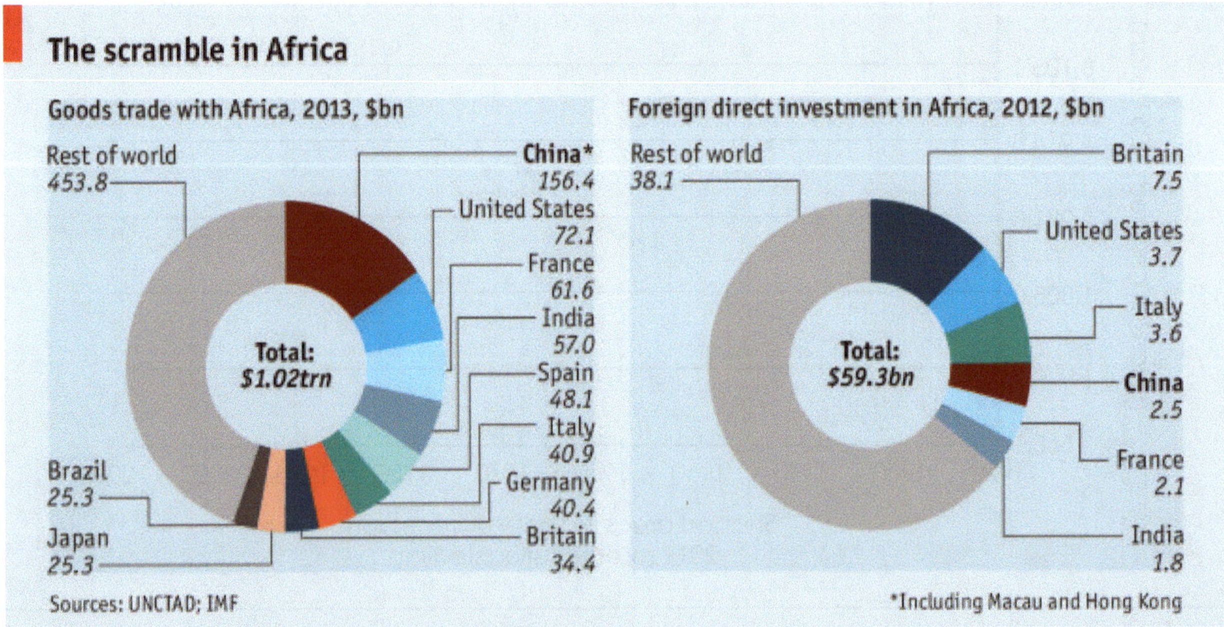

Figure 5.17

The immigration of manufacturing investments into Africa will over time help the economies of the continent escape an overreliance on natural resources exports for growth and begin to focus on the value-added transformational activities which will come with coupling manufacturing with natural resource advantages. African economies are not poised yet to become manufacturing tigers, but the economies are set with the right ingredients—demography, urbanization, a rising middle class, and strong service sector—to build a manufacturing base from to better service domestic consumption, domestic investment environments, living standards, and their established export channels.

QUESTIONS FOR CLASS DISCUSSION

1. At the start of the chapter, the following questions were proposed in regard to the predetermination of an economy's long-run growth path. Break into class groups and lead a discussion of the following questions.
   a. If human beings are born with genetics making some humans grow in height at a rate above, equal to, or below an average rate, then hasn't the course of a country's economy already been predetermined from the starting point of its resource and technological base?
   b. In what way can an economy alter the "mix of stars" that make up its destiny?
   c. What quality factors can be altered or even exploited from physical factors that cannot be altered so that an economy is growing above its long-run trend, and is this feasibly sustainable?

   As you and your group members discuss the above questions, realistically consider the short- and long-run challenges that are problematic for most predominate policy approaches to tackle. As such, does this mean most Western-style economic development policies and programs have been just "panaceas" to a developing economy's woes and unable to alter the economy's long-run growth path? Explain why or why not.

2. In this chapter, the Solow growth model was introduced and covered. The focus of the model is how well an economy translates savings into capital investment per worker over time to reach a steady state of capital and corresponding level of output per worker. However, the model presumes that for economies to grow, such economies just need to save more and invest in more capital per worker. Yet is it realistic that economies can make long-run growth sustainable off the accumulation of machines? Explain reasons why and why not.

   Finally, read the following article from the *Economist* magazine, "Manufacturing in Africa: 'An Awakening Giant'" (*Economist*, February 8, 2014), and discuss the content and coverage of the article against the assumptions and workings of the Solow growth model. As you and your class reconcile the news report's coverage of manufacturing in Africa, consider what the model accounts for and what it does not account for.

   a. Would offshored manufacturing into Africa be the "key" ingredient needed for the economies of this continent to experience an economic takeoff? Why or why not?
   b. What else is absent in these economies that would be needed to help generate a sustainable change in Africa's long-run economic picture?

3. Using what you have learned in this chapter about the savings-investment identity for an open economy, interpret and discuss the following statement within the context of the identity. Statement: *"If I owe you $100,000, you own my blood, but if I owe you $1,000,000,000, I own your soul."*

   a. What does this statement say about the debt leverage high-indebted economies have in the global economy?
   b. How does a highly indebted economy's external borrowing of savings from the rest of the world (financed by running large trade deficits as a share of the global economy) impact other economies' abilities translate domestic savings into domestic investment if such domestic savings is being lent to larger-indebted economies?
   c. Would such external financing by highly indebted economy crowd out domestic private investment in such smaller economies? Why or why not?
   d. Finally, does this suggest countries that save the least and borrow the most for investment will grow much faster than countries that save the most?

IMAGE CREDITS

- Fig. 5.1: www.economicshelp.org. Copyright © by EconomicsHelp.org.
- Fig. 5.2: www.fivethirtyeight.com, "Un and Underemployment Since December 2007," Burea of Labor Statistics; FiveThirtyEight.
- Fig. 5.3: "GDP Per-Capita Top 25 Countries 2011," www.econographics.wordpress.com.
- Fig. 5.4: Krugman and Wells, Macroeconomics, 3rd edition. Copyright © 2012 by Worth Publishers.
- Fig. 5.5: measuringworth.com; visualizingeconomics.com; www.ritholtz.com.
- Fig. 5.6: www.heritage.org. Copyright © 2005 by The Heritage Foundation.
- Fig. 5.7: Federal Reserve Bank of St. Louis. Copyright in the Public Domain.
- Fig. 5.15: CIA Long-Term Growth Model; www.famguardian.org. Copyright © 2015 by Family Guardian.
- Fig. 5.16: Karl Smith, www.economist.com. Copyright © 2001 by The Economist Newspaper Limited.
- Fig. 5.17: Manufacturing in Africa: "An Awakening Giant" (The Economist, 02/08/2014). Copyright © 2014 by The Economist Newspaper Limited.

CHAPTER 6

THE KEYNESIAN CROSS AND THE MULTIPLIER

Figure 6.0

The long run is a misleading guide to current affairs. In the long run, we are all dead. Economists set themselves too easy, too useless a task if in tempestuous seasons they can only tell us that when the storm is past the ocean is flat again.

—John Maynard Keynes

6.0 OVERVIEW

In Chapter 5 it was suggested that over the long run, the growth picture of an economy was predetermined by the amount and effectiveness of current resources available, as well as the level of existing technology available to support transformational activities with the employment of such resources. Without changes to the resource base or level of technology, there is a future potential level of output attainable to an economy if resources are being fully utilized in the most optimal way and the right incentives for the use of resources and technology are being full exploited. Due to the constant returns to scales exhibited over the long-run behavior of a production function, as the economy approaches its long-run potential level of output, the growth rate in income earned by the factors of production—capital and labor—would also exhibit constant returns-to-scale with respective growth rates approaching close to but never reaching zero.

It is also inferred that changes in the stock of resources in the economy, in terms of quantity and quality, along with technological change would help alter an economy's future course, raising real GDP growth and real earnings paid to the factors of production. But this may not always be the case. For example, take any two countries with relatively equal savings rates and corresponding domestic investment spending rates, and these same two countries may experience different growth rates (one faster and one slower) in terms of employment and real GDP per capita as well as a narrowing or even widening of income and wealth gaps. What may explain this difference?

As concluded at the end of Chapter 5, differences in other qualifying factors (in an expanded list)—*quality of public and private infrastructure, level of educational attainment of the workforce, R&D spending levels per worker, level of entrepreneurship, allocation and protection of property rights, differences in business regulatory and tax structures, political openness, levels of corruption, growth rates in inflation, depth and breadth of capital and debt markets, depth and breadth of financial intermediaries, type of economic system influencing the management of private and public choices, level of government intervention in the marketplace, openness to trade and international financial flows, and so forth*—may help explain more of the reasons why the short-run deviations of a countries economic growth rates in terms of real income per capita may vary by trend above, at, or below long-run growth trends.

This begs two important questions. First, can favorable or unfavorable deviations away from the long-run growth path be sustained or altered through active policy intervention? Or, second, is the market as a larger system naturally just correcting on its own in response to broader market forces less sensitive to policy activism?

In the end, the economic fluctuations in a business cycle characterized as economic expansion trending toward a peak and economic contraction trending toward a trough are seen visibly as output gaps above and below an economy's long-run output potential. To what degree such expansions and contractions are market driven by market participants—households, firms, government, and rest of the world—responding to new private incentives in the use of the wealth base, responding to shifts in macro policy, responding to a combination of the two, or responding to unplanned positive and negative shocks to the system are hotly debated among economists.

The coverage of the business cycle in Chapter 5 showed that economies tend to go through periods of economic expansion and contraction (of varying duration), often overshooting or undershooting long-run growth trends. An important idea to consider is how such deviations of an economy in the short run from its long-run path may be influenced to alter an economy's long-run path for both closed and open market systems. This means the future, as the long run is always changing in relation to the size and persistence of short-run fluctuations in the economy, making it difficult to tame and predict. So does the short run matter more, since the long run as the future is always in flux? Is it possible to exploit a favorable short-run trend and turn it into a desirable long-run course? And is it even possible to "tame" the business cycle like a lion in cage?

Stage Characteristics a Typical Business Cycle			
Expansion (Recovery/Boom)	**Contraction**		**Trough (Recession/Bust)**
Economics activity rebounds (GDP, employment,	Growth peating	Growth moderating	Falling economic activity
Credit Begins to grow	Credit growth strong	Credit begins to tighten	Credit dries up
Profit grow rapidly	Profit growth peaks	Componate earnings under pressure	Profits decline
Policy effects still stimulative	Policy effects neutral	Policy effects are contractionary	Policy effects ease
Inventories low, sales improve	Inventories, sales grow; equilibrium reached	Inventories grow; sales growth falls	Inventories, sales fall

Table 6.1

In this chapter a visual framework will be developed to invite discussion to the questions above and consider reasons why an economic system will often deviate from its long-run trend, and how such deviations in the short-run will affect where the economy will end up in the long-run, provided such deviations run a finite course of time.

To start this process, an income-expenditure model called the Keynesian cross will be introduced, covering the sectors of consumption expenditures and investment expenditures without government involvement as a buyer of goods and services. This model will be used to analyze how changes in economic expenditure components in the national income identity will support larger changes in short-run equilibrium levels of output through a process of affecting unplanned changes to inventory balances, provided certain qualifying assumptions of a multiplier process fairly hold and/or are controlled for.

The results of this model will be used in Chapter 7 to construct a graphical identity of an aggregate demand curve, and coverage will be given to explore the factors that will support increases and decreases in aggregate demand; including how aggregate demand will be expected to respond to positive and negative demand shocks.

To complete the model, a short-run aggregate supply and long-run aggregate supply curve will be introduced, along with coverage of factors that will lead to increase and decreases in overall short-run aggregate supply; along with how the supply side of the market will be expected to respond to positive and negative shocks.

Finally, using the complete AD-AS-LAS model that has been constructed, examples will be covered to consider how well a market system on its own, without macro policy intervention, may self-correct for output gaps (recessionary and inflationary) and trend the economy to future equilibrium levels in output and price along the long-run path. This leaves open for discussion, in Chapter 7, if such natural market corrections will attain long-run equilibriums that are desirable or not desirable.

6.1 THE NATIONAL INCOME IDENTITY, THE KEYNESIAN CROSS, AND THE RELEVANCE OF MULTIPLIERS

The Keynesian Cross and the Consumption Function

The national income identity (closed economy) up to this point has been a simple summation of gross aggregate expenditures—consumption spending, domestic investment spending, and government spending on final goods and services—equating to a final market value of gross national output, GDP, and equal to gross national income in the economy (wages + interest + rent + profits) as shown in Chapter 4.

$$Y = C + I + G$$

Excluding government spending for the time being in this chapter and considering the private market only, then $Y = C + I$, such that income that is not allocated to consumption spending is allocated as savings toward investment spending

Very simply, any changes in gross aggregate expenditure components, C+ I—the demand side— will increase an output response from the supply side by an equal amount to satisfy an equilibrium condition. With that said, then in equilibrium every Dollar of gross aggregate expenditures spent on output to be produced should be equal to every Dollar of gross income earned, Y, before taxes and will constitute an infinite number of points along a 45-degree line (Figure 6.1) that the economy will wish to attain the highest level of output (income) along. From the national income identity, the summation of the aggregate expenditures, AE, and GDP, Y, can be expressed as follows:

$$Y = C + I$$

$$AE = C + I$$

$$Y = AE$$

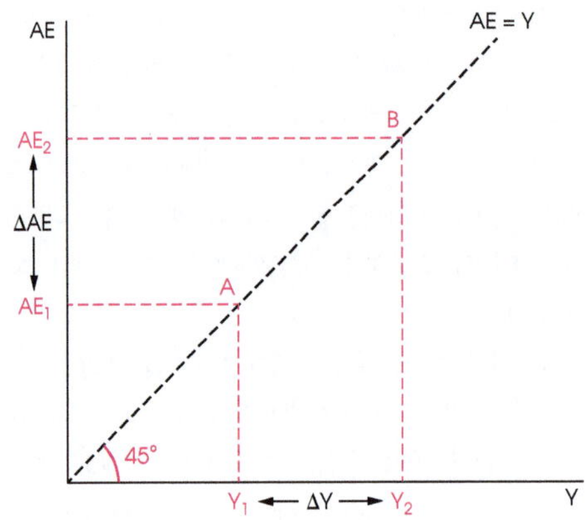

Figure 6.1. The 45-degree line of the Keynesian cross. The line shows that along every point, gross aggregate expenditures spent on output demanded will equal the final market value of gross output produced = gross income, Y. This will occur in the long run as short-run deviations between expenditures and output produced are arbitraged out.

As a concept, equilibrium represents a steady state (with no growth or change) or simply a state of rest. Covered in Chapter 3 (supply and demand analysis), all micro markets are in a constant degree of flux or motion. *This means at any time in all micro markets, deviations from equilibrium is the norm and ongoing, and all these markets responding to market pressure from disequilibrium (shortages and surpluses in the short run) are trending to new short-run equilibrium points (possibly equal to long-run equilibrium points) in terms of prices and corresponding quantities that will shape expectations about future prices and future quantities.*

Since markets are never in a state of rest in the short run—being the present—output supplied does not equal output demanded

$$Y > C + I \text{ or } Y < C + I$$

With this being the case in the short run, the above inequalities show there is either a savings surplus or deficit taking place in the marketplace, which will show up as an unplanned buildup of inventory balances or an unplanned decline of inventory balances.

Short-Run Disequilibrium to Long-Run Equilibrium in the Keynesian Cross: Adjusting for Investment Spending Unplanned

To account for why at any point total expenditures in the marketplace do not equal total output supplied, the aggregate consumption function will show of the total disposable income (Y – T) available for consumption, a fraction of this income will be spent toward consumption and the remaining fraction of the income will be saved for future consumption or investment. A typical consumption function is described as follows.

$$C = C_A + MPC\ (Y - T)$$

In this consumption function, the value MPC—marginal propensity to consume—is a value between 0 and 1 and designates the share of disposable income (Y – T), which is gross income less all taxes paid, to be spent on consumption. The MPC will also be equal to the slope of the consumption function: slope = $\Delta AE/\Delta Y$. If the MPC in the consumption function were equal to 1, then the slope of the consumption would be equal to the slope of the 45-degree line, communicating to the market every disposable Dollar is being spent on final output allowing for no accumulation or decumulation of savings showing up in the form of inventory imbalances.[1]

However, due to the uncertainty of risk and available opportunities in the marketplace, consumers will save a fraction of disposable income for speculative purposes, savings, and investment purposes as well as to smooth out consumption over multiple periods of time.

1 – MPC will be the marginal propensity to save, MPS, or the fraction of income saved that will be allocated into financial markets and used for gross investment expenditures.

The value C_A designates a level of consumption existing and is independent of the level of disposable income. In the identity, when Y – T = 0, C_A represents a positive value equal to the level of savings held in liquid form (or stored in wealth that can be liquidated) and can be drawn from for consumption purchases. With this insight, Figure 6.2 provides a new description of the Keynesian cross for a closed economy, introducing the planned expenditure function, PE = C + I, where $C = C_A + MPC\ (Y - T)$.

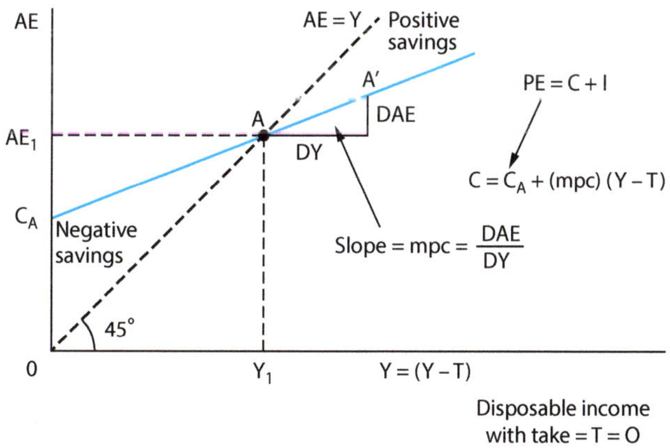

Figure 6.2. shows at a short-run equilibrium level of output of Y_1 planned expenditures in the economy equals total output produced in the economy resulting in unplanned inventory balances equaling zero. At output levels below equilibrium, planned expenditures exceed total output produced resulting in negative saving balances, and this will be reflected in an unplanned decumulation of inventory balances. At output levels greater than equilibrium, total output produced exceeds planned expenditures resulting in positive saving balances, and this will be reflected in an unplanned accumulation of inventory balances.

[1] Any and all savings will have been allocated to investment spending, leaving net private savings in the economy equal to zero.

As stated previously, if MPC = 1, then the slope of the planned expenditure would be equal to the slope of the 45-degree line such that AE = Y = PE and all savings in the economy will be used in the form investment spending. But since consumers do hold back a share of disposable income as savings, the slope of the planned expenditure function is greater than 0 and less than 1 and will not be equal to the slope of the 45-degree line.

Also as stated, the income-expenditure model as described by the use of the Keynesian cross as shown provides points where short-run equilibrium levels of output are equal to, less than, or greater than total expenditures.

At point, A, the intersection of the planned expenditure line and the 45-degree lines shows that PE = AE = Y_1. This short-run equilibrium level of output, Y_1, demonstrates savings to be equal to investment spending in a closed economy. With no excess or shortage of savings at this equilibrium output level, unplanned inventory balances will be equal to zero as all output produced has been consumed.

When disposable income, Y – T, is equal to zero, the planned expenditure function has an intercept of C_A along the AE axis. At output levels below short-run equilibrium level Y_1, where PE > AE = Y, results in a negative savings balance in the market. This would show up in the market as firms experiencing an unplanned decumulation of inventory balances by more than they had accounted for to be produced in production.

In order for the economy to return to equilibrium point A, where PE = AE = Y, firms will increase production of output, Y, by the amount needed to cover the shortfall in inventories. The increase in output by firms will increase disposable income, (ΔY – T), to the factors employed in the production as shown from the production function covered in Chapter 5.

In response to the rise in disposable income (provided taxes are held constant and greater than and equal to zero), the factors of production spend MPC(ΔY – T) on the new output produced and save 1 – MPC of (ΔY – T). The increase in consumption by MPC(ΔY – T) increases overall GDP, Y, by the same amount and will start a new cycle and consecutive cycles of consumption and savings.

Over time the marginal increases in Y—increasing at a declining rate equal to the change corresponding consumption from slower marginal increases in MPC(ΔY – T)—will filter through multiple rounds of consumption and saving until the change in total consumption from additional increases in MPC(ΔY – T) approaches zero. Simply put, one person's share of income spent as expenditures on output produced and added to inventory becomes another person's income that they will spend a fraction of on goods in inventory and will save a fraction. The fraction of savings along the way is used by firms for inventory investment until the change in inventory investment = change in savings balances = change in total consumption = 0 at equilibrium point, A, where PE = AE = Y.

This theoretical exercise also shows that any increase in disposable income from an increase in production (ΔY – T) will constitute a movement up and along (down and along) the planned expenditure function at the rate of the marginal propensity to consume, MPC. As such, the savings rate of consumers, 1 – MPC, acts as constraint on the rate (speed of time) it takes for the market to go from PE > AE = Y to PE = AE = Y.

Finally, the figure also shows at short-run level of output above equilibrium, Y1, the market is experiencing an accumulation of savings in which PE < AE = Y. In this case, for the market to return to equilibrium level, Y1 at point A, the above process works in reverse. With an unplanned buildup of inventories, firms cut back on production and lower prices on existing inventory in order to drawn down the excess inventory buildup. As firms decrease production, GDP, Y, decreases (as we would expect to see in the production in Chapter 5), and the effect filters through successive cycles of consumption and savings until the change in total consumption and change in GDP, Y, is equal to zero.

Without changes to autonomous consumption and autonomous investment spending (investment spending that is taking place at every interest rate level in the market determined by noninterest rate determinants such as profitability, risk, and so on), the adjustments shown in the figure describe behavior taking place in the short-run business cycle and similar to what would expected to be observed at the micro level of the economy adjusting to market pressures born from market shortages and market surpluses.

At any time, the figure illustrates in short-run equilibriums where expenditures exceed or fall short of output (disposable income) levels. The level of investment spending in the economy must account for these unplanned inventory buildups or shortfalls that may emerge. Therefore, investment spending in the planned expenditure function will be: $I = I_{planned} + I_{unplanned}$.

$I_{planned}$ will account for the output produced by firms that they expect to sell out of inventory, and $I_{unplanned}$ will account for inventory imbalances when expenditures are greater than or less than inventory held.

This now makes the planned expenditure function:

$$PE = C_{planned} + I_{planned} + I_{unplanned}$$

$$PE = C_A + MPC(Y\text{-}T) + I_{planned} + I_{unplanned}$$

As shown in Figure 6.3, at equilibrium point A, Y = AE = PE so that $I_{unplanned} = 0$. Therefore, any level of $I_{unplanned}$ unplanned can be solved for as follows:

$$Y = PE$$

$$Y = C_{planned} + I_{planned} + I_{unplanned}$$

$$Y - C_{planned} - I_{planned} = I_{unplanned}$$

$$Y - [C_A + MPC(Y - T) + I_{planned}] = I_{unplanned}$$

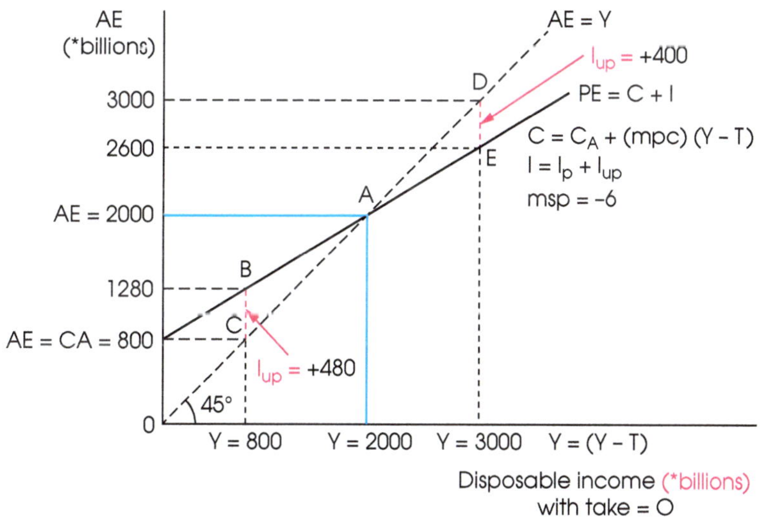

Figure 6.3. Different levels of unplanned investment at different level of output, Y, for the associated planned expenditure function PE = 800 + .6(Y – T) + $I_{planned}$ + $I_{unplanned}$ and taxes in the economy set equal to zero, T = 0.

According to Figure 6.3, when the short-run output (disposable) income level is Y = \$800 billion, planned expenditures at this level, PE = \$1,280 billion, creates an unplanned shortfall of inventories, $I_{unplanned}$ = –\$480 billion, which will be equal to the negative savings balance in the economy. As well, at a higher level of output (disposable income), such as Y = \$3,000 billion, corresponding planned expenditures, PE = \$2,600 billion result in an unplanned accumulation of inventories equal to $I_{unplanned}$ = \$400 billion. In response to these emerged inventory imbalances, production by firms will adjust accordingly—filtering the effects through a number of consumption cycles—in order to bring unplanned inventory balances to a zero level.

The Multiplier

As shown in the Keynesian cross, short-run changes in disposable income only constitute a movement along the planned expenditure line, resulting in inventory imbalances. As these inventory imbalances emerge as positive or negative changes in unplanned investment levels, firms will adjust production accordingly to match with the current consumption expenditures in the marketplace in order to bring inventory investment unplanned to zero.

This means without autonomous (independent) changes in consumption and investment spending, the economy will not achieve higher (or lower) short-run equilibrium levels of output. These important expenditure changes the market is looking for are changes in consumption (increases or decreases) occurring independently of changes in disposable income and changes in investment spending (increases or decreases) occurring independently of given market interest rates. Of course, increases in autonomous consumption and investment are preferred to decreases.

In this section the concept of a spending multiplier is introduced. The thought process is: Can an increase in autonomous consumption spending (an increase in the value of C_A in the consumption function) or an increase in autonomous investment spending (above what is planned) increase the short-run equilibrium level of output by a larger amount and move the real GDP growth of an economy above its long-run trend?[2]

Take again the national income identity for a closed economy without government spending.

$$Y = C + I$$

$$Y = C_A + MPC\ (Y - T) + I$$

As described in the identity, any increase in autonomous consumption or overall investment spending will increase GDP, ΔY, by an equal amount. But the effect does not stop there.

With the increase, ΔY, disposable income increases, increasing consumption by $MPC(\Delta Y - T)$, and increasing GDP, ΔY again by that amount. This will continue through multiple rounds of consumption until the marginal increases in consumption by $MPC(\Delta Y - T)$ reaches zero, holding all other factors in the market constant and assuming certain conditions of this multiplier process hold.

Deriving the Consumption and Investment Spending Multiplier

Deriving the consumption and spending multiplier uses a simple calculus approach by taking the first order differentiation of the national income identity with respect to consumption to solve for the consumption spending multiplier or with respect to investment spending to solve for the investment spending multiplier.

Taking the first derivative of the national income identity with respect to autonomous consumption derives the following.

$$Y = C_A + MPC\ (Y - T) + I$$

$$\partial Y/\partial C_A = 1 + MPC\ (\partial Y/\partial C_A)$$

$$\partial Y/\partial C_A - MPC\ (\partial Y/\partial C_A) = 1$$

$$\partial Y/\partial C_A\ (1 - MPC) = 1$$

$$\partial Y/\partial C_A = 1/(1 - MPC)$$

[2] The application of the AD-AS-LAS in Chapter 7 will consider if this type of trend is sustainable considering other market forces may be putting pressure on the economy to trend closer to its long-run growth trend as part of an overall system correction.

The final expression gives the consumption spending multiplier for a given value of MPC. Since the derivative of a function examines the rate of change of the dependent variable to a change in an independent variable holding all other independent variables constant, the final expression can be rewritten as:

$$\partial Y/\partial C_A = 1/(1 - MPC)$$

$$\Delta Y/\Delta C = 1/(1 - MPC)$$

$$\Delta Y = \Delta C[1/(1 - MPC)]$$

The expression considers how responsive a change in output will be from a change in consumption, suggesting that the change in output, Y, will be a multiple of the change in consumption and a given calculated multiplier = 1/(1 – MPC) = 1/(1 – MPS).

Affecting the size of the multiplier will be the value of MPS = 1 – MPC. If consumers save a greater fraction of every disposable Dollar, then the size of the multiplier will be smaller and the overall increase in output, Y, from an increase in consumption, C, will be smaller than it would be if consumers saved a smaller fraction of every disposable Dollar. From a policy standpoint, this would suggest that growth is demand driven by consumers who save less and spend more autonomously, using savings and borrowed funds at every disposable income level.[3]

The Investment Spending Multiplier

The derivation of the investment spending multiplier is done the same way, but in this case taking the derivative of the income identity with respect to investment.

$$Y = C_A + MPC\,(Y - T) + I$$

$$\partial Y/\partial I = MPC(\partial Y/\partial I) + 1$$

$$\partial Y/\partial I - MPC(\partial Y/\partial I) = 1$$

$$\partial Y/\partial I\,(1 - MPC) = 1$$

$$\partial Y/\partial I = 1/(1 - MPC)$$

The final expression gives the investment spending multiplier for a given value of MPC. Since the derivative of a function examines the rate of change of the dependent variable to a change in an independent variable holding all other independent variables constant, the final expression can be rewritten as:

$$\partial Y/\partial I = 1/(1 - MPC)$$

$$\Delta Y/\Delta I = 1/(1 - MPC)$$

$$\Delta Y = \Delta I[1/(1 - MPC)]$$

The expression considers how responsive a change in output will be from a change in investment spending, suggesting that the change in output, Y, will be a multiple of the change in investment spending and a given calculated multiplier = 1/(1 – MPC) = 1/(1 – MPS).

Affecting the size of the multiplier will be the value of MPS = 1 – MPC. If consumers save a greater fraction of every disposable Dollar, then the size of the multiplier will be smaller and the overall increase in output, Y, from an increase

[3] It will be considered in Chapter 7 whether demand-driven macro policies are sufficient to drive growth within an economy's given production constraint and technology constraints.

in investment spending, will be smaller than it would be if consumers saved a smaller fraction of every disposable Dollar.

But is this not counterintuitive to the savings and investment identity covered in Chapter 5, suggesting at higher savings rates an economy should see higher investment spending rates? How can this be reconciled? Consider what has been derived so far:

$$\Delta Y = \Delta C[1/(1 - MPC)]$$

$$\Delta Y = \Delta I[1/(1 - MPC)]$$

Setting both expressions equal derives:

$$\Delta C[1/(1 - MPC)] = \Delta I[1/(1 - MPC)]$$

This equality shows as the marginal propensity to consume increases, this decreases both sides of the equality. Dividing both sides by $[1/(1 - MPC)]$ to cancel out the terms shows that $\Delta C = \Delta I$, and as such a decrease in consumption spending from a higher marginal propensity to save, $MPS = 1 - MPC$, will be followed by a decrease in investment spending. Simply put, one person's consumption is another person's investment. The investment side of the market takes it cues from the consumption side of the market of where to invest more for production for sale. So why might the MPC increase?

In his famous work, *General Theory of Employment, Interest and Money*[4] (1936), British economist John Maynard Keynes proposed the paradox of thrift. According to the paradox, in anticipation of tough times, households and producers cut spending. These aggregate actions end up leaving households and firms worse off than if they had chosen to spend prolifically during the tough times. Although the act of savings is seen as "good" at the individual level, at the aggregate level, excessive savings makes everyone worse off.

Applying the Multiplier

Again, the multiplier process described so far suggests increases or decreases in overall consumption and investment expenditures will change short-run equilibrium output/income by a larger amount.

$$\Delta Y = \Delta C[1/(1 - MPC)] + \Delta I[1/(1 - MPC)]$$

$$\Delta Y = (\Delta C + \Delta I)[1/(1 - MPC)]$$

$$\Delta Y = \Delta AE[1/(1 - MPC)]$$

Figure 6.4 illustrates the impact of a change in investment of spending, ΔI = \$500 billion, when $MPC = 0.5$ for a planned expenditure function, $PE = 1000 + 0.5(Y - T) + I$ with taxes, T = \$0.

[4] *General Theory of Employment, Interest, and Money* was John Maynard Keynes's outright rejection of Say's law that stipulated supply created its own demand. According to John Maynard Keynes: "In the short period, level of national income and so of employment is determined by aggregate demand and aggregate supply in the country. The equilibrium of national income occurs where aggregate demand is equal to aggregate supply. This equilibrium is also called effective demand point."

Keynes also proposed it was improbable for an economy to reach full employment of resources for the attainment of a long-run level of output. According to Keynes, the equilibrium level of employment and output in the economy would trend above or below the full employment level (output level).

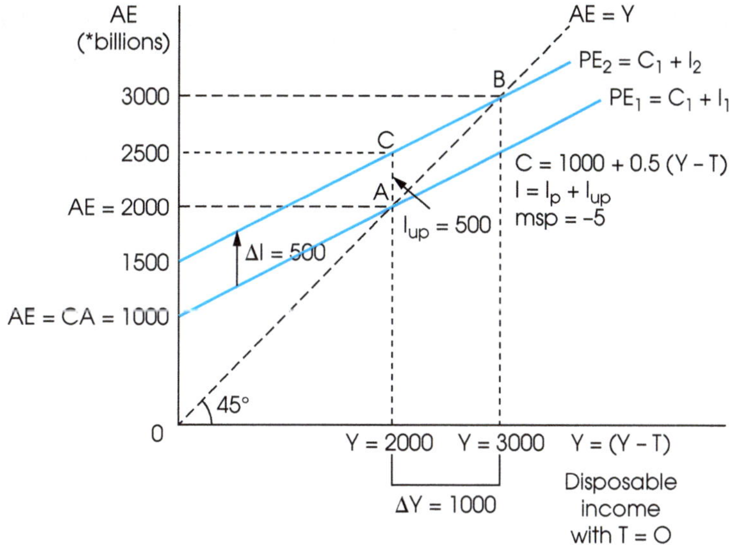

Figure 6.4. The Keynesian cross and the multiplier process in practice.

In the figure, the economy is at equilibrium point A, with Y = \$2,000 billion, with corresponding planned expenditure function, PE_1 with an intercept on the AE axis at C_A = \$1,000. At the equilibrium point, $I_{unplanned}$ = \$0. If investment spending in the economy increase by \$500 billion, the planned expenditure line and its intercept shifts upward by the full amount of the increase in investment spending resulting in an unplanned level of investment spending,

$I_{unplanned}$ = –\$500 billion.

With the increase in investment spending of \$500 billion, GDP, Y, increases first by the initial amount. This then also increases disposable income by the same amount and starts off a cycle of consumption and savings as the economy moves from point C to the new higher short-run equilibrium level at point B of Y = \$3,000 billion. The final result of the increase in investment spending has supported successive rounds of consumption to trend the economy to a higher growth in output (disposable income) greater than the initial increase in investment spending. This is sound, provided no obstructions in the domestic economy are present that would prevent the multiplier effect from reaching all levels of the economy. Such obstructions in a closed economy may be in the form of tax, regulatory, geographical, and technological obstructions.

As a calculation, the change in equilibrium income from the increase in investment spending can be solved as follows with Table 6.2 providing a summary of the successive rounds of consumption that take place until the final round when the change in total consumption spending has reached zero and at the new equilibrium level (point B), $I_{unplanned}$ = \$0.

$\Delta Y = \Delta I[1/(1 - MPC)]$

$\Delta Y = \$500 \text{ billion } [1/(1 - 0.5)]$

$\Delta Y = \$500 \text{ billion } [1/.5]$

$\Delta Y = \$500 \text{ billion } [2]$

$\Delta Y = \$1{,}000 \text{ billion}$

Rounds of Increase in RGDP from on Increase in Investment Spending of $500 Billion when MPC = .5		
	Increase in RGDP ($Billions)	Increase in Total RGDP ($Billions)
Round 1	500	500
Round 2	250	750
Round 3	125	875
Round 4	62.5	937.5
	.....	
Final Round	0	100

Table 6.2

A look at Figures 6.4 and Table 6.2 helps explain why short-run deviations in the business cycle away from an economy's long-run growth trend can be observed. A second look at the figure begs the question: If this is the case, then why do real GDP growth predictions often overshoot or undershoot their mark?

The beginning answers lie in the assumptions of the spending multiplier at the time of its inception during the Great Depression of the United States. During this time, unemployment had risen as high as 27 percent. The deflation in economic activity was driven by a bust in consumption and investment spending contracting the domestic price level by almost 30 percent.

These associated busts (along with a drying up of liquidity creating solvency issues for banks) raised the default rate on loans making them highly illiquid supporting the conditions for a collapse of the banking system. And coupled with all this was a contraction in international trade driven by retaliatory tariffs worldwide.[5] In summation, the US economy was a "bottomed-out" economy with excessive slack in production capacity and an economic experience that was counter to the classical macroeconomic thinking of Say's law: Market supply created its own demand. There was a lot of excess supply (unsold inventories that become permanent) without the expected derived demand to clear it out.

Taking the above into context—excess slack in production capacity, high unemployment, a highly deflated price level in the economy, inefficient levels of consumption and investment spending, a fairly closed economy driven by high retaliatory tariffs, and very low marginal tax rates[6] aiding and abetting the income and wealth divide (with the highest tax rates for the top earners at 24 percent)[7]—this backdrop derives the assumptions of the multiplier process that economists of the day used to better understand the collapse in overall demand leading to the Great Depression and helps explain the demand side–policy fiscal and monetary approaches in years since to better manage business cycle behavior. The assumptions of the multiplier derived against the backdrop of the Great Depression are as follows:

1. ***Changes in overall spending lead to changes in output (demand creates its own supply).*** Large decreases in overconsumption and investment spending lead to large decreases in real output by a multiplied amount. The price level is fixed in the short run.

---

5 The US Smoot-Hawley Tariff Act passed in 1930 raised the effective tax rate on 3,200 imported products to 60 percent. "According to government statistics, US imports from Europe decreased from a 1929 high of $1,334 million to just $390 million during 1932, while US exports to Europe decreased from $2,341 million in 1929 to $784 million in 1932. Overall, world trade decreased by some 66 percent between 1929 and 1934." Source: http://future.state.gov/when/timeline/1921_timeline/smoot_tariff.html.

6 At this time many social insurance programs of today—Social Security, Medicare, and Medicaid—had not come into being.

7 Figure 6.7.

2. ***With the price level fixed in the short run due to the rigidity ("stickiness") in wages, the risk of inflation in the short run is low, leaving the risk of interest rate increases low.***[8] For the short run, the interest rate will be treated as fixed.
3. ***Taxes, government transfers, and government purchases are zero.*** Without income being taxed to be used in the redistribution of income and for government purchases, wealth and income inequality is much wider. Without government transfers to the public through redistribution schemes to stabilize economic participation in the purchase of goods and service in the private sector, consumption and investment will be overall weaker and overall prices will be much lower.

   Without government participation in the economy as a purchaser of goods and services, the government spending multiplier on output and income is absent. This additional spending multiplier is helpful in supporting successive rounds of consumption in an economy to help clear out an excess supply of goods and services when inventory imbalances have become highly illiquid, production is inadequately low in response to the lack of consumption and investment spending, and savings balances in the economy are locked into highly illiquid assets, making it difficult for the financial system to extract such savings to be used as borrowed funds for consumption and investment.

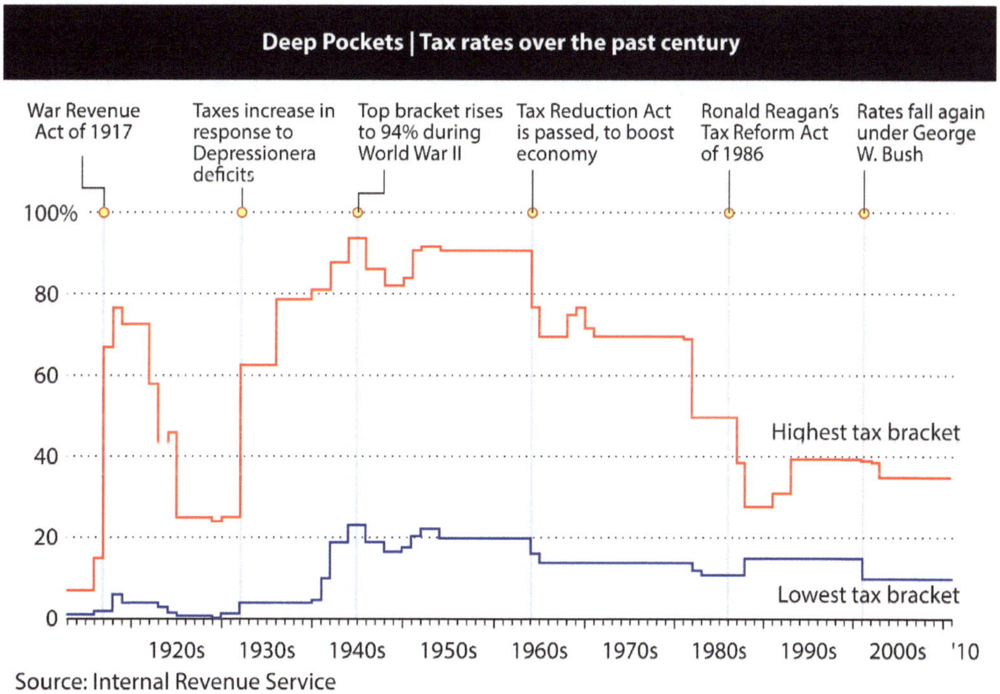

Figure 6.5. A history of income tax rates in the United States over the last 100 years. Between the 1920s and the onset of Depression-era deficits, the highest tax bracket on income was 24 percent and the lowest tax bracket on income was slightly above 0 percent. This suggests tax on income during this period was minimal, with the majority of US households taking home nearly all their earned income after taxes. Because of this, the treatment of taxes is set equal to zero in the simple multiplier model.

[8] In response to the market crash of 1929, the Federal Reserve elected to contract the money supply, which caused interest rates to rise and real debt burdens to increase and drove a wave of loan defaults and precipitous banking collapse. With the rise in nominal interest rates coupled with deflation, real interest rates rose ($r = i - \pi^e$), raising the propensity to save or "hoard" money.

4. ***Exports and imports are both zero.*** There is no trade. Every Dollar spent in the economy will stay in the economy. With imports equal to zero, increases in spending will be only on domestic goods, preventing the possibility of expected domestic economic growth from shifting into foreign markets. With trade highly restricted, the full gains from trade that would aid in increasing the overall welfare of the economy are nullified. As well, as a closed economy, the effects of the economic crisis are deepened through weaker consumption and investment spending. As with an open economy, the pressures of the crisis can be transferred through cross-border trade and financial flows.

6.2 CONCLUSION: "IN THE LONG RUN, WE ARE ALL DEAD"

Looking at how much the US economy and the world economy have changed since 1929 does require a consideration of the relevancy of multipliers as covered in principles courses. As is, the assumptions of the multiplier and multiplier process derived against the backdrop of the Great Depression weakly hold in today's macro economy and may help explain some of the visible slower growth effects from fiscal and monetary policy approaches to raise overall consumption and investment spending. Here are some reasons to suggest the questioned relevancy of the simple spending multiplier as covered in this chapter.

1. *As output changes, the price level changes in the short-run as a fraction of sellers in the short run adjust their offered prices in response to changes in equilibrium income led by changes in overall market demand or overall market supply.*
2. *Since there is some flexibility in some prices making up the price level in the short run, consumers and firms will adjust their expectations about future inflation based on observable price movements seen today. The rise and fall in the price of goods and business capital will have an impact on redirecting consumption and investment spending with short-run inflation behaving as an implicit tax.*
3. *Interest rates are not fixed in the short run, as yields on tradable debt instruments are bided up or down, putting market pressure on private market interest rates to rise or fall. Behavior of short-run interest rates today will shape the expectations of interest rates in the future and the expected capital gains/losses on such tradable instruments with different lengths to maturity.*
4. *The redistribution of income from taxes collected is done through a number of economic entitlement programs, and the government has significant presence in the economy not only as a buyer of goods and services for national defense and nondefense uses but also as a regulator. The presence of regulation is necessary for a number of reasons, but excessive regulation can impede the use of resources and the allocation of investment and other spending in the most optimal way.*
5. *Finally, economies run trade balances. This means leakages and injections will occur through trade and cross-border financial flows, impacting the size of the multiplier and the expected outcomes of the multiplier process. Economies with free cross-border financial capital mobility are able to import and export inflationary pressures and booms and busts through trade and international financial flows channeled through foreign exchange rate–systems in which countries participate.*

As well, the content of this chapter has suggested with the best efforts, an economy can only influence the short-run level of its output, and not the long-run. Because the multiplier process driven by a single change in an aggregate expenditure cannot be controlled in a vacuum with other market conditions remaining constant, these variable market conditions can amplify a short-run expansion and short-run contractions, making it difficult to identify the true peak and trough the short-run changes in the business cycle.

As for the long-run potential output and employment in the economy, this is dependent on a full employment of resources, and this potential level will change with changes in the quantity and quality (productivity) of the economy's capital and labor stock coupled with changes in technological innovation. As a result, the broader economy as a system responding to changes in the exploitability of its wealth base in emerged output gaps will go through a natural self-correction process. The output gaps will close in response to market forces and demand side policies may be inadequate to manage to speed up or delay the system correction.

And, as John Maynard Keynes purported in his *General Theory*, the economy is always in the short run and will be operating below or above long-potential output. Finally, as stated in his famous quote at the start of this chapter, according to Keynes, the only thing that is certain is we are all dead in the long run. What this means is when the economy reaches its long-run equilibrium, the growth rate in the economy will have approached zero.

For Keynes, what matters more is the short run, and an economy trending above or below its potential still means the economy is growing at some rate and has opportunities to be exploited. This certainty about the future and the uncertainty about everything else in-between as the economy moves from one short-run period to another (never reaching the long run) will be examined in the Chapter 7 coverage of the short-run and long-run aggregate demand and aggregate supply model.

CASE STUDY: THE MULTIPLIER AND THE SERVICES ECONOMY

It is very important to note here the limitations of the application of the Keynesian multiplier. Recall from this chapter that an important assumption of the multiplier is a closed economy with no trade. Any increases/decreases in aggregate consumption and investment expenditures affect domestic unplanned inventory balances in the domestic economy only; leaving unplanned inventory balances in overseas markets unaffected. The passage of the Smoot-Hawley Tariff Act in 1930, which drove global reciprocity in the passage of similar punitive import tariff barriers by other countries against the United States and one another, contracted global trade by some 67 percent, turning the United States and much of the world into closed economies.

In the model's purest form, with all assumptions of the model held as fixed, increases in domestic consumption and investment expenditures would in the short-run affect the size of unplanned inventory balances. As unplanned inventory balances adjusted to new expenditure levels to bring unplanned inventory balances to a zero level, the economy would move to a higher or lower equilibrium level of output/income in the short-run adjustment.

Keep in mind during the Great Depression when this multiplier model was derived, manufacturing was a large percentage share of US GDP. The multiplier model helped explain the accelerated buildup of inventory balances in durable and nondurable goods becoming highly illiquid as a result of the investment and consumption busts following the 1929 stock market crash and the collapse in the banking system in the years that followed.

So, what is the relevance of this simplified multiplier model in the US economy today, which is a highly open and service-driven economy? In today's US economy, manufacturing accounts for 12 percent of total GDP, leaving 88 percent of manufacturing output produced by outside emerging and developing markets.[9] All services sectors in the US economy account for almost 90 percent of GDP, and as shown in Chapter 4, changes in domestic inventory balances accounted for less than 1 percent of GDP for 2012–2014, with imports accounting for 16 percent to 17 percent of GDP for the same period.

Reconciling this with the multiplier model implies a share of increases/decreases in consumption and investment expenditures are affecting unplanned inventory balances abroad and shifting a share of domestic short-run growth/contraction abroad to overseas manufacturing economies. This begs an important question as to whether fiscal and monetary policy approaches used to a combat a future recession will overemphasize a calculated

---

[9] *Economist*, "Manufacturing: 'A Hard Pounding,'" 2016.

multiplier that will be counting on higher inventory turnover rates in a service economy carrying little private inventory balances to turnover. Retail sales can only prop up the US economy and overseas manufacturing economies so much.

QUESTIONS FOR CLASS DISCUSSION

1. An important idea to consider is how such deviations of an economy in the short run from its long-run path may be changed to alter an economy's long-run path for both closed and open market systems.

   This means the future as the long run is always changing in relation to the size and persistence of short-run fluctuations in the economy, making it difficult to tame and predict. So does the short run matter more, since the long run, as the future, is always in flux? Is it possible to exploit a favorable short-run trend and turn it into a desirable long-run course? Finally, is it even possible to "tame" the business cycle like a lion in cage? As a class, explain and discuss each question.
2. John Maynard Keynes's quote is spot on about the physics of market systems. All systems in motion will eventually return to a state of rest. This explain why Keynes stated "in the long run, we are all dead." However, the long run never arrives!! Discuss and explain why the long run is never reached in the context of the simple spending multiplier presented in this chapter.
3. The assumptions of the spending multiplier were derived against the backdrop of the Great Depression. Using the Keynesian income and expenditure model, discuss and explain the reasons for this deep economic depression that emerged in terms of changes in consumption, investment, government spending, and net trade flows that multiplied through the economy. How do the income-expenditure model and the multiplier process relate well the global systems view and "layers of an onion" analogy presented at the start of the textbook? Finally, use the income-expenditure and spending multiplier model to compare and contrast the Great Depression with the Great Recession of 2007–2009.
4. Reconcile the assumptions of the spending multiplier against the backdrop of today's modern economy. What makes the assumptions of the multiplier limiting and unrealistic for when formulating macro policy, and does this mean that "multipliers" are irrelevant? Why or why not? Take the time to research and find a more updated spending multiplier. What makes it different from the spending multiplier taught at this principle's level? What does it account for that the spending multiplier you have learned does not?

IMAGE CREDITS

CHAPTER 7

THE AGGREGATE DEMAND AND AGGREGATE SUPPLY MODEL: SHORT RUN TO THE LONG RUN

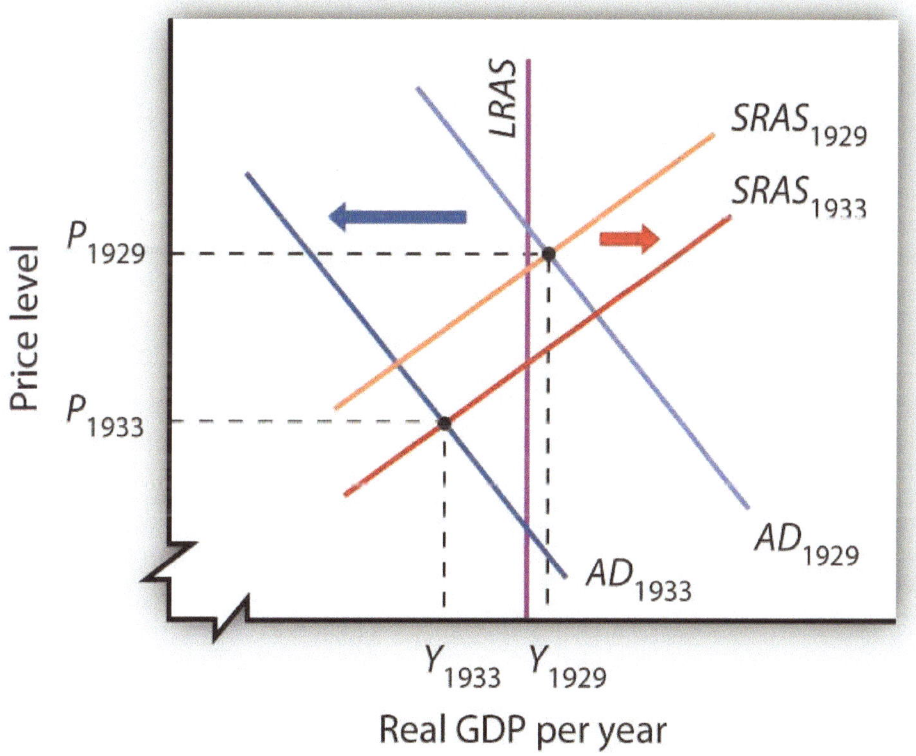

Figure 7.0. demonstrates using an aggregate demand and aggregate supply model the theoretical short-run to long-run adjustment the economy would have taken on its own without intervention to close the output gap of The Great Depression and help return the economy to its 1929 output level. The model suggests, without market intervention, allowing the economy to self-correct for deviations away from its long-run potential level of output will be accomplished through supply-side market adjustments over a number of short-run periods until the output gap is closed. The question to ask is whether taking our "hands off the wheel" and allow the market to self-correct on its own is desirable.

7.0 OVERVIEW

In Chapter 6 the Keynesian Cross and the multiplier process were introduced. These models were useful during the Great Depression to help explain how collapses in consumption and investment, deepened by a collapse in the banking system and contraction in world trade from high retaliatory tariff barriers, resulted in declines in output and income by large magnitudes, deflating economic activity and killing employment opportunities.

At the time of the Great Depression (pre-New Deal era), the level of government participation in the market as a taxer, regulator, and buyer of goods and services was minimal. Financial panics (the Panic of 1907) and recessions (brought on by busts in agriculture prices during the pre- and post-Civil War years) were not a new experience for the economy, and the economy tended to rebound from these events without much market intervention. So what made the Great Depression different?

As a modern manufacturing economy of the day, as opposed to a large agriculture economy of the pre- and post-Civil War years, the output composition of the United States had transitioned away from heavy production in nondurable goods to durable goods. Unlike nondurable goods such as agriculture, where supply side corrections can help to stabilize or rebound depressed market prices stimulating new agriculture production, durable manufactured goods will often sit idle and become illiquid in inventories when consumption and investment decline.

At depressed inventory prices for goods now illiquid, the circular flow of income and loanable funds becomes disrupted, making it more difficult to drive income streams off inventory that is not turning over. As well, in response to the market fallout from the stock market crash of 1929, the federal government imposed fiscal austerity,[1] and the Federal Reserve elected to contract the monetary base, which contracted the money supply, affecting the liquidity and solvency of the banking system (Figure 7.1).

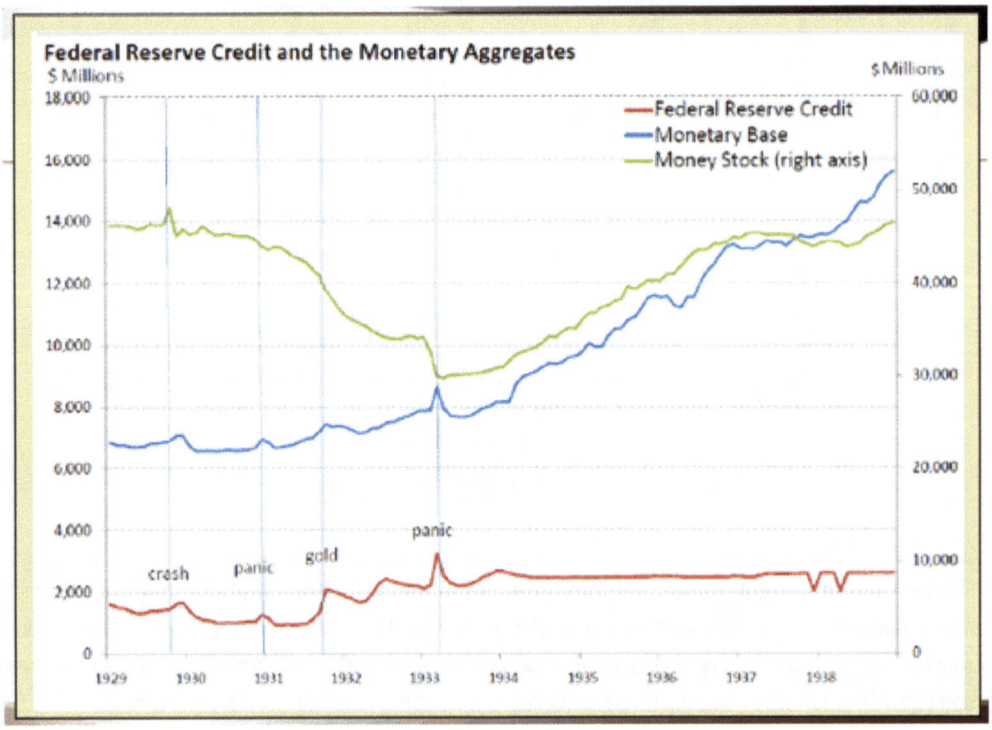

Figure 7.1

[1] Krugman, P., and R. Wells. 2012. *Macroeconomics*. 3rd ed. New York: Worth.

With excess inventories and low demand, the current classical macroeconomic thinking of the time could not reconcile why supply in the market was not creating its own demand. Keep in mind that as consumption and investment spending fell, so did production, affecting the supply side of the market. So does this mean that demand creates its own supply, or does supply create its own demand? According to Keynes's general theory:

> *In the short period, level of national income and so of employment is determined by aggregate demand and aggregate supply in the country. The equilibrium of national income occurs where aggregate demand is equal to aggregate supply. This equilibrium is also called effective demand point. (Keynes,* General Theory of Employment, Interest, and Money, *1936).*

In other words, effective demand is the equilibrium between aggregate demand and aggregate supply in the short run. This short-run equilibrium position indicates firms neither have a tendency to produce more or less than what is effectively demanded of their output. Firms will produce and supply a quantity of output equal to the expenditures to be made (demand). As well, this implies the long-run level of output (full employment) of the economy is not attainable. The economy will be at an equilibrium level of output and employment either above or below the long-run level. And, according to Keynes, "in the long run, we are all dead."

What does his statement mean in terms of the economy? Was he suggesting the adjustment from the short run to the long run was less than desirable? Or the adjustment to the long run would take longer than the lives of every human being?

If Keynes is correct, then some level of macro policy intervention is needed in order to manage or sustain given fluctuations in the business cycle to keep the economy trending to but never reaching its long-run growth average. In the long run, all systems are approaching a steady state of rest, in which at this point of rest no growth is taking place.

If this is the case, then one can infer from Keynes's statement why the long run is not desirable, because all systems are approaching a death rate. However, it does not answer the question as to whether policy intervention is strong enough to delay or push further out the market correction that will move the economy closer to its inevitable long-run outcome.

But for every deviation away from the initial conditions defining an equilibrium, the power of market forces will cultivate, eliminate, and exploit conditions setting the system on a different course. And, as Keynes purports, this will either be above or below the long trend but never at it.

To explore this thought process, an aggregate demand and aggregate supply model, like the one shown in Figure 7.1 at the introduction of the chapter, will be introduced to examine how an economy corrects for short-run economic fluctuations to move the economy above or below its long-run potential level of output. To start, the aggregate demand side of the market will be explored, and coverage will be given to explore the factors that will support increases and decreases in aggregate demand, including how aggregate demand will be expected to respond to positive and negative demand shocks (i.e., a financial panic or a housing boom).

To complete the model, a short-run aggregate supply and long-run aggregate supply curve will be introduced, along with coverage of changes in determinants generating increases and decreases in overall short-run aggregate supply. The model will also show how the supply side of the market will be expected to respond to positive and negative shocks affecting output/income in the short run.

Finally, using the constructed AD-AS-LAS model, examples will be covered to consider how well a market system on its own, without macro policy intervention, may self-correct for output gaps (recessionary and inflationary) and trend the economy to future equilibrium levels in output and price that are either predetermined or are ever changing in response to economy-wide fluctuations. This leaves open for discussion at the end of this chapter whether such natural market corrections will attain long-run equilibriums that are desirable or not.

7.1 AGGREGATE DEMAND

Unlike the demand curve in Chapter 3, which only considered the inverse relationship between the price of a single good and the quantity demanded of the good at a given price, aggregate demand explores the inverse relationship between the economy's overall price level and total quantity of real output demanded. We can infer from this relationship as prices of goods in micro markets increase (or decrease), causing an overall increase (or decrease) in the economy's average price level, there will be an associated increase (or decrease) in the quantity demanded of goods in respective micro markets, constituting a change in the overall quantity of real output demanded throughout the economy.

The aggregate demand curve for an open economy is composed of the following economic aggregates:

$$Y^{AD} = [\,C_A + mpc(Y - T)] + I(i) + G + (EX - IM)(e)$$

$$Y^{AD} = [C_A + mpc\,(Y - T)] + I(i) + G + NX(e)$$

Consumption Expenditures on Final Goods and Services

Like the demand curve for a single good, the aggregate demand curve slopes downward but for different reasons best explained by the supply and demand for real money balances—$(M/P)^S$ and $(M/P)^D = L(i, Y)$—where the demand for real money balances is a function of the interest rate, i, and income, Y, and the supply of real money balances is predetermined fixed level set by an economy's central monetary authority. Using these identities, the negative slope of the aggregate demand curve can be explained in terms of the price effect and interest rate effect to validate the inverse relationship between the economy's price level and quantity of output demanded.

As the price level falls (holding the nominal supply of money, M, constant) → the supply of real money balances will increase → causing the interest rate to fall → increasing the quantity of investment demanded → increasing the quantity of output demanded. And as the price level falls (holding the nominal supply of money, M, constant) → the supply of real money balances will increase → causing the interest rate to fall → causing the exchange rate to depreciate → resulting in an increase in exports relative to imports → causing the quantity of output demanded to increase.

Factors That Shift the Aggregate Demand Curve

The role of money in an economy is an important factor influencing an overall level of consumer, investor, government, and foreign participation in an economy. It can be observed that an increase in the money supply, M, at a given price level, P, and velocity of money, V (the rate a unit of currency turns over to support a given number of transaction), will increase the aggregate demand curve at every price level and lead to a higher level of output, Y. This resulting increase in output is driven by an increase investment spending from a lower resulting nominal interest rate, i, from the increase in the money supply.

$$MV = PY$$

$$\uparrow M/P = (1/v)(Y)\uparrow$$

As well, any autonomous increase in the aggregate spending components—consumption, investment, government spending, and net exports supported by an increase in the money supply—will shift aggregate demand to the right. Figure 7.2 provides a summary of the factors that when changed will result in increases or decreases in aggregate demand at the current price level.

Factors That Shift the Aggregate Demand Curve

Factor	Shift in Aggregate Demand Curve	Change
Autonomous net exports, $\overline{NX}$	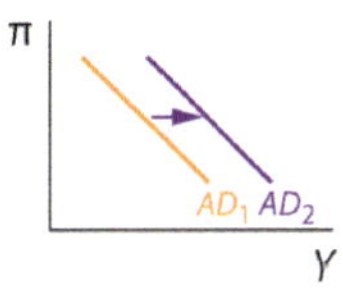	↑
Autonomous consumption expenditure, $\overline{C}$	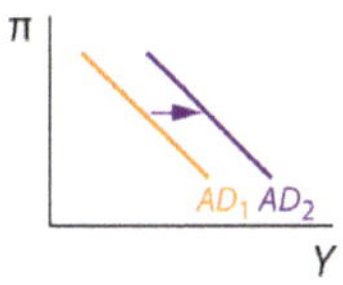	↑
Autonomous investment, $\bar{I}$	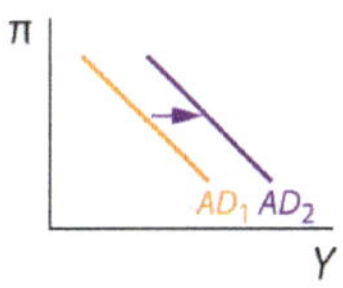	↑
Financial frictions, $\bar{f}$	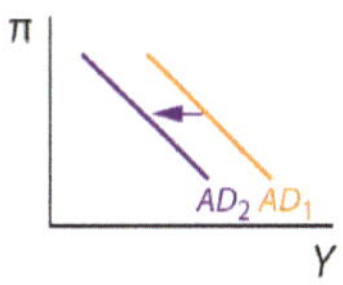	↑
Autonomous monetary policy, $\bar{r}$	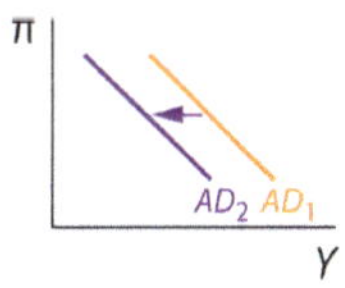	↑
Government purchases, $\overline{G}$	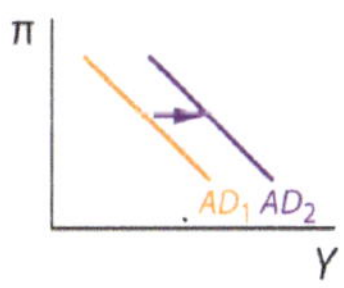	↑
Taxes, $\overline{T}$	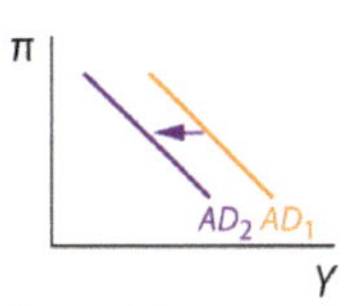	↑

Note: Only increases (↑) in the factors are shown. The effect of decreases in the factors would be the opposite of those indicated in the "Shift" column.

Figure 7.2

7.2 AGGREGATE SUPPLY AND LONG-RUN AGGREGATE SUPPLY

The supply side of the economy consists of two parts: (1) a long-run supply curve that describes the long-run potential level of real output for an economy with a full employment of resources for a given level of technology in the economy, and (2) a short-run supply curve that describes the positive relationship between the price level and the quantity of output supplied. This short- run supply curve represents all firms in the market supplying different quantities of output in their respective markets at different prices. Like the positive relationship between the market price and the quantity supplied for a given good in a micro market, the short-run aggregate supply curve expresses the same relationship representing the total quantity of real output supplied at different price levels in the overall economy.

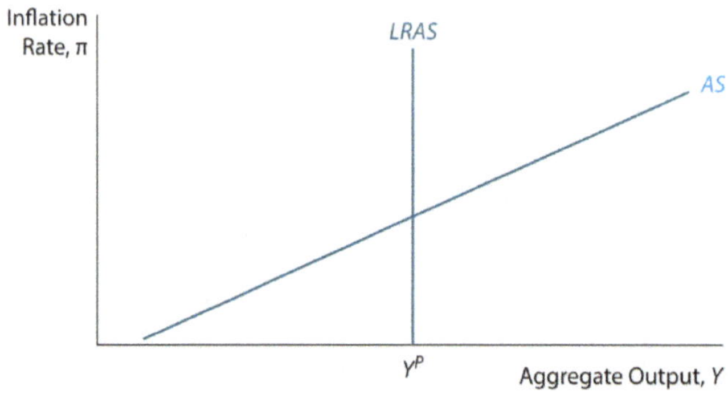

Figure 7.3. The long-run aggregate supply curve and short-run aggregate supply curve.

Source: Mishkin, Frederic. 2012. *Economics of Money, Banking, and Financial Markets.* 10th ed. Upper Saddle River, NJ: Prentice Hall.

As shown in Figure 7.3, the vertical nature of the long-run aggregate supply curve (LRAS) describes a given long-run potential level of output, Y^P, for the full employment of resources—capital and labor—using the best available technology. At the vertical intercept of the LRAS, at Y^P, the economy generates a natural rate of unemployment that is absent of any cyclical unemployment. The LRAS curve will shift to the right when the following takes place[2]:

- *There is an increase in the capital stock in the economy. This may be generated domestically or enter the economy via foreign direct investment.*
- *There is an increase in the stock of labor in the economy. This can occur as retirees reenter the labor force, a share of the population reaches working age and enters the workforce, or through immigration of labor.*
- *There is technological progress that creates a stronger intermediation between capital and labor as well as raising total productivity of capital and labor inputs.*
- *There is a decline in the natural rate of unemployment. This occurs when the rate of job separation and the rate at which workers find new employment starts to narrow. Is more evident when the amount of job creation exceeds the amount of job seekers seeking employment. Also, the LRAS will shift to the right from an expansion in entrepreneurial enterprises.*
- *Changes in production regulation that allow for a stronger optimal use of existing capacity, exploitation of resources, and more suitable technology.*

For the short-run supply curve (AS), the upward sloping nature of the curve represents "stickiness" in wages and prices. To take advantage of improved profitability, firms will respond to short-run increases in prices by supplying a greater quantity to raise total revenue. Factors that will shift the AS curve are as shown in Figure 7.4 are:

- *Expected inflation in wages and input prices*
- *Unanticipated price shocks domestically or imported in from abroad*
- *A persistent recessionary gap or inflationary gap*

[2] Opposite moves in the variables will cause the LRAS to shift to the left.

Factors That Shift the Short-Run Aggregate Supply Curve

Factor	Shift in Supply Curve	Change
Expected inflation, π^e	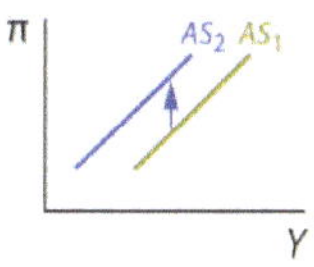	↑
Price shock, ↑	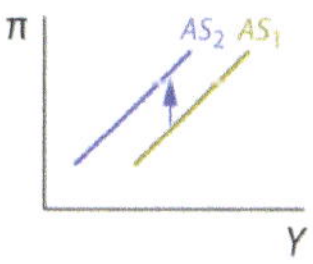	↑
Output gap, $(Y - Y^P)$	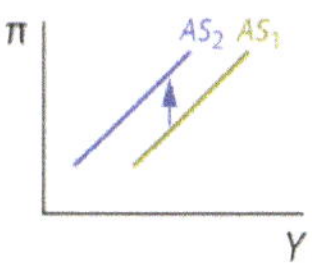	↑

Note: Only increases (↑) in the factors are shown. The effect of decreases in the factors would be the opposite of those indicated in the "Shift" column.

Figure 7.4

Source: Mishkin, Frederic. 2012. *Economics of Money, Banking, and Financial Markets.* 10th ed. Upper Saddle River, NJ: Prentice Hall.

7.3 LONG-RUN ADJUSTMENT FROM CHANGES IN SHORT-RUN EQUILIBRIUM LEVELS OF OUTPUT

According to Keynes's general theory, the equilibrium level of output and employment for an economy will be where aggregate demand equals short-run aggregate supply. This will either be below or above the economy's long-run potential output but never at the long run, only trending close to it.

If the economy's short-run level of output and employment was below potential output, a recessionary gap would emerge, and if the economy's short-run level of output and employment was above potential output, then an inflationary gap would emerge. If these gaps were persistent and there were no other changes in the aggregate expenditure components that would change aggregate demand causing these gaps to widen, then how would the economy on its own naturally self-correct and close the output gaps? And what would be the new expected observed level of output, employment, and the price level?

Due to the rigidity of prices and wages in the short run, the presumption in the long run is that as all resources become variable, wages and prices become fully flexible. The vertical nature of the LRAS curve shows no matter what the short-run price level converges to in the long run, the potential level of output of the economy will remain unchanged as this output level is dependent on the full employment of resources using the best available level of technology.

Therefore, if an economy's natural tendency is to trend toward a long-run output level, then this suggests the system uninhibited on its own can create some market adjustment in response to market forces to trend the economy to full employment and close recessionary and inflationary output gaps. Figure 7.6a and 7.6b provide two examples of an economy's long-run adjustment when the short-run equilibrium level of output is above potential output (inflationary gap) and when the short-run equilibrium is below potential output (recessionary gap).

The Economy Self-Correcting to Close an Inflationary Gap

To keep the analysis as simple as possible, for the time being, the long-run level of output, Y^P, will remain unchanged, keeping the LRAS curve constant. In Figure 7.5a short-run equilibrium level of output, Y^1 (intersection of AD and AS_1), is above potential output and creating an inflationary gap equal to $Y_1 - Y^P$. At this level of short-run output, employment in the economy is below the natural rate. With output in the present greater than potential, the excess tightness in labor markets creates an expectation of higher inflation in the future greater than π_1.

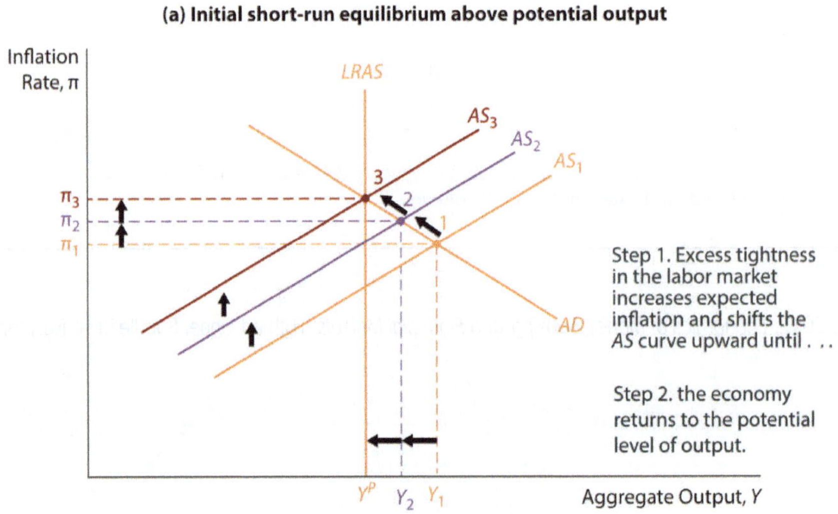

Figure 7.5a

Source: Mishkin, Frederic. 2012. *Economics of Money, Banking, and Financial Markets.* 10th ed. Upper Saddle River, NJ: Prentice Hall.

With an output level being produced above potential, the higher quantity demand for resources to produce a higher-quantity level of output places pressure on future prices of resources to be bid higher. Over time, contracts for the use of the labor, capital, and other inputs paying fixed payments begin to expire, and new payments are negotiated. The higher expectations of inflation causes a bidding up of nominal wages, coupled with a bidding up in prices of other inputs. As a result, the AS curve shifts up and along AD to AS_2 and AS_3. Further supporting this contraction in AS is also the onset of a decline in productivity due to diminishing returns in production producing above capacity.

Over time, the inflation in wages and input prices and the decline in productivity closes the output gap through a supply side contraction over a number of short-run periods, returning the economy to it long-run potential level of output but at a higher level of inflation, π_3. As a result of the inflation-driven supply side market correction, unemployment will rise to the natural rate, but with the economy now at a higher price level.[3] In this case the economy is experiencing stagflation, in which unemployment and inflation are both higher and coupled with a decline in real GDP per capita.

[3] During this correction process, as the inflation rates rise, real interest rates decline. In order to keep real interest rates from becoming negative ($r = i - \pi^e$), nominal interest rates are increased above the rate of inflation. The increase in the interest rate will reduce the quantity of borrowing for investment spending, causing output and employment to decline.

The Economy Self-Correcting to Close a Recessionary Gap

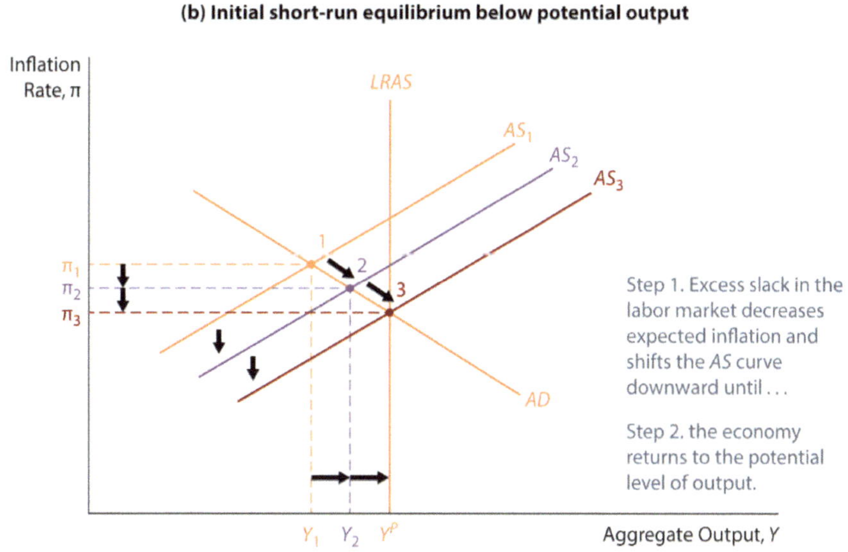

Figure 7.5b

Source: Mishkin, Frederic. 2012. *Economics of Money, Banking, and Financial Markets.* 10th ed. Upper Saddle River, NJ: Prentice Hall.

In the second example (Figure 7.6b), the economy's short-run level of output is below potential at Y_1 (intersection of AD and AS_1), creating a recessionary gap equal to $Y_1 - Y^P$ and an unemployment level above the natural rate. During recessions, higher levels of unemployment, coupled with an underutilization of resources, creates excess slack in the labor market, generating expectations that future inflation will be lower than π_1. With the quantity of output demanded being lower than potential in the short run and unemployment of resources higher, over time labor and capital owners bid down nominal wages and rental rates they will accept to secure employment.

As well, to keep from becoming unemployed, employed resources may also voluntarily accept cuts in payments. In addition, other future input prices are bid down, and productivity begins to rise. The reason productivity begins to rise is that as unemployment rises, labor remaining in employment has more available capital units to work with. This will occur provided fewer workers working with extra capital resources available to them are able to keep output unchanged or increase it to prevent a diminishment returns to capital.

The final result is a supply side market expansion that is deflation driven, as shown with the shift in the AS down and along the AD from AS_1 to AS_3. Through deflation of wages and other input prices, firms are able to expand supply, which closes the output gap and lowers the unemployment rate to the natural rate at output level, Y^P. As result of the deflation in the price level from π_1 to π_3, real GDP per capita increases. However, at Y^P, real GDP at this level may be unchanged from what it was when output was lower at Y_1 with higher price level at π_3.[4]

7.4 DEMAND AND SUPPLY SHOCKS

With a better understanding of the distinction between short-run and long-run equilibrium and how an economy uninhibited is able to close persistent recessionary and inflationary gaps through a supply side

[4] During this correction process, as the price level declines and expected inflation falls, real interest rates rise, as nominal interests are greater than the expected rate of inflation. As the price level falls over time, so will nominal interest rates. At lower interest rates the quantity of funds borrowed for investment spending will increase, supporting the increase in employment and output back to the natural rate.

correction process that is bidding up or bidding down inflation to return the economy to a level of full employment, let's now consider what happens when positive and demand shocks cause aggregate demand to change.

Such shocks are usually a response to ongoing or unanticipated market events causing a change in the autonomous expenditure components deriving the aggregate demand curve. These shocks may come in the negative form of financial market fallout (i.e., financial fallout from an abrupt market correction such as the stock market crash of 1929) or in positive form such as an investment led housing boom. Regardless of the type and form of the demand shock, the shock has an impact on the wealth base affecting the confidence and level of participation of consumers and investors; often creating herd effects.

Supply shocks, on the other hand, are much different than demand shocks. Supply shocks that are negative and usually in the form of a supply disruption may be temporary. In this case, once the supply disruption has run its course and supply levels become normalized again and/or production having been suspended is brought online, the AS curve returns to its initial level. However, if the negative supply shock is permanent, this will not only affect the short-run supply equilibrium, it will also negatively affect the long-run potential level of output in the economy.

Positive supply shocks are preferred, as they often raise real GDP per capita. Such shocks may come in the form of technological progress rapidly filtering through the economy and raising total factor productivity. Not only will this be beneficial to short-run growth, it will also alter the long-run potential level of the outcome. Most shocks of this nature are purely private market driven, exploiting unique opportunities creating positive network externalities (i.e., the evolution of the Internet and e-commerce).

The following figures provide a description of different types of demand and supply shocks; including a step-by-step walkthrough of the shock from the short-run to the long-run adjustment.

A Short-Run Positive Demand Shock and the Corresponding Long-Run Adjustment

In Figure 7.6, suppose the positive demand shock is driven by an investment-led housing boom. This type of boom raises the value of homes in the hands of homeowners and improves homeowner net worth. With the increase in the real value of the wealth base (supported by higher home values), households may become more confident returns on home ownership will continue to rise in the future. As a result, autonomous consumption increases and with increases in autonomous investment in new private residential housing starts, aggregate demand shifts from AD_1 to AD_2.

In the short run, this moves the economy above full employment to short-run equilibrium level, Y_2. With output above potential and unemployment below the natural rate of unemployment, tightness in labor, capital, and input markets create expectations of higher future inflation. Over time, factor and input prices are bid up, coupled with a decline in productivity from diminishment returns in production and inflation pressure bid present and future prices higher. The AS curve shifts up and to the left from AS_1 to AS_2.

The inflation-driven supply side correction causes output to contract, closing the gap and returning the economy to the higher natural rate of unemployment and higher level of inflation at π_3. The stagflation experience of the economy—higher unemployment and higher inflation—leads to a decline in real GDP per capita. In this case a demand shock that was a boom has become an inflationary bust.

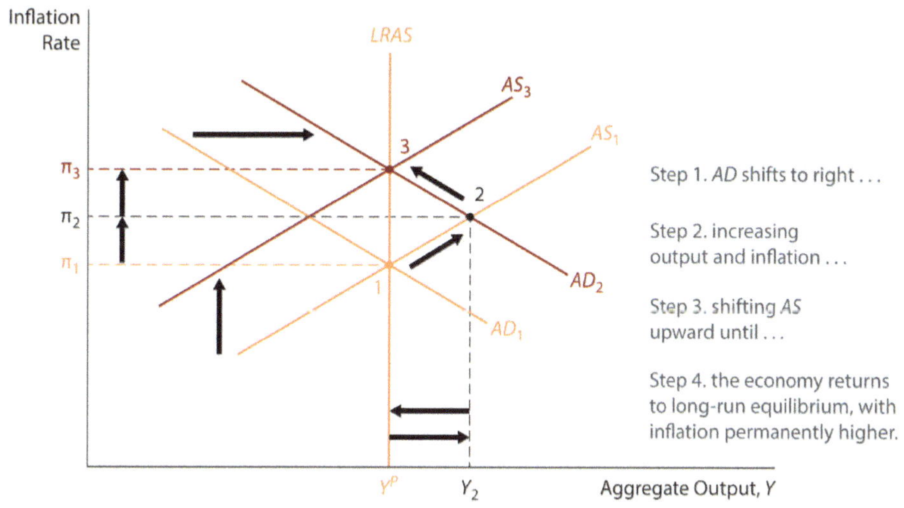

Figure 7.6

Source: Mishkin, Frederic. 2012. *Economics of Money, Banking, and Financial Markets.* 10th ed. Upper Saddle River, NJ: Prentice Hall.

Negative Demand Shock (2001–2004) and the Corresponding Long-Run Adjustment

Figure 7.7 describes the negative demand shock from the 2001–2004 recession caused by a market "bust" from overinvestment in information technology and the dot-com market. As portfolios and returns on financial and physical capital lost value, investment declined decreasing aggregate demand, as shown in the figure with the shift from AD_1 to AD_2, moving the economy into recession as short-run equilibrium output (income) fell below the natural rate, causing unemployment to rise from 4.0 percent in 2000 to 5.5 percent in 2004. Over time, the slackness in factors market created by the recessionary gap bid down factor prices and inflation, sustaining a supply side market correction (shift in AS from AS_1 to AS_2), closing the output gap and helping return the economy to full employment.

Positive Supply Shock (1995–1999)

Figure 7.8 describes the positive supply shock driven by the technological progress (1995–1999) from the rapid dissemination of the Internet, e-commerce, and other complementary information technology at the firm and household level. This type of technology progress not only sped up transactions and lowered transaction costs but also provided businesses opportunities to exploit new production economies of scale to serve more domestic and global markets at a lower average cost. As shown in the figure, the technological progress raised total factor productivity and permanently increased long-run potential output and permanently decreased inflation.

Temporary Supply Shock (1973–1975 and 1978–1980)

Figure 7.9 describes the temporary negative supply shock from the oil and energy crisis in the early and late 1970s, derived from cuts in oil supply by OPEC coupled with political and security disruptions in the Middle East. Both shocks raised unemployment and inflation, but neither shock was permanent. Between 1975 and 1978, as the first shock dissipated and supply normalized to new levels, unemployment and inflation fell. Graphically, this would be represented as the AS curve trending back to its initial short-run equilibrium level.

(a) Aggregate Demand and Aggregate Supply Analysis

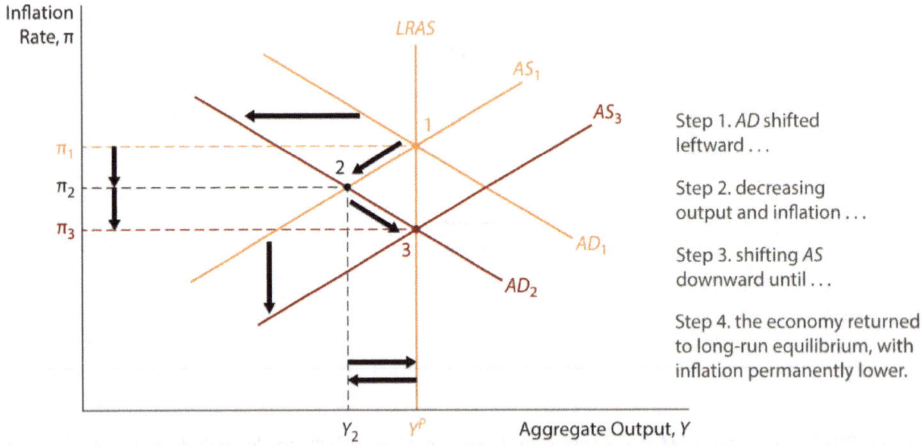

(b) Unemployment and Inflation, 2000–2004

Year	Unemployment Rate (%)	Inflation (Year to Year) (%)
2000	4.0	3.4
2001	4.7	2.8
2002	5.8	1.6
2003	6.0	2.3
2004	5.5	2.7

Figure 7.7

Source: Mishkin, Frederic. 2012. *Economics of Money, Banking, and Financial Markets.* 10th ed. Upper Saddle River, NJ: Prentice Hall.

Source: Economic Report of the President.

A Permanent Negative Supply Shock

Figure 7.10 presents a worst-case scenario, in which a temporary supply shock becomes more permanent. As a result, long-run potential output is permanently lower and inflation is permanent higher.

7.5 CONCLUSION: IF MARKETS CAN TAKE CARE OF THE CORRECTION, THEN WHY IS THERE INTERVENTION?

Any system in motion will eventually come to rest. The same goes for the economy. Regardless of the initial position of the short-run equilibrium level of output, the economy will return to its natural rate. This would only take place if the level of economic activity approached or got even close to a zero growth rate.

Since an economy is always in motion, Keynes was right to say an economy will never reach its long-run growth level of output. For this to be, growth would have to reach zero, and in his famous words, "in the long run, we are all dead." Fortunately, the economy is always in motion and will trend above, below, or close to its long-run growth

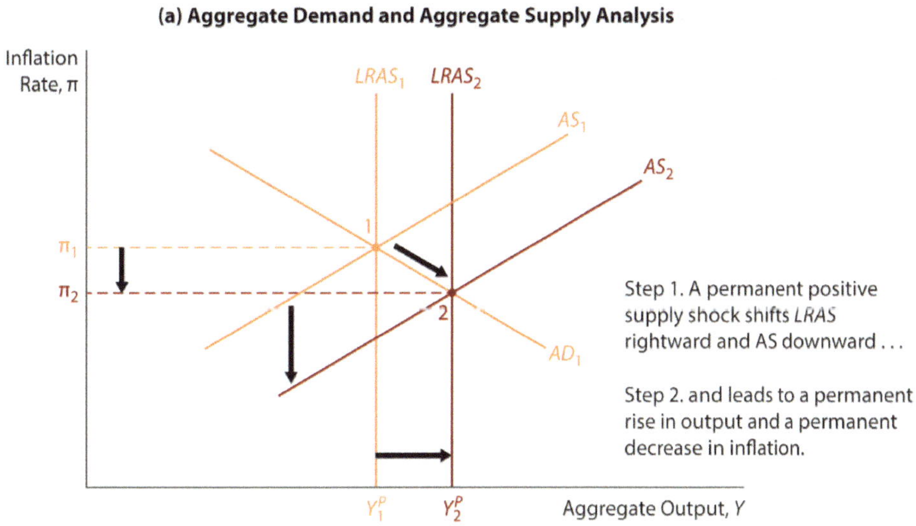

(b) Unemployment and Inflation, 1995–1999

Year	Unemployment Rate (%)	Inflation (Year to Year) (%)
1995	5.6	2.8
1996	5.4	3.0
1997	4.9	2.3
1998	4.5	1.6
1999	4.2	2.2

Figure 7.8

Source: Mishkin, Frederic. 2012. *Economics of Money, Banking, and Financial Markets.* 10th ed. Upper Saddle River, NJ: Prentice Hall.

Source: Economic Report of the President.

average. This constant motion trending to but never arriving at a point of rest has plenty to do with the simple spending multiplier process covered in Chapter 6.

But if the economy is always on its own acting as an opposing force to create a market correction to return to its natural state, is it even possible for macro policy to steer the economy in a different direction or accelerate the correction if it is desirable in the interest of welfare? A review of this chapter would show an economy self-correcting to close recessionary gaps and inflationary gaps will either return the economy to a level of full employment as either a deflated one or an inflated one. Neither situation seems desirable.

So the question to ask is, in what way would macro policy be beneficial? If wages and prices are fully flexible at some future point, then there should be no need for fiscal or monetary policy intervention. Any such intervention would not only accelerate the correction process but also run the risk of overshooting the "mark"; perhaps turning a recessionary gap into an inflationary one or an inflationary gap into a recessionary one. However, if wages and prices are inflexible due to some persistent obstruction in the marketplace, then macro policy intervention may be warranted.

This chapter's coverage of aggregate demand and aggregate supply analysis yields two important conclusions to take into Chapter 8, which covers fiscal and monetary policy.

- *Shifts in the aggregate demand curve will affect output only in the short run and have no effect on output in the long run.*
- *The economy's self-correcting mechanism will return the economy to its potential output and the natural rate of unemployment, despite the initial position of the short-run equilibrium level of output.*

(a) Aggregate Demand and Aggregate Supply Analysis

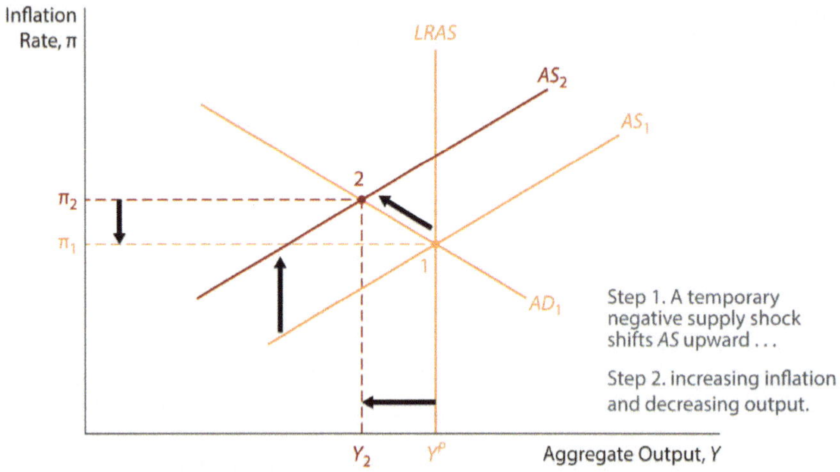

(b) Unemployment and Inflation, 1973–1975 and 1978–1980

Year	Unemployment Rate (%)	Inflation (Year to Year) (%)
1973	4.8	6.2
1974	5.5	11.0
1975	8.3	9.1
1978	6.0	7.6
1979	5.8	11.3
1980	7.1	13.5

Figure 7.9

Source: Mishkin, Frederic. 2012. *Economics of Money, Banking, and Financial Markets.* 10th ed. Upper Saddle River, NJ: Prentice Hall.

Source: Economic Report of the President.

The first point suggests that even with the best effort, demand side macro policies can not alter the long-run course of the economy, only the short-run course. In this case macro policy will have to make trade-offs between inflation and unemployment. And once the effects of any policy begin to ease, the economy will revert to its normal course, heading to its long-run equilibrium as stipulated in the second point.

From lessons learned from the Great Depression and the multiplier process, macro policy in the post–New Deal era has been quite demand sided in the form of fiscal and monetary policy activism. As point one stipulates, such approaches to the management of business cycle behavior cannot alter the long course of an economy. So, this leaves supply side approaches that are contrarian to Keynesianism and brings the discussion full circle back to the classical macroeconomics of Say's market law: Supply creates its own demand.

If macro policy is ineffective in altering an economy's long-run growth path, then such policy approaches are used for different purposes to sustain or meet different goals or even avoid a less-than-desirable long-run market correction occurring if no macro policy intervention was present. In Chapter 8, fiscal and monetary policy will be covered, and consideration will be given to the design and role of such policy approaches in the economy and if one approach is more effective than another. In the end, can macro policy effectively tame the business cycle—the lion in the cage?

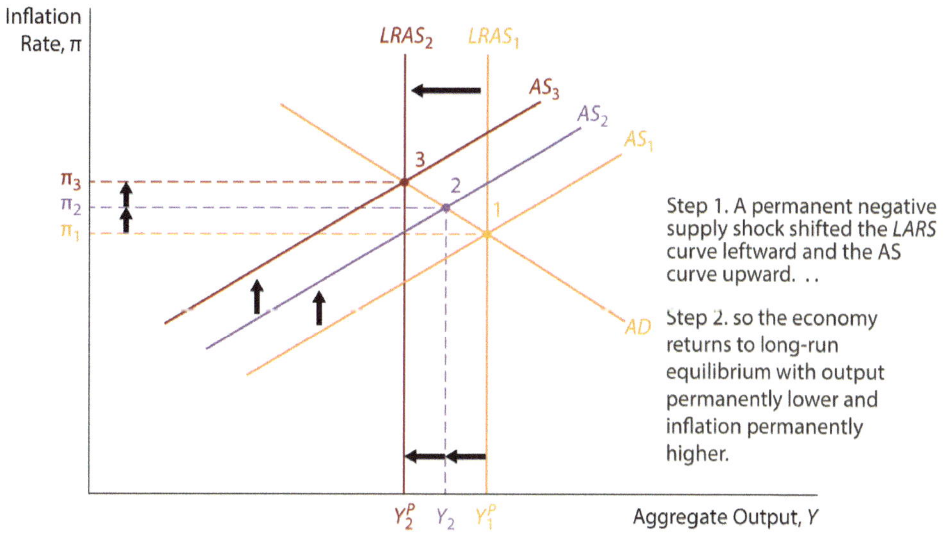

Figure 7.10

Source: Mishkin, Frederic. 2012. *Economics of Money, Banking, and Financial Markets.* 10th ed. Upper Saddle River, NJ: Prentice Hall.

CASE STUDY: FINAL NOTE ON THE AGGREGATE DEMAND AND AGGREGATE SUPPLY MODEL

The graphical model covered in this chapter to describe the behavior of the macro economy in the short run around a long-run potential level output is not without limitations. Keep in mind the model in its purest form considers an economy that is closed rather than open. The model considers how the economy overall would self-correct for recessionary gaps and inflationary gaps over a number of short-run periods to return to a long-run level of output that is treated as fixed.

One inherent problem in the model is that it is quite difficult to nail down an economy's long-run potential level of output for both closed and open economies. This is because short-run changes in the economy may alter a country's long-run potential level of output. How might this be so?

For example, making changes in investment expenditures in the model that would increase aggregate demand to raise output/income in the short run does not consider how such investment expenditures in the model may add net additions to the economy's capital stock. Growth in the economy's capital stock would shift the economy's LAS curve out and to the right by an ambiguous amount. As investment expenditures add to national income, the increase in national income would also support corresponding increases in consumption expenditures which would play through successive rounds of consumption in the multiplier process. In the end, the resulting inflationary gap which emerges may suggest a larger or much smaller supply side market correction needed over a number of short-run periods to close the gap. How much overall higher the price level would be in the long run is ambiguous.

Finally, the model in its examination of the short-run to long-run adjustment of the economy holds all exogenous factors constant. For a closed economy, the model does not account for obstructions in the marketplace, such as taxes, geography, level of technology, level of population growth and changes in demographics, and level of regulatory barriers that may impede the economy's adjustment to close a recessionary and/or inflationary gap. In the model these factors are treated as constant. For an open economy, the model does not account for a share of short-run growth/contraction that would be shifted abroad or imported in via trade and international financial channels. Such external factors may accelerate or impede a market correction from the short run to the long run.

The long-run level of output for an open economy may also change as a result of the migration of foreign direct investment and labor in and out of the economy across borders.

So is the model still highly useful? The answer is yes. This is provided the user of the model understands the predictive constraints of the model and does not treat causal effects between the independent variables and the dependent variable (output/income) as being always highly correlated and statistically significant. This type of error may result in the use of the model to prescribe a fiscal and/or monetary policy response incorrectly to a market problem. In the end, the model is a predictive guide only of the short-run direction of the economy around a long-run average. Adaptions will be needed to improve its predictive power to explain and address specific market problems and how fiscal and monetary policy responses may be used to influence the short run to avoid the less-than-desirable long-run outcomes if "hands were taken off the wheel."

QUESTIONS FOR CLASS DISCUSSION

1. Review the following statement from this chapter:

   "if the economy is always on its own acting as an opposing force to create a market correction to return to its natural state, is it even possible for macro policy to steer the economy in a different direction or accelerate the correction if it is desirable in the interest of welfare? A review of this chapter would show an economy self-correcting to close recessionary gaps and inflationary gaps will either return the economy to a level of full employment as either a deflated one or an inflated one. Neither situation seems desirable."

   Lead a class discussion on why the adjustment of an economy from the short run to the long run without government macro policy intervention to steer the economy away from the long-run level of potential output or to aid the economic correction in a controlled way is not desirable. Explain why or why not.
2. Discuss reasons why the long-run level of potential of output cannot be treated as static and this long-run level of output is always changing in response to short-run changes in aggregate supply and aggregate demand. Present and illustrate a hypothetical or real-world case for your group or class response.
3. Using what you have learned about economic growth from Chapter 5, it is arguable that supply side economic policy is potentially more powerful in altering an economy's long-run economic path. Explain why or why not and illustrate and debate your argument using an AD-AS-LAS model. Finally, from what you and your class have learned in Chapters 6 and 7, discuss the reasons why supply side economics has regained renewed interest within macro policy circles.

IMAGE CREDITS

- Fig. 7.1: Gary North, "Federal Reserve Credit and Monetary Aggregates," www.garynorth.com. Copyright © by GaryNorth.com, Inc.
- Fig. 7.2: Adapted from Frederic Mishkin, Economics of Money, Banking, and Financial Markets. Copyright © 2012 by Pearson Education Limited.
- Fig. 7.3: Adapted from Frederic Mishkin, Economics of Money, Banking, and Financial Markets. Copyright © 2012 by Pearson Education Limited.
- Fig. 7.4: Adapted from Frederic Mishkin, Economics of Money, Banking, and Financial Markets. Copyright © 2012 by Pearson Education Limited.
- Fig. 7.5a: Adapted from Frederic Mishkin, Economics of Money, Banking, and Financial Markets. Copyright © 2012 by Pearson Education Limited.

CHAPTER 8

FISCAL AND MONETARY POLICY: SHORT-RUN MANAGEMENT OF THE BUSINESS CYCLE

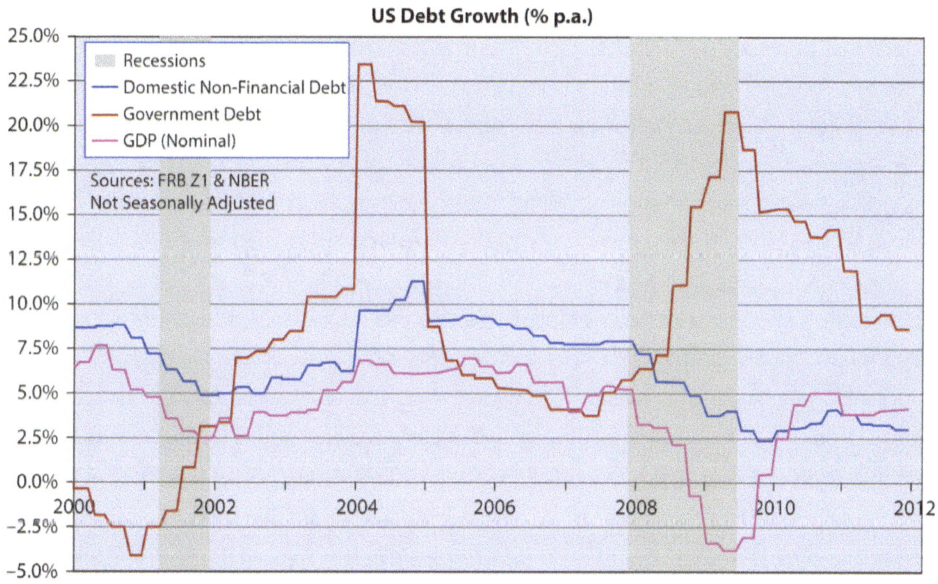

Figure 8.0. With the exception of the wars in Iraq and Afghanistan in response to the al Qaeda terrorist attacks on the US World Trade Center on September 11, 2001, in which US government debt soared from increases in defense spending and the establishment of the US Department of Homeland Security, the figure shows the growth in government debt trended inversely to the growth rate in Nominal GDP from 2000 to 2002 and 2008 to 2012.

8.0 OVERVIEW

An important conclusion in Chapter 7's coverage of aggregate demand and aggregate supply analysis was changes in overall aggregate demand from changes in the expenditure components would have no effect in altering the long-run path of an economy. In the short run, the economy's short-run equilibrium level of employment and output will either be above or below the natural rate. This means at any given time an output gap of some type in size and form (recessionary or inflationary) is present in the economy.

Because of the presence of such output gaps, the economy as an overall system is naturally trending to its long-run level. This means in the short run, fiscal and monetary policy are attempting to steer the economy along a desirable short-run path (making trade-offs between unemployment and inflation), through the management and influence of the aggregate demand expenditure components to steer the growth rate in output in a desired direction. As shown in Figure 8.0, the government attempts to steer the domestic economy out of a recession through increases in government expenditures accommodated by autonomous expansionary monetary policy. This level of fiscal and monetary intervention is done in an attempt to positively influence market expectations that will help to serve increases in domestic consumption and investment expenditures to close a recessionary output gap and steer the economy away from a less than desirable long-run market correction had no intervention taken place. However, even with the best application of fiscal and monetary policy measures, policy planning cannot account for demand and supply shocks, which may widen recessionary and inflationary gaps and make macro policy management more difficult. As well, policy makers are often criticized over what degree macro policy is a contributive ingredient to the boom and bust cycles occurring over time.

All the blame cannot be placed on macro policy for the generation of boom and bust cycles. Keep in mind boom and bust cycles are often a result of demand shocks and sometimes coupled with supply shocks. Such shocks will transmit signals throughout the market economy that private households and firms will see as scarce opportunities to be exploited. Even without macro policy intervention, boom and bust cycles are a "necessary evil" of the economy's natural self-correction mechanism, helping communicate which opportunities are more or less optimal to exploit using the limits of the economy's ability to exploit such opportunities with existing production, technological, and financial capabilities. Market booms and busts prior to the Great Depression are a case in point.

Thinking of it differently, fluctuations in the business cycle around a long-run growth rate is a natural tendency for the system to eliminate exploitable opportunities having become no longer efficient to exploit in terms of productivity and returns. Through this weeding-out process, the market structure of incentives will change, helping reallocate resources and funds to opportunities that are more growth optimal. Eventually, these opportunities will be crowded out by new exploitable opportunities, often through the creative destruction from technological progress.

In the short run, such creative destruction may raise structural unemployment in resources but in the future reemploy these unemployed resources in a more specialized way, provided market opportunities are available, improving resource specialization and the matching of resources with supply side opportunities. Even in storm or crisis, there is a silver lining highlighting better opportunities to be exploited.

Thinking of the economic system as a very large sailing vessel, policy makers are making use of a steering wheel that at times is quite flexible and at other time quite sticky to navigate the calm and rough waters of the economy. The challenge to macro policy is to capitalize on headwinds to help steer the system into waters representing growth in terms of strong employment and low inflation, and to avoid waters that would kill prosperity and make the trade-offs between unemployment and inflation more challenging.

This is not a perfect science, as in the short-run, policy makers will have to make trade-offs between inflation and unemployment, and sometimes fiscal and monetary policy goals can be opposing. Since unemployment and inflation rates should trend inversely to one another, fiscal policy activism focusing on stabilizing employment growth of creating short-run growth may conflict with current monetary policy focusing on price stability and low inflation at the expense of employment.[1]

---

[1] This chapter will show the primary goal of fiscal policy is to raise short-run growth through expenditure changes to increase overall aggregate demand in the short run that stabilizes or lowers unemployment, but at the cost of higher inflation. The primary goal of monetary policy is short-run price stability (stable inflation), with long-run employment a secondary goal.

As suggested in the Chapter 7, if the long-run corrections in an economy without macro policy intervention are less than desirable—a deflated or inflated economy at full employment—then macro policy goals are very short run in order to push a market correction into the future or steer the economy through a market correction in the best way manageable to create as much of a soft landing as possible.

This chapter's coverage of fiscal and monetary policy is done together because in response to emerged output gaps, fiscal and monetary policy should be complementary and not conducted independently. In this chapter, examples will be provided to describe reasons an economy would need temporary or permanent macro policy intervention The problem lies in fiscal and monetary policy that is more permanent and can possibly transform a recessionary gap into an inflationary one or an inflationary gap into a recessionary one, creating an overshooting/undershooting of the long-run growth trend.

In terms of fiscal policy, this chapter will examine the efficacy of changes in government spending, taxes, and transfer payments, to address recessionary and inflationary gaps along with which output gap fiscal policy may be more effective in addressing. As well, this chapter will show that income redistribution through taxation will only help stabilize output and employment and is not an effective tool to create short-run growth. For growth to occur, additions have to be added (supply side), and redistribution fails to accomplish this in the form of redistribution of exploitable opportunities. Redistribution has its own problems that negatively affect the incentives to exploit opportunities. Redistribution works great until you run out of something to redistribute!

In terms of monetary policy, this chapter will examine the role of the banking system and financial markets in the economy as an instrument of financial intermediation to transform liabilities into different types of assets to support the creation of investments in production for the creation of callable opportunities. This level of intermediation is accomplished through the money-creation process. This chapter will also examine a central bank's role in supporting the money-creation process through open market operations for the management of the broader money supply and interest rates affecting price stability and investment spending levels.

In conclusion, this chapter will consider the limits of macro policy intervention and policy activism in steering the course of the economy away from an inevitable market correction or toward one in a managed way.

8.1 A QUICK OVERVIEW OF THE 2007–2009 RECESSION

The economic recession of 2007–2009 was considered to be one of the deepest global recessions of the past twenty-five years. This recession was considered to be a "perfect storm" of a coupling of a negative supply shock, from a rise in energy and commodity prices worldwide, and a negative demand shock in the form of a bust in housing and mortgage-backed securities.

Applying the aggregate demand and supply analysis model from Chapter 7, Figure 8.1 shows the impact of these combined demand and supply shocks on the short-run equilibrium level of output and employment. The residual effects of the crisis are still being felt today in a public and private sector debt overhang that has acted as an implicit tax on growth in real GDP and household media incomes (Figure 8.2).[2]

[2] As of October 2014, the most recent job report numbers from the US Department of Labor showed 216,000 jobs added and economy growing at 2.3 percent. However, growth in real median income has been trended flat at around $51,000 (Figure 8.3).

Short-Run Impact of Negative Demand and Supply Shocks (2007–2009)

(a) Aggregate Demand and Aggregate Supply Analysis

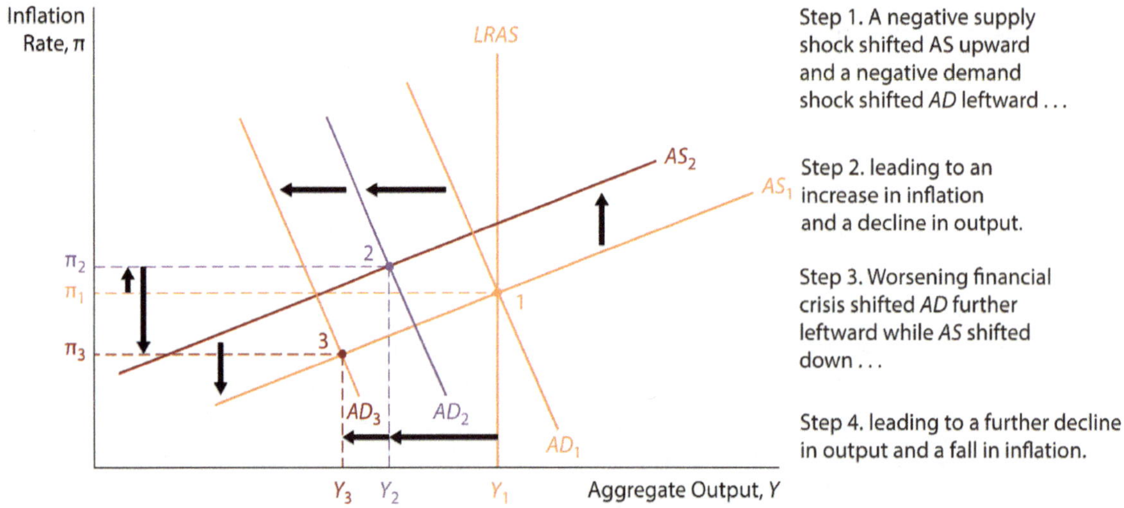

(b) Unemployment and Inflation During the Perfect Storm of 2007–2009

Year	Unemployment Rate (%)	Inflation (Year to Year) (%)
2006	4.6	2.5
2007	4.6	4.1
2008, June	5.5	5.0
2008, Dec.	7.2	0.1
2009, June	9.5	−1.2
2009, Dec.	10.0	2.8

Figure 8.1

Source: Mishkin, Frederic. 2012. *Economics of Money, Banking, and Financial Markets.* 10th ed. Upper Saddle River, NJ: Prentice Hall.

Source: Economic Report of the President.

Since this recession is considered to one of the worst since the Great Depression, it needs to be put into perspective with the Great Depression (Figure 8.3).

A quick look at the figure shows the depth and severity the 2007–2009 Great Recession and the Great Depression are far different. Keep in mind that during the Great Depression, the initial macro policy response to the crisis was fiscal austerity in terms of government spending cuts and tax increases, and monetary policy contracting the monetary base and accompanying money supply by the Federal Reserve supported a banking crisis and bank failure that followed (Chapter 7). The 2007–2009 recession—despite the contraction in GDP, rise in unemployment without price deflation[3]—may attest to the success of fiscal and monetary policy to stabilize output, employment, and inflation along with the presence of social insurance schemes, which were nonexistent in the economy during The Great Depression, that helped smooth consumption of unemployed workers and households to stabilize their participation in the economy.

Interesting to note, though, is that this recession was somewhat anticipated (Figure 8.4 and Figure 8.5). According to Figure 8.4, the US median home value peaked in 2006 and then corrected downward. It was not until the bust in subprime mortgages 2007, affecting the risk and quality of mortgage-backed securities, that a pullback in fixed residential investment and consumption (highly tied to the wealth base of housing) began. The associated decline

[3] Deflation was seen as a risk, so monetary policy addressed this risk with increases in the money supply to support higher-than-expected inflation.

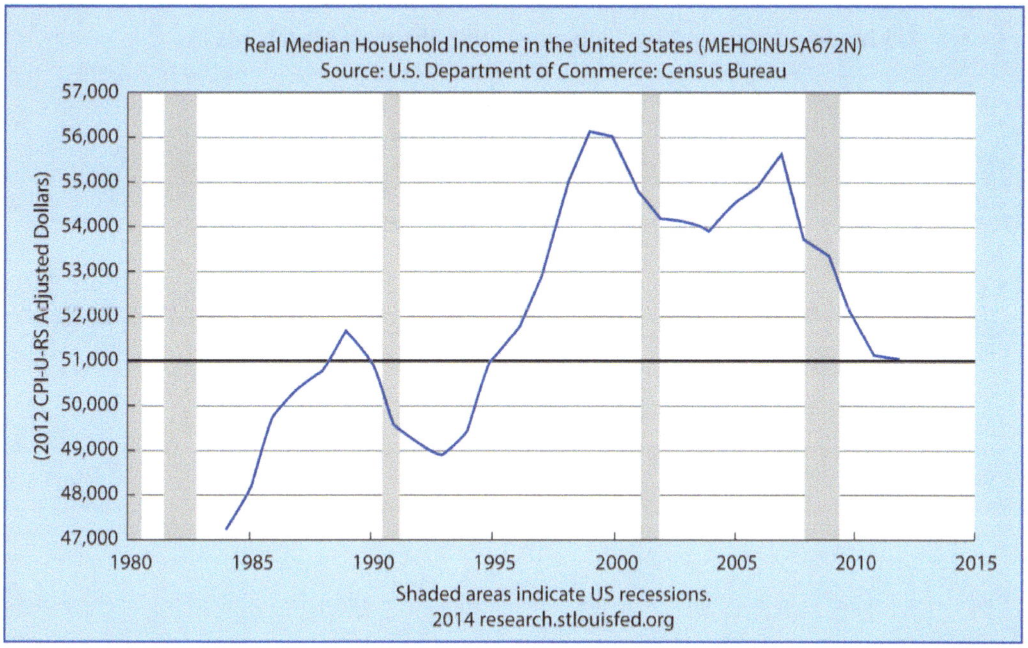

Figure 8.2

Source: www.mybudget360.com.

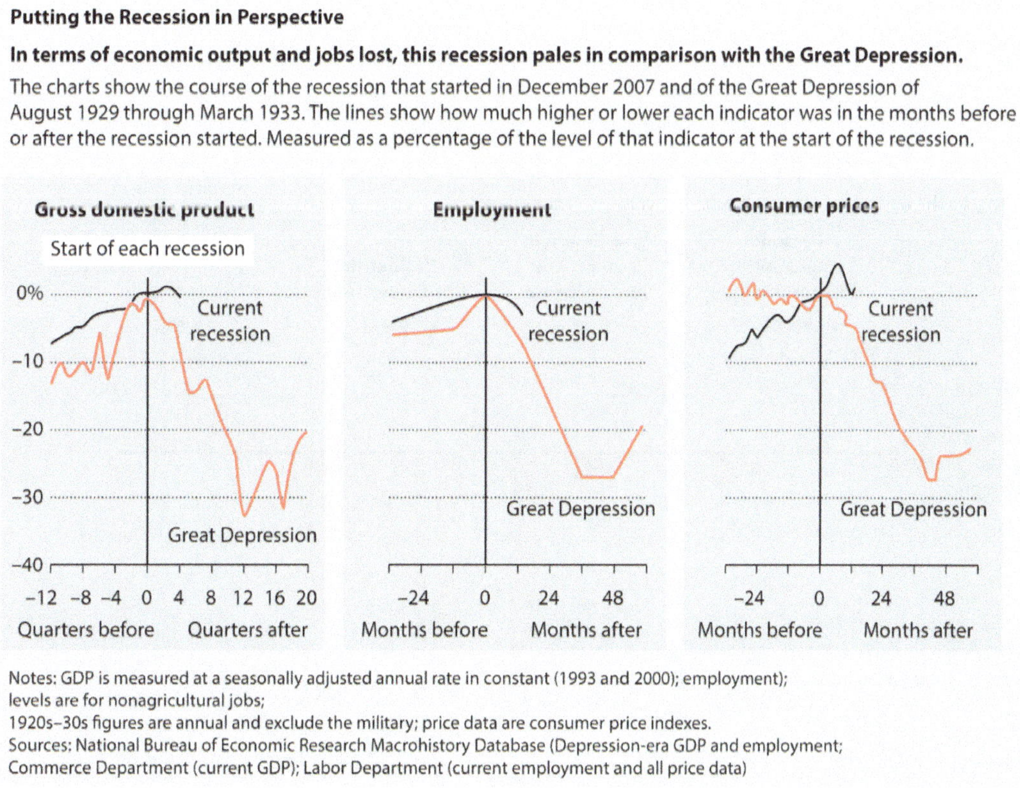

Figure 8.3

Source: *Economist*, 2009.

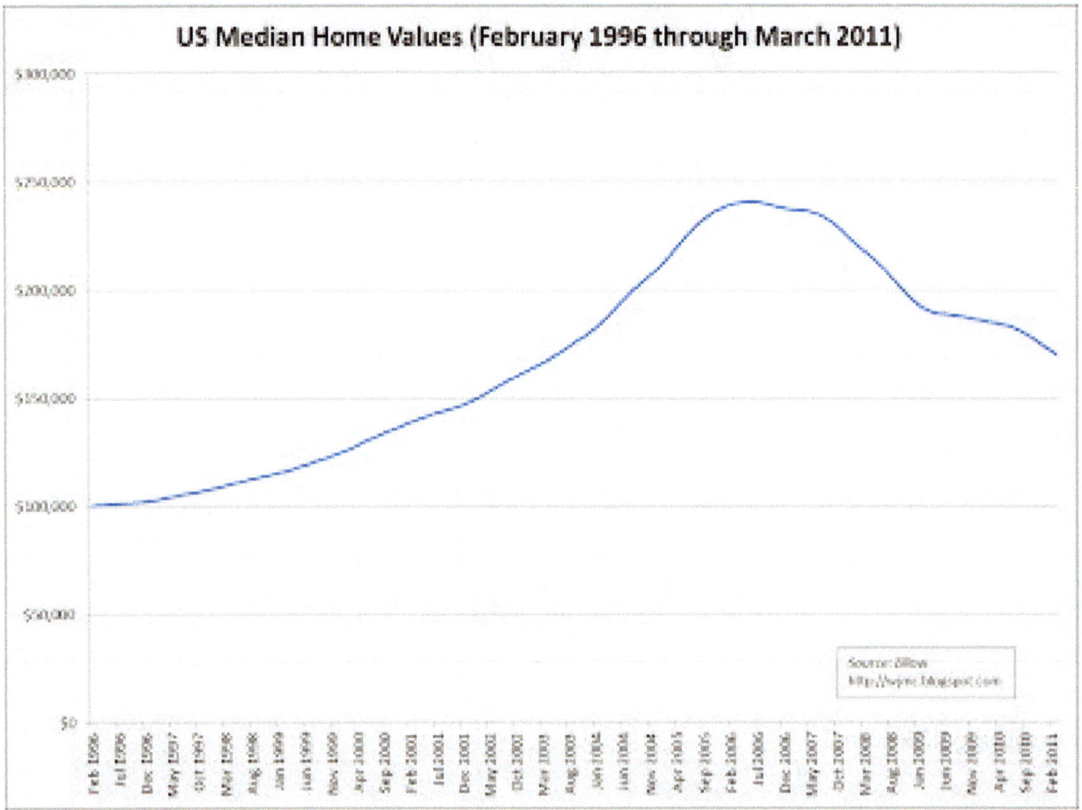

Figure 8.4

Source: www.lorajost.org.

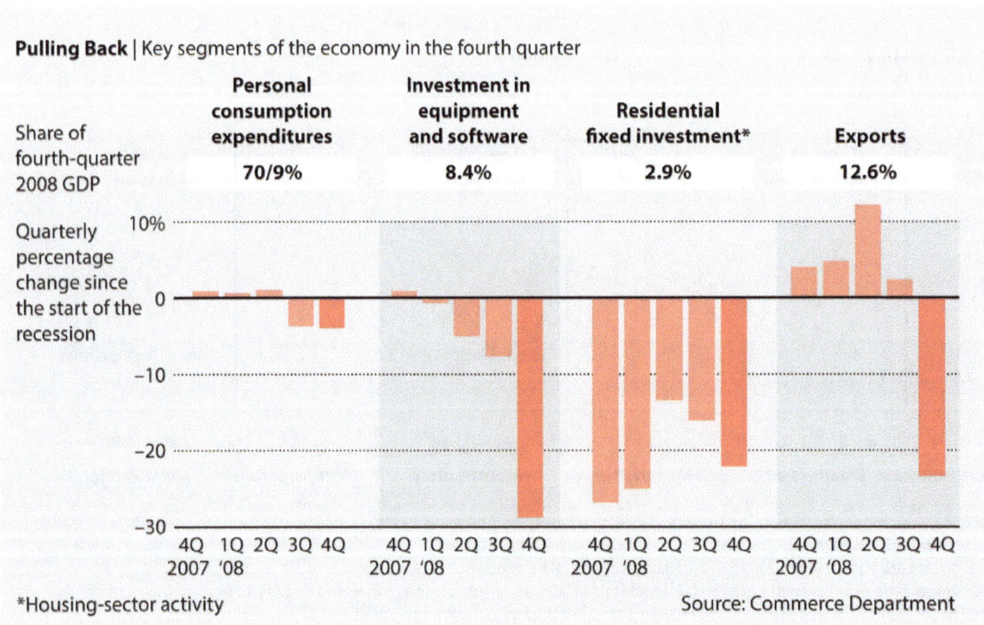

Figure 8.5

Source: *Economist*, 2009.

in US net exports in fourth quarter 2008 (Figure 8.5) and in countries worldwide not only affected world trade but also disrupted cross-border international financial flows used for external financing of domestic investment and credit creation, making the US financial crisis a global one.

In response to the housing and associated final crisis, fiscal and monetary policy took action to stabilize output, employment, and investment. It is here that this chapter begins its examination of fiscal and monetary policies to address demand shocks to manage changes in the aggregate expenditure components affecting the size and depth of the multiplier process.

8.2 FISCAL POLICY: RESPONDING TO OUTPUT GAPS THROUGH CHANGES IN GOVERNMENT SPENDING, TAXES, AND TRANSFER PAYMENTS

The Government Spending Multiplier and Tax Multiplier

In the post-New Deal era, addressing output gaps (often recessionary) from short-run fluctuations has been accomplished through changes in government spending, taxation, and transfer payments. Lessons learned from the Great Depression show that fiscal austerity responses in the form of government spending cuts and higher marginal tax rates deepen negative effects on consumption, the after-tax cost of investment, and trade on the economy through a multiplier process.

A Hypothetical Theoretical Example

Using the national income identity for a closed economy with government spending and taking the first-order derivative of the income identity derives the government spending multiplier.

$$Y = C_A + MPC\,(Y - T) + I + G$$

$$\partial Y/\partial G = MPC(\partial Y/\partial G) + 1$$

$$\partial Y/\partial G - MPC(\partial Y/\partial G) = 1$$

$$\partial Y/\partial G\,(1 - MPC) = 1$$

$$\partial Y/\partial G = 1/(1 - MPC)$$

With the derived government spending multiplier, it now provides the following expanded identity to show how changes in government expenditures by an initial amount will increase aggregate expenditures by the initial amount and multiply growth to a higher short-run equilibrium GDP by an amount equal to the size of the spending multiplier, 1/(1 – MPC).

$$\Delta Y = \Delta C[1/(1 - MPC)] + \Delta I[1/(1 - MPC)] + \Delta G[1/(1 - MPC)]$$

$$\Delta Y = (\Delta C + \Delta I + \Delta G)[1/(1 - MPC)]$$

$$\Delta Y = \Delta AE[1/(1 - MPC)]$$

Where in a private economy, consumption and investment spending are tightly linked through income and savings channels, such that changes in the size of autonomous consumption affect correlated investment spending levels over the short run, and vice versa, the level of government spending is treated as exogenous since such spending is determined through a budget process through the congressional legislative system. This means any pullback in consumption expenditures causing a pullback in investment expenditures, and vice versa, can be offset by an increase in government expenditures to do the following:

- *Stabilize aggregate demand in order stabilize output and employment.*
- *Or, through larger increases in government expenditures (well above the decreases in consumption and investment spending levels), to increase aggregate demand to raise short-run equilibrium output, disposable income, and also savings from short-run growth to be allocated to investment spending.*

The following describes the empirical thought process of this multiplier process, provided "looser assumptions" of the multiplier process hold, of how government spending on goods and services may help support investment expenditures in a weaker consumption environment:

- *The price level is fairly "sticky" or fixed in the short run.*
- *Interest rates in the short run are fairly fixed or neutral to reduce an anticipated short-run rise that would cause a decrease in investment spending.*
- *Taxes are held constant. Transfer payments are held constant in the short-run, and the fairly fixed price level in the short run keeps expectations of future inflation unchanged.*
- *Trade is balanced and there is open cross-border capital mobility.*

To stabilize output from the decrease in consumption spending and investment spending (by equal amounts) is done by an equal amount to keep short-run output unchanged.

$$\Delta Y = \downarrow\Delta C[1/(1 - MPC)] + \downarrow\Delta I[1/(1 - MPC)] + \uparrow\uparrow\Delta G[1/(1 - MPC)]$$ [4]

Or, to increase short-run equilibrium level of output (income) by a larger amount to offset the multiplied decrease in consumption and investment spending, the government spends more:

$$\uparrow\Delta Y = \downarrow\Delta C[1/(1 - MPC)] + \downarrow\Delta I[1/(1 - MPC)] + \uparrow\uparrow\uparrow\Delta G[1/(1 - MPC)]$$

Although the increase in deficit spending in the short run would cause interest rates to rise and crowd out investment spending (Chapter 5), if the increase in government spending raises short-run equilibrium level of output (disposable income), then the private savings balance in the market will rise over short-run growth and cause the interest rate to fall or remain fairly unchanged. This will help support the investment environment through government expenditures having help to increase aggregate demand. This makes logical sense, as investment expenditures will follow consumption and government expenditures in the marketplace.

The Tax Multiplier

Without borrowing, government spending has to be financed with taxes. Figure 8.6 shows the sources of tax revenue in the U.S. economy for fiscal year 2013. The pie chart shows that individuals represent the largest tax base to finance all federal outlays; including social insurance schemes. Because of the existence of taxes in the consumption function of the aggregate demand identity, taking the first derivative of the national income identity with respect to taxes derives the tax multiplier.

$$Y = C_A + MPC\,(Y - T) + I + G$$

$$\partial Y/\partial T = MPC(\partial Y/\partial T) - MPC\,(\partial T/\partial T)$$

[4] With balanced trade, the change in net exports, ΔNX, is equal to zero, also making the change to capital inflows, ΔKI, equal to zero.

$\partial Y/\partial T = MPC(\partial Y/\partial T) - MPC$

$\partial Y/\partial T - MPC(\partial Y/\partial T) = -MPC$

$\partial Y/\partial T\ (1 - MPC) = -MPC$

$\partial Y/\partial T = -MPC/(1 - MPC)$

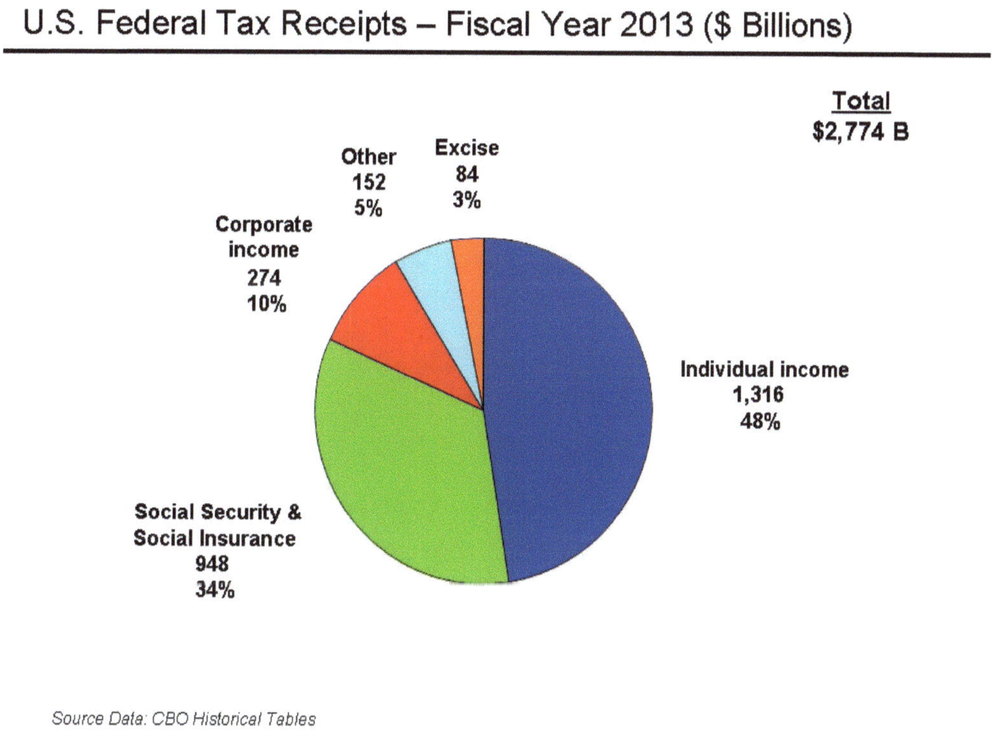

Figure 8.6

The size of the tax multiplier, $-MPC/(1 - MPC)$, is much smaller than the government spending multiplier $1/(1 - MPC)$. As such, taxing the growth in income will reduce the size of the multiplier process. For example, suppose for a closed economy the government elects to increase defense spending by $100 billion and elects to finance the increase in defense spending by raising taxes equal to $100 billion. What will be the growth in short-run equilibrium output (income) if the MPC in the economy is equal to .8?

First, applying the government spending multiplier, the calculated change in equilibrium output from the increase in government defense spending of $100 billion is:

$\Delta Y = \Delta G\ [1/(1 - MPC)]$

$\Delta Y = \$100 \text{ billion } [1/(1 - .8)]$

$\Delta Y = \$100 \text{ billion } [5]$

$\Delta Y = \$500 \text{ billion}$

Next, applying the tax multiplier, the calculated change in equilibrium output from an increase in taxes of $100 billion to finance the increase in defense spending of $100 billion is:

$\Delta Y = \Delta T[-MPC/(1 - MPC)]$

$\Delta Y = \$100 \text{ billion } [-.8/(1 - .8)]$

$\Delta Y = \$100 \text{ billion } [-.8/.2]$

$\Delta Y = \$100 \text{ billion } [-4]$

$\Delta Y = -\$400 \text{ billion}$

As a result, the net change in short equilibrium GDP is only \$100 billion.[5] Because the derived tax multiplier will always be a negative value, any increase in taxes will decrease equilibrium output by a large multiplied amount and any decrease in taxes will increase equilibrium output by a large multiplied amount.

This explains why during recessionary periods, government spending increases and taxes are cut to increase aggregate demand in an attempt to close the output gap, and during inflationary periods government spending is cut and taxes are increased in order to decrease aggregate demand to close the gap.[6] However, with the presence of taxes on income growth and the redistribution of taxes and borrowed money through transfer payments, the size of the expected changes in equilibrium output through the multiplier process will be diminished.

5 $\Delta Y = \Delta G[1/(1 - MPC)] - \Delta T[-MPC/(1 - MPC)]$.

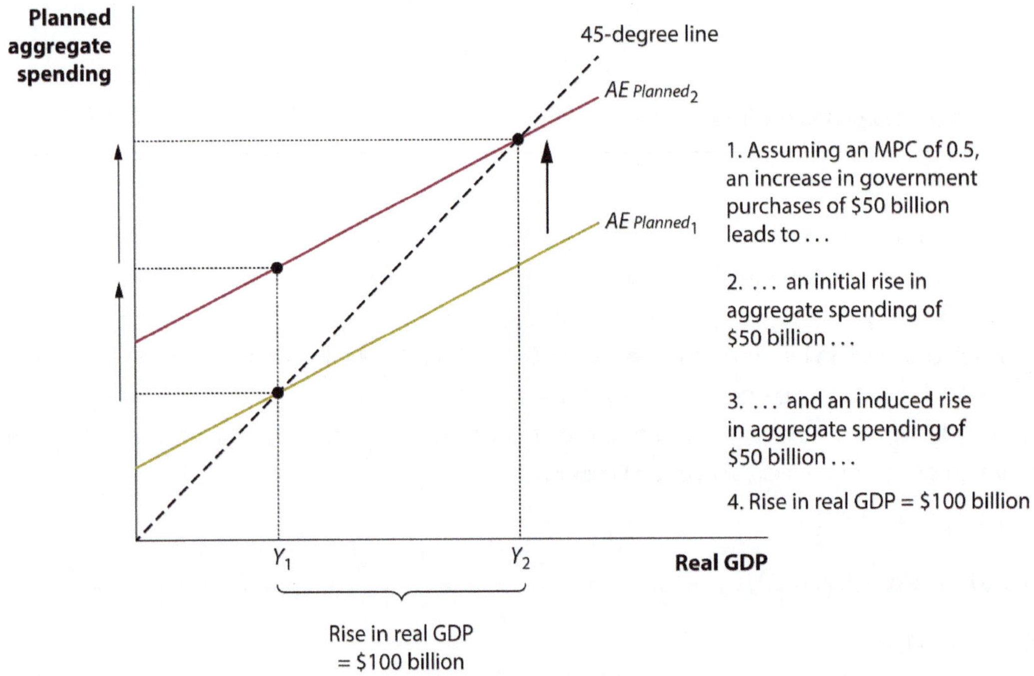

Figure 8.7

Source: Krugman, P., and R. Wells. 2012. *Macroeconomics*. 3rd ed. New York: Worth.

6 Fiscal expansion in inflationary environments would increase aggregate demand and widen the inflationary gap, inevitably leading to a more severe market correction with higher future inflation once the policy effects have eased.

8.3 FISCAL POLICY AND CLOSING OUTPUT GAPS

Depending on the type of output gap, fiscal policy approaches can be used to close the gap through a combination of changes in government spending and taxes. Applying the Keynesian cross, Figure 8.7 shows how increases in government spending will increase short-run equilibrium output by a multiplied amount, depending on the size of the multiplier.

Expansionary Fiscal Policy and the Multiplier Process

Closing Recessionary and Inflationary Output Gaps

Since in the long run wages and prices are fully flexible, there is no telling at what point in the future the long run will come. Figure 8.8 considers this as a case in point for an economy that is experiencing a persistent recessionary gap making short-run unemployment a potential long-run problem. The long-run adjustment that closes this type of output gap through a short-run supply side correction over a number of short-run periods will cause deflation in wages and the price level, with the deflation in the price level making overall sales revenue and profitability of firms much lower.

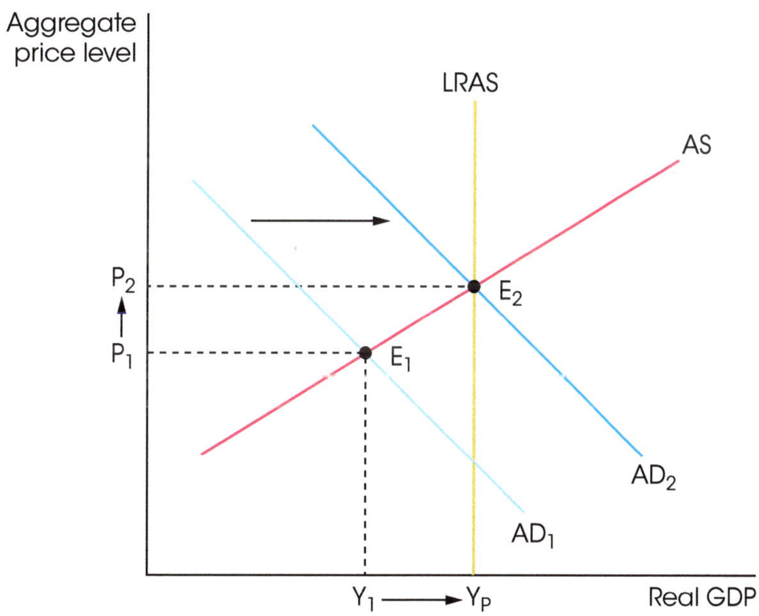

Figure 8.8

Source: Krugman, P., and R. Wells. 2012. *Macroeconomics*. 3rd ed. New York: Worth.

Use of Expansionary Fiscal Policy to Close a Recessionary Gap

In order to prevent wage deflation and the associated price deflation, the government can close the recessionary gap by increasing aggregate demand through a combination of increases in government spending on final goods and services accompanied with tax cuts on income and other earnings. In this example, fiscal policy has to make a trade-off between inflation and unemployment, and in this case having to accept lower unemployment in exchange for higher short-run inflation.

However, changes in government spending and taxation have to be done in an exact way so that multiplier effects filter through rounds of consumption approaching zero at the exact time the gap closes. Otherwise, the multiplier process will continue and move the economy above the natural rate of output and an inflationary gap will emerge. This will most likely occur because the multiplier process occurs over an infinite number of rounds of consumption and the change in consumption will never reach zero.

Use of Contractionary Fiscal Policy to Close and Inflationary Gap

In Figure 8.9, the economy is at a short-run output level above the long-run level, generating an inflationary gap. Since the long-run adjustment to close the gap would be a contractionary process through a number of short-run supply side corrections, driving inflation higher and raising unemployment, the government has to make a trade-off between inflation and unemployment in order to avoid the emergence of a stagflation environment.

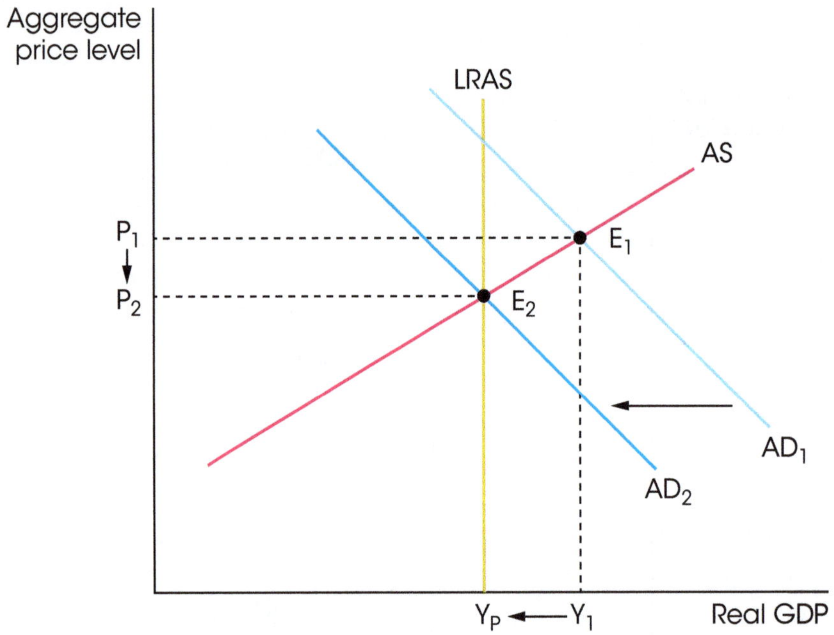

Figure 8.9

Source: Krugman, P., and R. Wells. 2012. *Macroeconomics*. 3rd ed. New York: Worth.

In this case, fiscal policy is stuck "between a rock and hard place." If the goal is to bring unemployment down, then fiscal expansion would increase aggregate demand and cause the inflationary gap to widen. This would only create a recipe for a future negative supply shock of runaway inflation in resource and factor prices. The market at some point would force an adjustment and this would often take place first in debt markets.

So the best policy option available is to contract government spending and raise taxes in order to decrease aggregate demand; making again another trade-off between inflation and unemployment. The expected higher future inflation will be less preferred to maintaining employment above the natural rate. But, as in the case shown in Figure 8.9, the contractionary fiscal policy used to close the inflationary gap will likely overshoot the long run and create the emergence of a recessionary gap, as changes in consumption over an infinite number of consumption rounds will cause the change in consumption to approach zero but never reach zero. Whether fiscal expansion or fiscal contraction to close associated output gaps will create an overshooting of the natural rate of output depends on how rigid wages and prices are over the short run.

What about Transfer Payments?

During recessionary periods, transfer payments through social insurance and other entitlement schemes often increase for smoothing out the instability in household consumption as a consequence of unemployment and other economic hardship. These payment schemes are not by design intended to drive short-run growth, but only to be used as a form of automatic stabilization through a redistribution of income. The graduated structure of the US tax system also acts as a similar automatic stabilizer. As household income rises with economic growth it is taxed at a higher rate, and as household income falls with economic contraction it is taxed at a lower rate.

Using the concept of the multiplier process, Table 8.1 compares the expected results of an increase in government spending versus an increase in transfer payments on equilibrium GDP in an economy with aggregate marginal propensity to consume, MPC = .5.

According to the results of the applied multiplier for this hypothetical economy, an increase in government spending on goods and services equal to $50 billion increases short-run equilibrium GDP to $100 billion; whereas just an increase in transfer payments by $50 billion just increases short-run GDP by the same amount of $50 billion. This is the effect of redistribution and other transfer payment schemes—they diminish the potential size of the multiplier process. Why is this the case? The answer lies in the size of the MPC of the consumption function.

Without transfer payments, the consumption function is:

$$C = C_A + MPC(Y - T)$$

With transfer payments, the consumption function is now:

$$C = C_A + MPC(Y + TR - T)$$

The new function shows when transfer payments increase by ΔTR, the change in consumption will only increase by a fraction of the total increase in disposable income equal to MPC(Y + ΔTR – T). So, with a marginal propensity to consume, MPC = .5, an increase in transfer payments by $50 billion will increase disposable income in the economy by $50 billion, but only increase total consumption by $25 billion. Taking the change in total consumption from the increase in transfer payment, the final expected change in short-run equilibrium GDP is $50 billion.

$$\Delta Y = \Delta C[1/(1 - MPC)]$$

$$\Delta Y = \$25 \text{ billion } [1/(1 - .5)]$$

$$\Delta Y = \$25 \text{ billion } [2]$$

$$\Delta Y = \$50 \text{ billion}$$

Hypothetical Effects of Fiscal Policy in an Economy with a Multiplier = (1/1 – MPC) = 2

Effects on real GDP	$50 billion rise in government purchases of goods and services	$50 billion rise in government transfer payments
First round	$50 billion	$25 billion
Second round	$25 billion	$12.5 billion
Third round	$12.5 billion	$6.25 billion
.	.	.
.	.	.
.	.	.
Eventual effect	$100 billion	$50 billion

Table 8.1

Source: Krugman, P., and R. Wells. 2012. *Macroeconomics.* 3rd ed. New York: Worth.

8.4 MONETARY POLICY: MANAGING AGGREGATE DEMAND THROUGH THE MONEY SUPPLY AND THE INTEREST RATE

An alternative approach to managing fluctuations in the business cycle is the use of monetary policy. Monetary policy is designed to influence the overall level of investment spending in the economy through the management of the domestic money supply and interest rates through the domestic banking system.

This is accomplished through a variety of monetary policy tools, with the most important being the buying and selling of domestic government debt securities in the open market. The monetary authority in an economy is the country's central bank, the Federal Reserve in the United States. An important function of a country's central bank is to oversee the health of the domestic banking system by acting as the lender of last resort to banks and making use of open market operations held to ensure bank liquidity and solvency during normal and tight credit environments. The monetary tools and structure of the Federal Reserve System are shown in Figure 8.10.

Federal Reserve Structure and Tools used in the Conduct of U.S. Monetary Policy

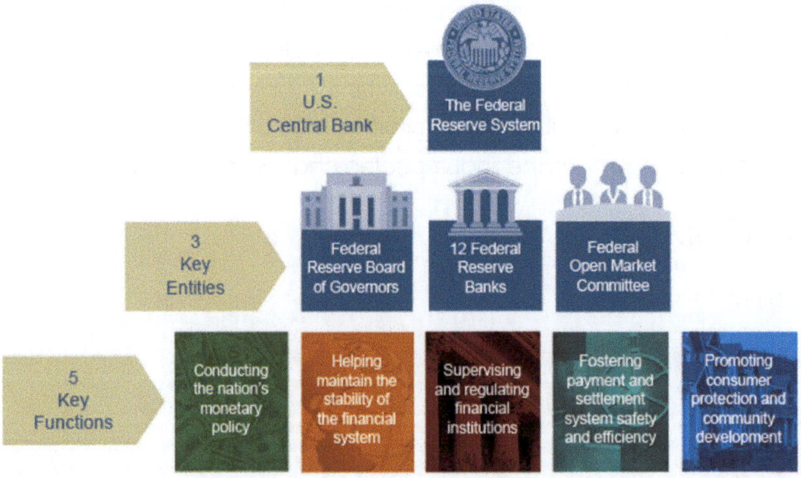

Figure 8.10. The structure and responsibility for tools used in monetary policy by the Federal Reserve. The Federal Open Market Committee (FOMC) plays an important role in the execution of monetary policy through financial markets and the banking system. An important tool of the FOMC is the buying and selling of US Treasuring through the US banking to the size of the broader money supply and key interest rates affecting borrowing for consumption, investment spending, and government spending.

Source: Mishkin, Frederic. 2012. *Economics of Money, Banking, and Financial Markets.* 10th ed. Upper Saddle River, NJ: Prentice Hall.

Affecting the Size of the Money Supply through a Multiplier Process

An important tool of the Federal Reserve is its ability to increase or decrease the money supply of printed money in circulation and on deposit in the banking system through the buying and selling of US government debt instruments in the open debt market. The buying and selling of such instruments will affect the size of total reserves in the banking system making up the monetary base and supporting the broader money supply as currency in circulation and money held on deposit in the banking system. Figure 8.11 shows any increase (or decrease) in the monetary base will also increase (or decrease) the money supply.

Money supply = Currency in circulation + Total demand deposits in the banking system

Monetary base = Currency in circulation + Total bank reserves in the banking system

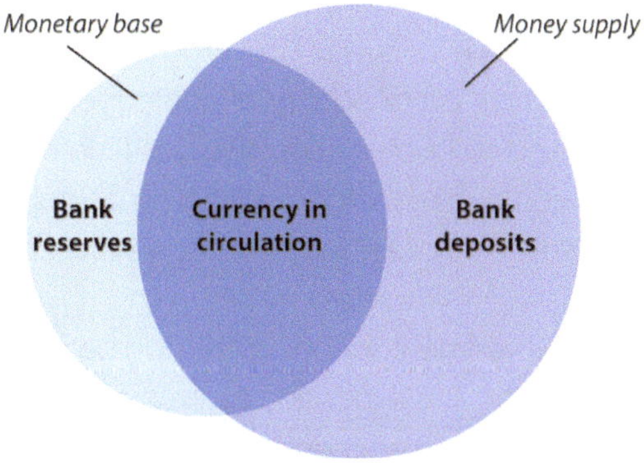

Creation of Deposits (assuming 10% reserve requirement and a $100 million increase in reserves)			
Bank	**Increase in Deposits ($)**	**Increase in Loans ($)**	**Increase in Reserves ($)**
First National	0.00	100.00m	0.00
A	100.00 m	90.00 m	10.00 m
B	90.00 m	81.00 m	9.00 m
C	81.00 m	72.90 m	8.10 m
D	72.90 m	65.61 m	2.29 m
E	65.61 m	69.05 m	6.56 m
F	69.05 m	53.14 m	5.91 m
.	.	.	.
.	.	.	.
.	.	.	.
Total for all banks	1,000.00 m	1,000.00 m	1,00.00 m

Table 8.2

Figure 8.11 shows the composition of the economy's monetary base and money supply. Transferring currency in circulation into bank deposits is important to increasing total bank reserves to increase the amount of excess reserves available in the banking system to lend out to support money supply expansion.

Through the employment of fractional reserve banking as a technique, the central bank is able to aid the money supply expansion/contraction process through a deposit multiplier process as shown in Table 8.2. Using a simple money multiplier that assumes every Dollar lent out into circulation will end up on deposit in the banking system, the calculated change in the money supply is $\Delta MS = \Delta C + mm(\Delta D)$, where the money multiplier, mm, is equal to 1 divided by the required reserve-to-deposit ratio, r. For example, with a reserve-to-deposit requirement equal to 10 percent, an increase in bank loans of \$100 million will increase bank deposits in the banking system by \$100 million and total bank reserves in the banking system by an equal amount. The increase in bank deposits by \$100 million, assuming all cash is held in the banking system, will support other loan and sequential deposit creation from lending and expand the total money supply = to total bank deposits = to total loans to \$1,000 million. $\Delta MS = \Delta C + mm(\Delta D) = \$0 + (1/.10)(\$100 \text{ million}) = \$1{,}000 \text{ million}$.

Using Monetary Policy to Close Output Gaps

A central bank with complete autonomy over the money-creation process through the banking system can affect key domestic interest rates to affect private rates for overall borrowing to be used for consumption and investment purposes. Figures 8.12 and 8.13 illustrate how expansionary or contractionary monetary policy is used to affect interest rates to influence investment spending levels for affecting short-run equilibrium output, employment, and income. Keep in mind monetary expansion and monetary contraction can also create overshooting effects in the form of recessionary gaps becoming inflationary ones and inflationary gaps becoming recessionary ones through the spending multiplier process.

If the central bank wishes to stimulate investment spending, this can be accomplished through the lowering of key interest rates via money-supply expansion. This expansion in the money supply by a multiplied amount is accomplished through the purchase of domestic government debt securities from banks. Using newly printed money as funds, the central bank will purchase these securities from commercial banks and place these funds in deposit accounts banks hold with one another.

As a result, the initial deposit of new funds from the open market government debt purchase by the central bank increases excess reserves in the banking system. This expands banking deposits and the corresponding money supply by a multiplied amount, $\Delta MS = \Delta C + mm(\Delta D)$. The expanded excess reserves, from deposit expansion, will be lent out in the form of loans that will circulate back into deposit accounts in the banking system via the CFI cycle.

Expansionary Monetary Policy Can Close a Recessionary Gap

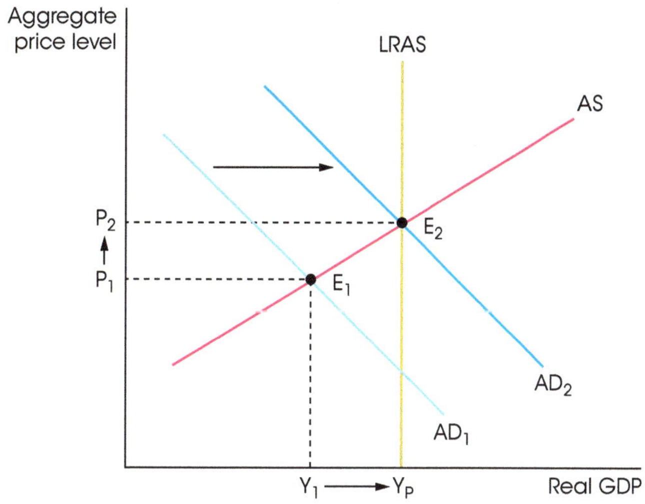

Figure 8.12

Source: Krugman, P., and R. Wells. 2012. *Macroeconomics*. 3rd ed. New York: Worth.

If the central bank wishes to contract investment spending, this can be accomplished through increasing key interest rates via money supply contraction. This contraction in the money supply by a multiplied amount is accomplished through the central bank's sale of domestic government securities to commercial banks.

Contractionary Monetary Policy Can Close an Inflationary Gap

The open market sale of domestic government debt instruments to banks is paid for out of deposit accounts commercial banks hold with each other. This results in a decrease in overall deposits in the banking system, which decreases the amount of un-borrowed excess reserves available to be lent for consumption and investment purposes; negatively affecting the deposit creation process.

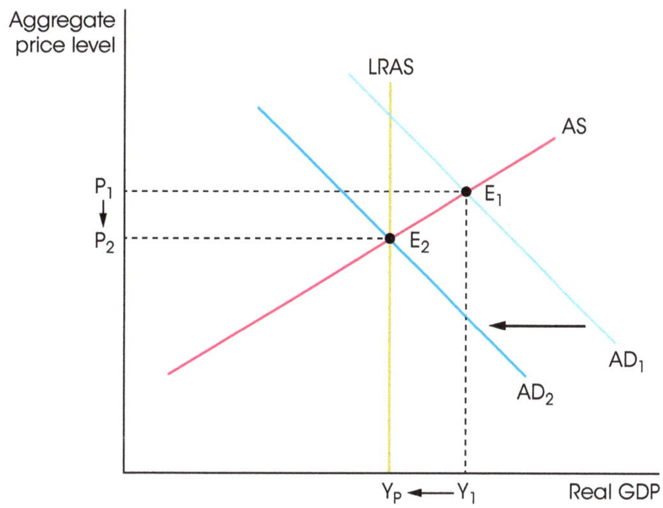

Figure 8.13

Source: Krugman, P., and R. Wells. 2012. *Macroeconomics*. 3rd ed. New York: Worth.

8.5 CONCLUSION: BOOM AND BUST TENDENCIES OF MACRO POLICY'S DANCE WITH THE LONG-RUN

This chapter's treatment of its coverage of fiscal and monetary policy begs two important questions. First, if macro policy can only influence the level of short-run output, income, and employment through changes in aggregate demand expenditures but cannot affect the long-run natural rate of output, employment, and income, then is macro policy fighting a losing battle against an inevitable future market correction? And second, doesn't this mean there are limits of debt-led growth?

Taking the first question, according to Keynes's *General Theory*, then the answer is yes. Macro policy makers are fighting a losing battle against the inevitable and only pushing a correction as much as possible into the future. However, thanks to a multiplier process never reaching zero and always keeping the circular flow of income on the move, then macro policy is best suited for short-run management of the economy's business cycle. But, with such a multiplier process without an expiration period and continually compounded by growth changes in fiscal expenditures and money supply management, macro policy may just be trading todays booms for future busts and vice-versa.

As for the second question, since it is the natural tendency for the economy to self-correct and self-regulate itself as a system of numerous orchestrated micro components, then there are limits to debt-led growth; especially since debt-driven growth can only affect the short run but never alter the course of the long run. This would suggest in today's modern economy more of the boom and bust cycles are debt led, driving consumption and investment levels to peaks and valleys around the economy's natural rate.

Keep in mind that spending from newly printed borrowed money today will filter through a spending multiplier process into infinity, as the multiplier effects through changes in total consumption get smaller and smaller but never approach zero. Also keep in mind that the Dollar's debt position in the world economy, share of global transactions it commands (i.e., the trade in petroleum and world energy), and as a premium global reserve instrument used by many other countries provides the US economy a unique ability to recycle debt coming due today into the future.

This makes the US global debt position an important economic tool for asset and wealth creation. But without innovation permanently altering the long-run picture and inflation in a favorable way, any lack of healthy real growth will limit any economy's strength derived from its global debt and asset position; raising the country's financial risk and weakening its ability to use debt as a tool for the exploitation of today's scarce opportunities. Until then, with a world awash with U.S. Dollars and its own securitization intensively tied to the liquidity and soundness of U.S. indebtedness, the world economy will continue to be susceptible to the boom and bust tendencies of U.S. macro policy's dance around its long-run growth path.

CASE STUDY: "MUCH ADO ABOUT MULTIPLIERS" (*ECONOMIST*, SEPTEMBER 24, 2009)[7]

Ever since the Great Depression, economists have hotly debated to what degree fiscal stimulus works to close recessionary gaps and spur short-run economic growth. This debate hinges on two key points: (1) the size of the fiscal multiplier and (2) how responsive the market is to increases in government spending (i.e., degree of market confidence in the policy approach).

[7] Economic Focus: "Much Ado about Multipliers." *Economist*, 2009.

When there is a case of overall weaker aggregate demand, a fiscal boost can spur an increase in aggregate demand if the boost in expenditures employs idle resources and excess production capacity and spurs and increases in inventory turnover rates. The size of the multiplier will vary according to economic conditions in the marketplace. For instance, if the economy is operating at full capacity, the size of the fiscal multiplier will be equal to zero, for in the economy there would be no spare idle resources to bring online to produce with. But during recessions, when there is idle capacity and idle inventory balances, the multiplier size can be greater than 1 if the fiscal boost creates a cascade of expenditures among consumers and businesses, helping spur production and draw idle inventory balances down.

The fiscal multiplier will also vary according to the type of fiscal intervention in the marketplace. For example, government expenditures to build roads and bridges may have a bigger multiplier impact than a temporary tax cut to consumers; especially if consumers save the increase in disposable income from the tax cut to pay for higher taxes in the future used to finance the temporary tax cut today.

Overall, how confident the market is in its response to fiscal stimulus is very important. For instance, if the market sees the fiscal stimulus as creating a "crowding in" of investment spending as opposed to a "crowding out" of investment spending, then the spending multiplier may rise as consumer and investment expenditures increase with the increase fiscal stimulus spending. This may likely happen if there is accommodative monetary policy expansion to prevent interest rates from rising.

However, the estimates of the size of the multiplier may be more overstated. In closed economies, as shown in this chapter, there is no openness to trade, which would diminish the size of the multiplier from an increased domestic expenditure on foreign imports. Therefore, the size of the multiplier for closed economies is much larger than open ones. And this is why, during recessions, there is tendency to be more trade protectionist.

In the past the test of the multiplier has been in an environment of military outlays that were economically expansive. World War II mobilized idle labor and production capacity around defense output expansion, which raised real growth and real income per household, and the Cold War years generated similar effects. This is why defense spending was always seen as healthy to an economy, or "war was good for the economy." However, in an economy that is more concentrated around services than manufacturing, then the focus of multiplier effects has centered more on spurring retail sales to move inventory off stores shelves at the expense of a larger trade deficit diminishing the overall size of the multiplier.

In a post-financial crisis environment, with an anticipated global recession on the horizon spurred by China's economic slowdown, the end of the "super commodities cycle," and a possible emerging market debt crisis, households may be saving more and using gained savings from tax cuts to pay down household liabilities as opposed to spending more at the retail level. In the end fiscal policy is perhaps "flying blind" in applying past fiscal prescriptions that are out of context for what the economy is today. For an economy today that is services driven and more highly indebted, without excess inventory balances to turn over, the size of the fiscal multiplier and the "economic punch" it is expected to bring will perhaps be smaller.

QUESTIONS FOR CLASS DISCUSSION

1. Using what you have learned from this chapter and all chapters presented so far, interpret and lead a class discussion on the following statement made in the opening paragraphs from this chapter:

   "Redistribution works great until you run out of something to redistribute!"

   From a policy perspective, using an AD-AS-LAS model, explain why fiscal approaches used to redistribute income over short-run fluctuations in the business cycle are done to stabilize output, income, and unemployment.

Lead a discussion on whether such policies are insufficient as economic growth tools, and examine why or why not.

2. Break into small groups and, for any given economic event, compare and contrast the power of spending intervention in the economy versus tax intervention. Why might the private sector not respond as expected in terms of changes in consumption spending and investment spending for any changes in fiscal spending and taxation?
3. From what you and the class have learned about monetary policy in this chapter, explain why the Federal Reserve since the 2007–2009 financial crisis initiated three different quantitative easing programs. What was each quantitative easing program intended for, and why? Did each quantitative easing program produce the intended results? Explain why or why not. Finally, using material from Chapters 5 through 8, discuss the limits of credit and debt-led growth. What are the limits of monetary and fiscal policy in the short run and long run?
4. Taking a global systems view, choose any economic event in the global economy and consider how such an event would impact the effectiveness and reach of fiscal policy and monetary policy within a home economy. For example, you and your classmates may wish to examine the impact of a recession in the Eurozone or the recession in China on US economic performance domestically and externally; considering the impact of such a recession(s) on the effectiveness of fiscal and monetary approaches to stabilizing associated fluctuations in the domestic business cycle.

IMAGE CREDITS

- Fig. 8.0: Federal Reserve Bank and National Bureau of Economic Research. Copyright in the Public Domain.
- Fig. 8.1: Adapted from Frederic Mishkin, Economics of Money, Banking, and Financial Markets. Copyright © 2012 by Pearson Education Limited.
- Fig. 8.2: www.budget360.com, ~1. Copyright © 2014 by budget360.com.
- Fig. 8.3: The Economist. Copyright © 2009 by The Economist Newspaper Limited.
- Fig. 8.4: www.lorajost.org. Copyright © 2011 by Lora Jost.
- Fig. 8.5: The Economist. Copyright © 2009 by The Economist Newspaper Limited.
- Fig. 8.6: Congressional Budget Office. Copyright in the Public Domain.
- Fig. 8.7: Adapted from Paul Krugman, Macroeconomics. Copyright © 2012 by Worth Publishers.
- Fig. 8.8: Adapted from Paul Krugman, Macroeconomics. Copyright © 2012 by Worth Publishers.
- Fig. 8.9: Adapted from Paul Krugman, Macroeconomics. Copyright © 2012 by Worth Publishers.
- Tbl. 8.1: Adapted from Paul Krugman, Macroeconomics. Copyright © 2012 by Worth Publishers.
- Fig. 8.11: Paul Krugman, Macroeconomics. Copyright © 2012 by Worth Publishers.
- Tbl. 8.2: Frederic Mishkin, Economics of Money, Banking, and Financial Markets. Copyright © 2012 by Pearson Education Limited.
- Fig. 8.12: Adapted from Paul Krugman, Macroeconomics. Copyright © 2012 by Worth Publishers.
- Fig. 8.13: Adapted from Paul Krugman, Macroeconomics. Copyright © 2012 by Worth Publishers.

CHAPTER 9

THE OPEN MACRO ECONOMY: A BRIEF SYNOPSIS OF THE WEDDED RELATIONSHIP OF INTERNATIONAL TRADE AND FINANCE

"If I owe you a $100,000 you own my blood. If I owe you a $1 Billion I own your soul."
—Anonymous

9.0 OVERVIEW

Up to now, this textbook has made an attempt to deconstruct the principles of macroeconomics using a bottom-up approach by examining the role microeconomic markets play in shaping the national economic picture. In Chapter 2, the concept of scarcity was used to define the important role differences in opportunity costs would make in determining the availability of exploitable opportunities to maximize the gains from trade and exchange that would filter through the numerous layers of the marketplace, impacting the distribution of national income through the market forces in domestic economic exchanges.

Since scarcity is always present, whether it be in goods and services, resources, loanable funds (savings), and so on, no economy is able to be 100 percent self-sufficient. Every economy, to some degree, is open to the rest of the world to obtain and borrow that which is scarce in order to maximize its domestic economic goals to generate economic growth and to raise its standard of living. The purpose of this chapter is to not explore an exhaustive breakdown and application of international trade and international finance theory and models being taught and applied, but to show how international trade and international finance are in a wedded relationship for driving economic growth and wealth building.

For example, in Chapter 5, the role of savings transformed into capital investments per worker to raise labor's share of national income to be created and captured was explored. The chapter (in its examination of the Robert Solow growth model) suggested closed economies that save more should have higher levels of investment spending and higher economic growth rates than closed economies that save the least. This would be correct if economies were closed, but all economies are open to the world to some degree. So why is the observable opposite true: Open economies that save the least grow faster than open economies that save more. How can this be so?

To answer this question, this chapter will examine theoretically how a country can use international trade and open financial markets to externally finance growth at home and abroad. This textbook has spent time deconstructing macroeconomic principles, and the conclusion of this chapter will stress the circular nature of a debt obligations creating a circular world of IOUs collateralized with IOUs and how the United States's level of indebtedness with the world is a source of economic clout reinforcing the Dollar's dominance in global financial markets. As the quote at the start of the chapter suggests, a large share of world debt denominated in Dollars anchors the world economy to the Dollar and US economic performance. Because of US Dollar global hegemony, the central nervous system of the global economy is defined by US Dollar pathways, making US Dollar government debt instruments a safe haven during global financial crises.

9.1 INTERNATIONAL TRADE: REVISITING TOM AND HANK FROM CHAPTER 2

Recall from Chapter 2 the basis of trade and exchange is determined by comparative advantage via the exploitation of differences in opportunity costs as reflected by the degree of scarcity in market environments. The chapter introduced two people, Tom and Hank, who each produce two identical goods—yards of cloth and bushels of wheat—for consumption.

An exploration of each of their respective markets showed Tom's opportunity cost of producing bushels of wheat in terms of yards of cloth forgone was much lower, compared to Hank's opportunity cost of producing bushels of wheat in terms of yards of cloth. On the flipside, it was also shown in the example that despite the fact Hank held no absolute advantage in the production of either good, he did hold a lower opportunity cost in the production of yards of cloth in terms of bushels wheat, as compared to Tom's opportunity cost of producing yards of cloth, which was much higher (Table 9.1).

	Opportunity Cost of Producing 1 Bushel of Wheat	**Opportunity Cost of Producing 1 Yard of Cloth**
Tom	¾ yards of cloth	$^4/_3$ bushels of wheat
Hank	2 yards of cloth	½ bushels of wheat

Table 9.1. Comparison of Tom's and Hank's opportunity costs.

Based on the above table, the respective differences in opportunity costs show Tom holds a comparative advantage in the production of bushels of wheat and Hank holds a comparative advantage in the production of yards of cloth. For Tom and Hank to completely specialize production in the good in which they hold a comparative advantage, each of them has to value the other's output more than before in order for a facilitation of exchange of bushels of wheat for yards of cloth to take place. If Tom and Hank each specialize production according to the principle of comparative advantage, the result is an increased total output between them (Table 9.2).

Before Trade and Without Specialization		**Before Trade and with Specialization**
Tom	28 bushels of wheat	40 bushel of wheat
	9 yards of cloth	0 yards of cloth
Hank	6 bushels of wheat	0 bushels of wheat
	8 yards of cloth	20 yards of cloth
Total Output	34 bushels of wheat	40 bushels of wheat
	17 yards of cloth	20 yards of cloth

Table 9.2. Output levels with and without specialization.

Table 9.2 reveals that with production specialization, there are 6 more bushels of wheat and 3 more additional yards of cloth available to Tom and Hank to exchange. Now, if Tom and Hank agree to exchange bushel of wheat for yards of cloth at a rate of exchange between their respective opportunity costs (market prices), for example,

1 bushel of wheat for 1 yard of cloth, the result is an improvement in their consumption profiles, as shown in Figure 2.4 in Chapter 2. This also shows that with a given set of resource constraints (the employment of their labor for a fixed amount of time per day), both Tom and Hank have been able, through trade and exchange, to raise their standard of living by being able to consume more of both goods beyond what their production constrain (PPF) allowed for.

The example also shows the facilitation of trade between Tom and Hank generated a level of savings each could invest, lend, or consume with. A look at the example again shows that at a rate of exchange of 1 bushel of wheat for 1 yard cloth, Tom saves $^1/_3$ bushels of wheat for every yard of cloth he imports, and Hank saves 1 yard of cloth for every bushel of wheat he imports. Figure 2.4 in Chapter 2 shows that with a complete exchange of 10 bushels of wheat and 10 yards of cloth traded between them, the resulting total savings materialize for Tom is 3.333 bushels of wheat and for Hank it is 10 yards of cloth (Table 9.3).

Savings Realized from Trade	
Tom	3.333 bushels of wheat
Hank	10 yards of cloth

Table 9.3. Tom's and Hank's savings realized from trade/exchange.

So the question is, now what? What do Tom and Hank do with their realized savings gained from trade? First and foremost, each of them may choose the following:

1. *Save the gain at some rate of interest and use the principle and interest earned to pay for consumption at a future date.*
2. *Consume the gain and forgo the future consumption, which would be financed with the investment of savings.*
3. *Lend the savings out domestically at a market rate of interest.*
4. *Transform the savings into capital investments in expanded production capacity to produce more of their comparative advantage good.*
5. *Borrow each's respective savings to finance domestic investment and consumption expenditures to facilitate future exchanges domestically in their markets and externally between them.*

9.2 EXTERNALLY FINANCING DOMESTIC CONSUMPTION, INVESTMENT, AND GOVERNMENT EXPENDITURES

The simplified Tom and Hank example shows their respective realized savings in their respective good produced provides them an opportunity to externally finance future transactions to support future trade and consumption between them.

Although the trade balances for Tom and Hank balance (exports = imports) in the long run, as the market prices of bushels of wheat and yards of cloth in their respective markets converge to the equilibrium trade price of 1 bushel of wheat for 1 yard of cloth, in the short run—based on timing of production and delivery—one of them could have run a trade surplus and the other could have run a trade deficit. It is in the short run that countries which save the least and run trade deficits use such trade deficits as an external tool to borrow savings from countries that save more and run offsetting trade balances.

For example, Table 4.1 from Chapter 4 provides a breakdown of the domestic aggregate expenditures and net foreign expenditures on US output for the years 2012 to 2014. For each year in the table, the United States ran a trade deficit, implying the borrowing of excess savings abroad in Dollars to finance domestic gross investment expenditures.

Unlike a closed economy, the national income identity for an open economy (as covered in Chapter 4) is:

$$Y = C + I + G + (EX - IM)$$

Rewriting the identity as investment spending in terms of national savings and the trade balance yields:

$$I = Y - C - G - (EX - IM)$$

$$I = S_{national} - (EX - IM)$$

$$I - S_{national} = IM - EX$$

The final expression of the identity shows countries that invest more and expend more in excess of available domestic savings balances will import more and export less and run a trade deficit to attract in capital inflows from the selling of domestic assets (debt securities and other marketable securities) to foreign countries running trade surpluses and holding excess savings to cover their respective investments spending and savings gap.

	2012 (Q4)	**2013 (Q4)**
Gross private domestic investment	2481.5	2745.2
Gross domestic product	16332.5	17078.3
Personal consumption expenditures	11222.6	11653.3
Government consumption expenditures and gross investment	3156.6	3142.7
National savings (private + public); Y – C – G	1953.3	2282.3
Gross private domestic investment – national savings (I – S)	528.2	462.9
Net exports = Exports – Imports (from Figure 4.7)	–528.2	–462.9

Table 9.4. United States's net savings borrowed through cross-border capital flows from running a trade deficit.

Table 9.4 shows for 2012 (Q4) and 2013 (Q4), the domestic gap between domestic investment expenditures and domestic savings balances was financed externally through running a trade deficit; or simply put, borrowing excess savings in Dollars held abroad accumulated in countries running trade surpluses with the United States. Taking this further, our revised investment and savings identity for the United States as an open economy is:

$$I - S_{national} = IM - EX$$

$$I = S_{national} + (IM - EX)$$

$$I = S_{national} + \textit{Capital inflows}$$

As seen from the table, the level of all domestic investment expenditures in the United States for these two time periods exceeded the level of domestic national savings able to support it. This means an economy that is the world's largest debtor nation must externally finance its excess domestic expenditures by structurally creating pro-trade arrangements.

This external financing is done via fixed foreign exchange rate arrangements with strategically valuable economies for the sole purpose of creating a surplus of savings held abroad in Dollars. The excess Dollars in these economies earned from trade with the United States allows for the United States to borrow cheaply in its own money to finance domestic savings and investment gaps. Securing these Dollars is accomplished through the sale of US government debt securities to these countries, with commitments by these countries to hold such US debt instruments on hand to defend an exchange rate arrangement favoring trade surpluses run for these countries. These trade surpluses (offset by our trade deficits) will be recycled through US financial markets in the sales of US assets to the rest of the world to raise external financing for domestic consumption and investment expenditures.

The strategic benefit of importing excess savings from abroad through trade helps reduce the propensity of domestic interest rates from rising abnormally higher from increases in domestic investment demand along with the demand for loanable funds to finance domestic consumption expenditures and expanding federal budget deficits adding to total national debt. As a result, our gross external liabilities as an economy will continue to rise and shift a surplus of excess savings abroad in Dollars via trade and fixed exchange rate arrangements. Figure 9.1 shows the behavioral trend of US gross external liabilities exceeding gross foreign assets held domestically for 1976 to 2012.

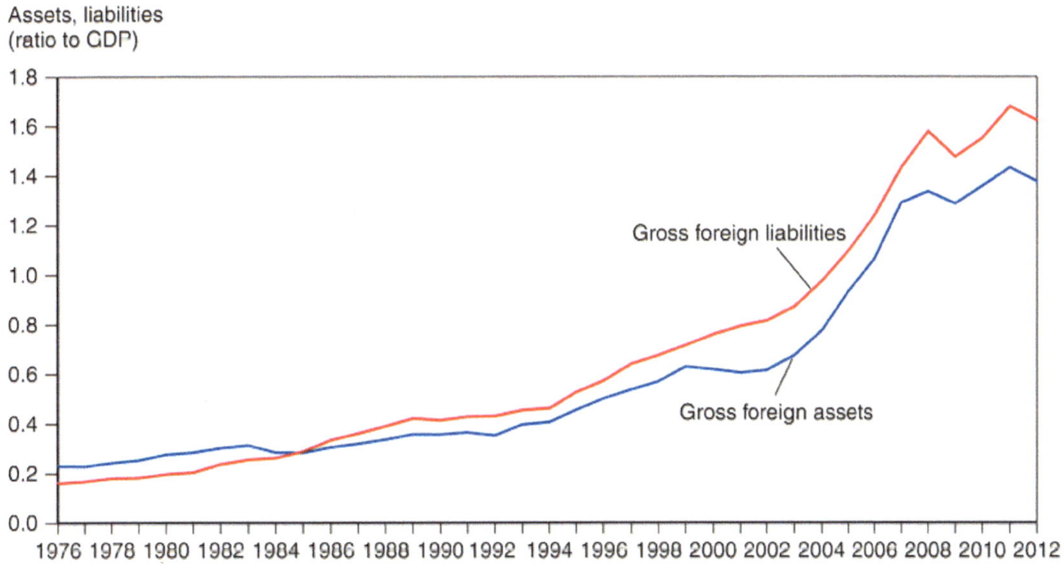

Source: U.S. Department of Commerce, Bureau of Economic Analysis, June 2013.

Figure 9.1

The key point to observe in Figure 9.1 is that the difference between gross foreign liabilities and gross foreign assets will be reflected as deficit in the US current account's trade deficit position and net foreign income receipts earned from abroad, but by a US financial account surplus. As stated earlier, in order to sustain an ongoing accumulation of excess savings held abroad in Dollars, which is often helpful with a global oil trade priced and remunerated in US Dollars, structurally creating fixed exchange rate arrangements with key economies to be anchored to the US Dollar promotes ongoing trade surpluses in US Dollars from these countries for the United States to borrow.

9.3 CONCLUSION

A big question is the sustainability of this form of external financing for the United States in the context of the systemic Dollar risk being seen in today's global economy. With depressed global oil prices in US Dollars, an economic slowdown in China—which is the largest external purchaser of US government debt securities—and threats of a looming emerging market debt crisis that would threaten foreign exchange rate arrangement vital to US external financing, is it quite possible the global economy would begin to decouple from the US Dollar and look for an alternative international financial architecture not so ordered in US Dollars?

Not at this time. Recent International Monetary Fund (IMF) forecasts for the global economy in 2016 show global growth to be weaker for the year and slowing more overall for emerging economies, but the United States economy outperforming the rest of the world (Figure 9.2).

Latest IMF projections

Global growth likely to be weaker this year than last, with improving prospects in the advanced economies but a fifth year of slowing in emerging markets. (percent change)

		Projections		Difference from July 2015 WEO update[1]	
	2014	2015	2016	2015	2016
World Ouput	3.4	3.1	3.6	-0.2	-0.2
Advanced Economies	1.8	2.0	2.2	-0.1	-0.2
United States	2.4	2.6	2.8	0.1	-0.2
Euro Area	0.9	1.5	1.6	0.0	-0.1
Germany	1.6	1.5	1.6	-0.1	-0.1
France	0.2	1.2	1.5	0.0	0.0
Italy	-0.4	0.8	1.3	0.1	0.1
Spain	1.4	3.1	2.5	0.0	0.0
Japan	-0.1	0.6	1.0	-0.2	-0.2
United Kingdom	3.0	2.5	2.2	0.1	0.0
Canada	2.4	1.0	1.7	-0.5	-0.4
Other Advanced Economies	2.8	2.3	2.7	-0.4	-0.4
Emerging Market and Developing Economies	4.6	4.0	4.5	-0.2	-0.2
Commonwealth of Independent States	1.0	-2.7	0.5	-0.5	-0.7
Russia	0.6	-3.8	-0.6	-0.4	-0.8
Excluding Russia	1.9	-0.1	2.8	-0.8	-0.5
Emerging and Developing Asia	6.8	6.5	6.4	-0.1	0.0
China	7.3	6.8	6.3	0.0	0.0
India	7.3	7.3	7.5	-0.2	0.0
ASEAN-5[2]	4.6	4.6	4.9	-0.1	-0.2
Emerging and Developing Europe	2.8	3.0	3.0	0.1	0.1
Latin America and the Caribbean	1.3	-0.3	0.8	-0.8	-0.9
Brazil	0.1	-3.0	-1.0	-1.5	-1.7
Mexico	2.1	2.3	2.8	-0.1	-0.2
Middle East, North Africa, Afghanistan, and Pakistan	2.7	2.5	3.9	-0.1	0.1
Saudi Arabia	3.5	3.4	2.2	0.3	-0.2
South Africa	1.0	1.4	1.0	-0.0	0.0
Low-Income Developing Countries	6.0	4.8	5.8	-0.3	-0.4

Source: IMF, *World Economic Outlook*, October 2015.
[1]Difference based on rounded figures for July 2015 *WEO Update*.
[2]Indonesia, Malaysia, Philippines, Thailand, and Vietnam.

Figure 9.2

And, although the US debt-to-GDP ratio has exceeded well above 100 percent of GDP (Figure 9.3), the focus right now is on the sustainability of even much higher debt-to-GDP ratios out of countries in the Eurozone and China. It's all about how well these and all countries use their domestic assets and comparative advantages to drive growth and income creation to sustain the repayment of obligations owed to securitize more obligations with which to create assets.

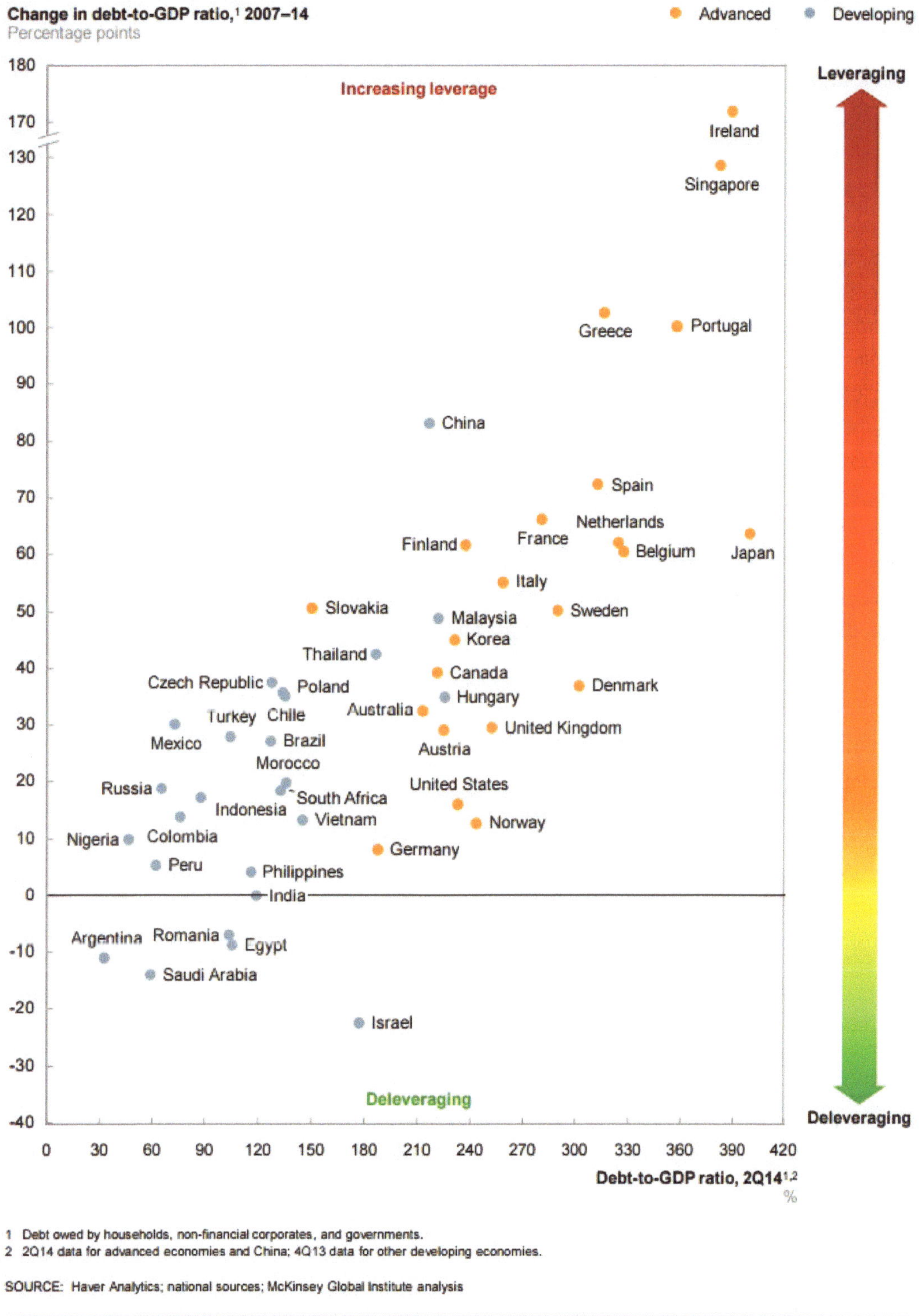

Figure 9.3. The ratio of debt to GDP has increased in all advanced economies since 2007.

For the time being, the Dollar is here to stay and will continue to be the anchor and collateral other countries raise their indebtedness and ability to repay against. It's a world of IOUs collateralized against a constant stream of IOUs. Whoever has the most global IOUs may claim the most economic clout.

CASE STUDY: GLOBAL MONETARY SYSTEM "THRILLS AND SPILLS" (*ECONOMIST*, OCTOBER 3, 2015)

In the late nineteenth century, the world economy was anchored to the economic prowess of the British Empire and London finance. Fast-forward to today: The global economy is orchestrated through US Dollar transactions and US Dollar asset trades, by the world's largest debtor nation. In a post-2007-2009 financial crisis environment, the United States and the US Dollar stand at the epicenter of an organized global monetary disorder.

The global monetary system has always been a headache to economies seeking to mitigate the risk of external imbalances in the global monetary order from disrupting the domestic balances supportive of healthy income and wealth creation. In a world of loose exchange rate arrangements and mobile financial capital sloshing across borders, countries have been challenged with offsetting trade deficits and surpluses with appropriate financial asset offsets without affecting economic growth and ballooning potential asset bubbles.

Countries that run very large and questionably sustainable trade deficits have been asked to impose austerity measures to adjust import balances downward at the cost of slowing growth for countries running trade surpluses and slimming world cross-border financial flows. Countries having attempted to devalue their currencies to gain export advantages invite a "beggar-thy-neighbor" environment as other challenging countries respond with competitive devaluations, creating trade and financial exchange benefits for no one. After twenty years of financial globalization, cross-border capital flows have exceeded global current account deficits and reinforced a US Dollar zone of some "60 percent of the world's population and 60 percent of world output" as shown in Figure 9.4.[1]

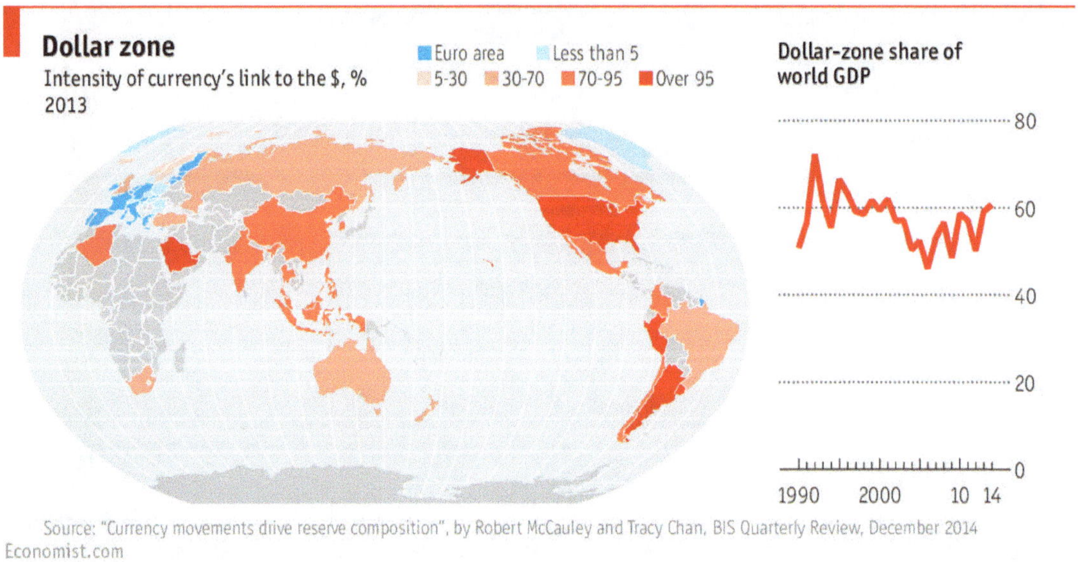

Figure 9.4

Figure 9.4 shows how the world economy is orchestrated to a US financial rhythm. With global oil markets priced in US Dollars, Saudi Arabia as shown in the figure has one of the highest currency intensity links to the US Dollar, reinforced by the US Dollar–Saudi Riyal currency peg. Large US trading partners such as China (fixed exchange rate arrangement with the US Dollar), Canada and Mexico (NAFTA and geographical proximity), and India score high in intensity link to the US Dollar. In emerging market economies, where much of the currency intensity link predominates,

[1] Global Monetary System: "Thrills and Spills." *Economist*, 2015.

these economies mimic US monetary policy to avoid the instability of excessive capital inflows and outflows as reflected in their banking systems' expansion and contraction to mimic the US financial environment.

But in a crisis-prone system, the lessons of 2007–2009 demonstrate why the United States should feel nervous about a global monetary order it anchors to what some see as artificial demand for its "safe" assets. It is wishful thinking to believe external surpluses in one economy will heal the external deficits of another. The though process goes like this:

> The imbalances between surplus countries in Asia and the Middle East and deficit countries, most notably America, will narrow now that oil exporters are earning less and China is trying to move away from its export-led model. Capital flows have gone over the top as central banks have tried to fend off a depression, but as the Dollar rises, emerging economies will use their reserves to stabilize their currencies. The system will start to look more normal. (Economist, October 3, 2015)

If China experiences a deeper domestic economic slowdown coupled with persistent depressed oil and commodity prices spurring an emerging market debt bust, two decades of financial globalization may unravel as emerging markets sell down Dollar reserves, driving a decoupling process from the US Dollar. This would be disruptive to US Treasuries; prompting a rise in interest rates and US government borrowing costs, bringing a looming fiscal crisis much closer to the present. The United States may find it more difficult to carry on than it has in the past.

However, with a global US Dollar zone of 60 percent of the world population and 60 percent of world output, the obvious and smart money would be to still pile into US Treasuries for safety. Why? Without an alternative reserve currency with an ability to replace the global US Dollar zone share, there is no place to go. This would continue to make US Dollar offshore markets subject to boom and bust cycles and more crisis prone, with the Federal Reserve remaining as the lender of last resort to a future world US Dollar crisis. If world economies continue to accumulate US Dollar reserve balances in line with their economic size, and US debt-to-GDP ratio remains steady, then it is estimated that by 2035 there will be a global shortage of US Treasuries for the Federal Reserve to work with, making it more difficult for the Fed to execute its duties as a lender of last resort through the US banking system through which the world is connected.

The present global monetary architecture is unsustainable and prone to harmful "beggar-thy-neighbor" reciprocity. As the 2016 US elections have the country looking more inward and disintermediated from the world, it leaves Federal Reserve monetary policy to go it alone in the management of the global payments system without an alternative entity able to do it much better.

QUESTIONS FOR CLASS DISCUSSION

1. At the beginning of the chapter, it is stated that open economies that save the least grow the fastest. This would seem contrary to most economic growth models' predictions, but the contrariness has not held. As a class or in small groups, pick a country that runs a trade deficit and, using the savings investment and spending identity for an open economy, explain how the country has used its trade deficit as an instrument to externally finance domestic consumption, investment, and government expenditures.

   Next, explain how the country's economy has or has not benefited from this external financing approach. Finally, explain how this external financing approach has given the United States an exorbitant privilege to global borrowing in its own money.
2. Discuss the following statement: "If larger economies are borrowing savings from smaller economies to prevent a crowding out of investment in their home economies, are they possibly crowding out investment spending in

these smaller economies?" Finally, how might a smaller economy lending its trade surplus to the United States go about preventing the crowding out of investment spending in its home market?

3. As a class or in small groups, discuss global emerging threats (economic and noneconomic) to US Dollar hegemony. Discuss reasons for or against IMF Special Drawing Rights becoming an alternative "safe asset" to the US Dollar. Finally, discuss reasons for or against a full decoupling of the Chinese Yuan from the US Dollar and becoming an alternative reserve currency to the US Dollar.
4. In December 2015 the Chinese Yuan was added to the official basket of reserve currencies constituting the IMF's Special Drawing Rights, a composite currency IMF member countries can use to pay one another. Discuss the importance of this move and what it says about China's place in the world financial order; does the currency's addition to the basket move the currency incrementally closer to being seen as a possible "safe asset" and competitive alternative to the Dollar? Finally, is there room for a Yuan zone? Why or why not?

IMAGE CREDITS

- Fig. 9.1: U.S, Bureau of Economic Analysis. Copyright in the Public Domain.
- Fig. 9.2: www.imf.org. Copyright © 2016 by International Monetary Fund.
- Fig. 9.3: Mckinsey Global Institute; Haver Analytics, www.secretsofthefed.com. Copyright © 2014 by Secrets of the Fed.
- Fig. 9.4: The Economist, Global Monetary System: "Thrills and Spills" (The Economist, October 3rd, 2015). Copyright © 2015 by The Economist Newspaper Limited.

CREDITS

CHAPTER 1

1. Fig. 1.0: Copyright © satanoid (CC by 2.0) at http://commons.wikimedia.org/wiki/File:2010_street_Lagos_Nigeria_4577464660.jpg.
2. Table 1.1: Source: http://www.naics.com/history-naics-code/.
3. Table 1.2: Source: Adapted from https://wikis.engrade.com/economicsystems.
4. Fig. 1.1: Source: Terry Miller, Anthony Kim, Kim Holmes, http://www.heritage.org/index/images/book/2014/in-2014-region-map-web-world.jpg.
5. Fig. 1.2: Source: Terry Miller, Anthony Kim, Kim Holmes, http://www.heritage.org/index.
6. Fig. 1.3: Copyright © Le0t (CC BY-SA 3.0) at http://commons.wikimedia.org/wiki/File:Circular_flow_of_income.png.
7. Fig. 1.4: Source: www.intellectualtakeout.org.

CHAPTER 2

1. Tbl. 2.4: Source: Canada Department of Foreign Affairs and International Trade, 2003.

CHAPTER 3

1. Fig. 3.7: Source: Paul Farnham, Economics for Managers.
2. Fig. 3.8: Source: Paul Farnham, Economics for Managers.
3. Fig. 3.9: Source: Paul Farnham, Economics for Managers.
4. Fig. 3.10:Source: Comex, "Copper Limbo: How Just How Low Can It Go" (The Wall Street Journal, 02/28/1998).

CHAPTER 4

1. Fig. 4.0: http://commons.wikimedia.org/wiki/File:Circulation_in_macroeconomics.svg. Copyright in the Public Domain.
2. Fig. 4.1a: Copyright © LeOt (CC BY-SA 3.0) at http://commons.wikimedia.org/wiki/File:Circular_flow_of_income.png.
3. Fig. 4.1b: Copyright © Shinkansen Fan (CC BY-SA 3.0) at http://commons.wikimedia.org/wiki/File:Circulation_in_macroeconomics-fr_es_en.svg.
4. Fig. 4.2: "Number of households for each county in the U.S. 2007–2011," U.S. Census Bureau. Copyright in the Public Domain.
5. Fig. 4.3: "Median Houshold Income in 2012 by county," U.S. Census Bureau. Copyright in the Public Domain.
6. Fig. 4.4: Source: www.american.com.
7. Fig. 4.5: "United States GDP and Government Spending," Budget of the United States Government. Copyright in the Public Domain.
8. Fig. 4.6: "U.S. Government Expenditure by level," U.S. Bureau of Economic Analysis; National Income and Product Acounts, December 2011, Tables 1.15, 3.16, 3.2, 3.3, and 5.10www.brookings.edu. Copyright in the Public Domain.
9. Tbl. 4.1: "US GDP 2012–2012," U.S. Bureau of Economic Analysis. Copyright in the Public Domain.
10. Tbl. 4.2: "US GDP Shares 2012-2014," U.S. Bureau of Economic Analysis. Copyright in the Public Domain.
11. Tbl. 4.3a: Adapted from Paul Krugman and Robin Wells, Macroeconomics, 3rd ed. Copyright © 2012 by Worth Publishers.
12. Tbl. 4.3b: Adapted from Paul Krugman and Robin Wells, Macroeconomics, 3rd ed. Copyright © 2012 by Worth Publishers.
13. Tbl. 4.3c: Adapted from Paul Krugman and Robin Wells, Macroeconomics, 3rd ed. Copyright © 2012 by Worth Publishers.
14. Table 4.4:Adapted from Paul Krugman and Robin Wells, Macroeconomics, 3rd ed. Copyright © 2012 by Worth Publishers.
15. Table 4.5a &b: Adapted from Paul Krugman and Robin Wells, Macroeconomics, 3rd ed. Copyright © 2012 by Worth Publishers.
16. Fig. 4.7: "U.S.Real GDP and Real Value Added by Sector," U.S. Bureau of Economic Analysis. Copyright in the Public Domain.
17. Fig. 4.8: Source: Thomas Sargent, www.cato.org.
18. Fig. 4.9: Source: Dr. Steve Hanke, John's Hopkins University, IMF World Economic Outlook Database.
19. Fig. 4.10: Source: "Putting the Recession into Perspective," National Bureau of Economics Research, Commerce Department, Labor Department, The Economist Magazine.
20. Fig. 4.11: Source: "U.S. core inflation, nominal wage growth and real wage growth," Federal Reserve Bank of San Francisco, www.frbsf.org.
21. Fig. 4.12: Source: "GDP Per Capita and Life Satsifaction," IMF World Economic Outlook Database, 2014; www.fruittreeblog.com.

CHAPTER 5

1. Fig. 5.0: MeFeKa, "Dubai 1990-2003," https://www.flickr.com/photos/mefeka/1242269952.
2. Fig. 5.1: Source: "The Business Cycle," www.economicshelp.org.
3. Fig. 5.2: Source: www.fivethirtyeight.com, Bureau of Labor Statistics.

4. Fig. 5.3: Source: "GDP Per-Capita Top 25 Countries 2011," www.econographics.wordpress.com.
5. Fig. 5.4: Adapted from Paul Krugman and Robin Wells, Macroeconomics, 3rd ed. Copyright © 2012 by Worth Publishers.
6. Fig. 5.5: Sources: measuringworth.com, visualizingeconomics.com, www.ritholtz.com.
7. Fig. 5.6: Source: Heritage Foundation, "Productivity and Real Compensation Grow Together," www.heritage.org.
8. Fig. 5.7: Source: Federal Reserve Bank of St. Louis.
9. Fig. 5.15: Source: "Regional GDP 1970–2016," CIA Long-Term Growth Model; www,famguardian.org.
10. Fig. 5.16: Source: Karl Smith, "Real Gross Domestic Product," www.economist.com.
11. Fig. 5.17: Source: Manufacturing in Africa: "An Awakening Giant" (The Economist, February 8, 2014).

CHAPTER 6

1. Fig. 6.0: http://commons.wikimedia.org/wiki/John_Maynard_Keynes#mediaviewer/File:Keynes_1933.jpg. Copyright in the Public Domain.
2. Fig. 6.5: Source: www.irs.gov.

CHAPTER 7

1. Fig. 7.0: Source: www.web-books.com.
2. Fig. 7.1: Source: Gary North, www.garynorth.com.
3. Fig. 7.2: Adapted from Frederic Mishkin, Economics of Money, Banking, and Financial Markets, 10th ed. Copyright © 2012 by Prentice Hall.
4. Fig. 7.3: Adapted from Frederic Mishkin, Economics of Money, Banking, and Financial Markets, 10th ed. Copyright © 2012 by Prentice Hall.
5. Fig. 7.4: Adapted from Frederic Mishkin, Economics of Money, Banking, and Financial Markets, 10th ed. Copyright © 2012 by Prentice Hall.
6. Fig. 7.5a: Adapted from Frederic Mishkin, Economics of Money, Banking, and Financial Markets, 10th ed. Copyright © 2012 by Prentice Hall.
7. Fig. 7.5b: Adapted from Frederic Mishkin, Economics of Money, Banking, and Financial Markets, 10th ed. Copyright © 2012 by Prentice Hall.
8. Fig. 7.6: Adapted from Frederic Mishkin, Economics of Money, Banking, and Financial Markets, 10th ed. Copyright © 2012 by Prentice Hall.
9. Fig. 7.7: Adapted from Frederic Mishkin, Economics of Money, Banking, and Financial Markets, 10th ed. Copyright © 2012 by Prentice Hall.
10. Fig. 7.8: Adapted from Frederic Mishkin, Economics of Money, Banking, and Financial Markets, 10th ed. Copyright © 2012 by Prentice Hall.
11. Fig. 7.9: Adapted from Frederic Mishkin, Economics of Money, Banking, and Financial Markets, 10th ed. Copyright © 2012 by Prentice Hall.
12. Fig. 7.10: Adapted from Frederic Mishkin, Economics of Money, Banking, and Financial Markets, 10th ed. Copyright © 2012 by Prentice Hall.

CHAPTER 8

1. Fig. 8.0: Source: Federal Reserve Bank and National Bureau of Economic Research.
2. Fig. 8.1: Adapted from Frederic Mishkin, Economics of Money, Banking, and Financial Markets, 10th ed. Copyright © 2012 by Prentice Hall.
3. Fig. 8.2: Source: www.budget360.com.
4. Fig. 8.3: Justin Lahart, "How a Modern Depression Might Look – If the U.S. Gets There," The Wall Street Journal. Copyright © 2009 by Dow Jones & Company, Inc.
5. Fig. 8.4: Source: Jost, Lora, "US Median Home Values (February 1996 to March 2011)," www.lorajost.org.
6. Fig. 8.5: Conor Dougherty and Kelly Evans, "Economy in Worst Fall Since '82," The Wall Street Journal. Copyright © 2009 by Dow Jones & Company, Inc.
7. Fig. 8.6: Source: "US Federal Tax Receipts-Fiscal Year 2013," CBO Historial Tables.
8. Fig. 8.7: Adapted from Paul Krugman and Robin Wells, Macroeconomics, 3rd ed. Copyright © 2012 by Worth Publishers.
9. Fig. 8.8: Adapted from Paul Krugman and Robin Wells, Macroeconomics, 3rd ed. Copyright © 2012 by Worth Publishers.
10. Fig. 8.9: Adapted from Paul Krugman and Robin Wells, Macroeconomics, 3rd ed. Copyright © 2012 by Worth Publishers.
11. Tbl. 8.1: Adapted from Paul Krugman and Robin Wells, Macroeconomics, 3rd ed. Copyright © 2012 by Worth Publishers.
12. Fig. 8.10: Adapted from Frederic Mishkin, Economics of Money, Banking, and Financial Markets, 10th ed. Copyright © 2012 by Prentice Hall.
13. Fig. 8.11: Adapted from Paul Krugman and Robin Wells, Macroeconomics, 3rd ed. Copyright © 2012 by Worth Publishers.
14. Tbl. 8.2: Adapted from Frederic Mishkin, Economics of Money, Banking, and Financial Markets, 10th ed. Copyright © 2012 by Prentice Hall.
15. Fig. 8.12: Adapted from Paul Krugman and Robin Wells, Macroeconomics, 3rd ed. Copyright © 2012 by Worth Publishers.
16. Fig. 8.13: Adapted from Paul Krugman and Robin Wells, Macroeconomics, 3rd ed. Copyright © 2012 by Worth Publishers.

CHAPTER 9

1. Fig. 9.1: Source: U.S. Bureau of Economic Analysis.
2. Fig. 9.2: Source: www.imf.org.
3. Fig. 9.3: Source: Mckinsey Global Institute; Haver Analytics, www.secretsofthefed.com.
4. Fig. 9.4: Source: "Global Monetary System: Thrills and Spills," The Economist, October 3rd, 2015. Copyright © 2015 by The Economist Newspaper Limited.

9 781516 514335

Printed by Libri Plureos GmbH in Hamburg,
Germany